RANGE

D0977963

NEW YORK CITY

TOP SIGHTS, AUTHENTIC EXPERIENCES

Regis St Louis, Michael Grosberg

Lonely Planet's
New York City

Plan Your Trip

Top Experiences......................35

Dining Out...................................119

Treasure Hunt 141

This Year in New York City

2018

LEV RADIN / SHUTTERSTOCK ©

New York City

No matter when you visit, there's always something happening in New York City, with music festivals, holiday markets and costume parades packing the year's calendar. Be sure to plan ahead for the bigger events.

Above: Village Halloween Parade (p15); Top Right: Independence Day fireworks (p12); Bottom Right: Cherry Blossom Festival, Brooklyn Botanic Garden (p9)

Central Park 🚇   🏛 Guggenheim Museum
              🏛 Metropolitan Museum of Art

Upper East Side
High-end boutiques, sophisticated mansions and Museum Mile – one of the most cultured strips in the world.
(Map p252)

Roosevelt Island

🏛 **Museum of Modern Art**
🏛 **Rockefeller Center**

🚇 Grand Central Terminal

MoMA PS1
              🚇

ire State Building

Union Square, Flatiron District & Gramercy
A bustling, vibrant park binds surrounding areas filled with good eats.
(Map p250)

East Village & Lower East Side
Two of the city's hottest 'hoods that lure students, bankers and scruffier types alike.
(Map p246)

r East Side
ement Museum

ridge

Bridge Park

Lower Manhattan & the Financial District
Iconic monuments, riverfront access and Wall St mingle at the island's southern end.
(Map p244)

🚇 Prospect Park (0.7mi)   ✈ John F Kennedy International Airport (10mi)

Welcome to New York City

Epicenter of the arts. Dining and shopping capital. Trendsetter in fashion and design. Home to an astonishingly diverse mix of peoples and cultures. Add it all up and you have one of the most dynamic destinations on earth.

With its compact size and streets packed with eye-candy of all sorts – architectural treasures, Old World cafes, atmospheric booksellers and curio shops – New York City is an urban wanderer's delight. Crossing continents is as easy as walking over a few avenues in this jumbled city of 200-plus nationalities. Every neighborhood offers a dramatically different version of NYC: from the 100-year-old Jewish delis of the Upper West Side to the meandering cobblestone lanes of Greenwich Village.

When the sun sinks slowly beyond the Hudson River and luminous skyscrapers light up the night, New York transforms into one grand stage. Well-known actors take to the legendary theaters of Broadway; world-class soloists, dancers and musicians perform at venues large and small across town. Whether high culture or low, New York embraces it all: in-your-face rock shows at Williamsburg dives, lavish opera productions at the Lincoln Center, and everything in between. This is a city of experimental theater, improv comedy, indie cinema, ballet, poetry readings, burlesque, world music, jazz and so much more. If you can dream it up, it's probably happening in NYC.

If you can dream it up, it's probably happening in NYC

Lower Manhattan skyline

★ NEW YORK CITY ★

Upper West Side & Central Park
Home to the premier performing arts center and the park that helps define the city. (Map p252)

Midtown
Times Square, Broadway theaters, canyons of skyscrapers, and bustling crowds that rarely thin. (Map p250)

Greenwich Village, Chelsea & Meatpacking District
Quaint, intimate streets plus trendy nightlife, shopping and art galleries galore. (Map p246)

SoHo & Chinatown
Soup dumpling parlors and hawkers selling bric-a-brac next door to cobblestone streets and stores with the biggest name brands in the world. (Map p246)

Lincoln Center ◎

Broadway ◎
Times Square ◎

Pennsylvania
(Penn) Station 🚇

🏛
Em

High Line ◐

Hudson River

◐ Washingto
Square Par

Low
🏛 Ten

◎ Chinatow

One World Trade Center ◎
🏛
National September 11 Memorial & Museum

◎ Brooklyn B

Liberty
State Park

◐ Brooklyn

◎ Ellis Island

*Upper New
York Bay*

Governors
Island

Statue of Liberty ❶

BLUEMOONPICS / SHUTTERSTOCK ©

T PHOTOGRAPHY / SHUTTERSTOCK ©

2018

★ Top Events & Festivals

Cherry Blossom Festival Apr 28–29 (p9)

Shakespeare in the Park Late May–Aug (p10)

SummerStage Jun–Aug (p11)

Independence Day Jul 4 (p12)

Village Halloween Parade Oct 31 (p15)

Plan Your Trip
This Year in New York City

January

The winter doldrums arrive following the build-up of Christmas and New Year's Eve. Despite the long nights, New Yorkers take advantage of the frosty weather, with outdoor ice skating and weekend ski trips to the Catskills.

🏊 New Year's Day Swim   Jan 1
What better way to greet the new year than with an icy dip in the Atlantic? Join the Coney Island Polar Bear Club for this annual brrrr fest (www.polarbearclub.org).

☆ Winter Jazzfest   Early Jan
In early January this four-day music fest (www.winterjazzfest.com) brings in over 100 acts playing at nearly a dozen venues around the city. Most of the action happens around the West Village.

🏊 No Pants Subway Ride   Mid-Jan
In mid-January (usually on the second Sunday), some 4000 New Yorkers spice things up with a bit of leg nudity on public transit (http://improveverywhere.com). Anyone can join in, and there's usually an after-party for the cheeky participants. Check the website for meeting times and details.

✗ Winter Restaurant Week   Late Jan–Early Feb
From late January to early February celebrate the dreary weather with slash-cut meal deals at some of the city's finest eating establishments during New York's Winter Restaurant Week (www.nycgo.com/restaurant-week), which actually runs for about three weeks. A three-course lunch costs around $30 ($42 for dinner).

2018

MANDRITOIU / SHUTTERSTOCK ©

02

February

The odd blizzard and below-freezing temperatures make February a good time to stay indoors nursing a drink or a warm meal at a cozy bar or bistro.

☆ Westminster Kennel Club Dog Show   Feb 12–13

Canine lovers from the four corners of the earth sweep into Manhattan during this showcase of beautiful breeds (www.westminsterkennelclub.org). Some 3200 dogs compete for top honors. The best in show judging takes place in Madison Square Garden.

🛍 Mercedes Benz Fashion Week   Mid-Feb

The infamous Bryant Park fashion shows (www.fashionweekonline.com) are sadly not open to the public. But whether you're invited or not, being in the city this week -- when the couture world descends upon

🎆 Lunar (Chinese) New Year Festival   Feb 17

One of the biggest Chinese New Year (www.explorechinatown.com) celebrations in the country, this display of fireworks and dancing dragons draws mobs of thrill seekers into the streets of Chinatown.

Manhattan to swoon over new looks – could provide a vicarious thrill, especially if you can find the after-parties.

✗ Valentine's Day   Feb 14

If you're traveling with a special someone, you'll want to reserve well ahead for a Valentine's Day dinner. Many restaurants offer special prix-fixe menus, and it's quite the popular night for going out.

From left: New Year's Day Swim; Lunar (Chinese) New Year Festival parade

Plan Your Trip

This Year in New York City

March

After months of freezing temperatures and thick winter coats, the odd warm spring day appears and everyone rejoices – though it's usually followed by a week of sub-zero drear as winter lingers on.

☉ Armory Show   Mar 8–11

New York's biggest art show (www.the armoryshow.com) brings together some of the world's top galleries, with art collectors and curators in a dazzling showcase of what's new on the art scene. It happens on Piers 92 and 94, off Twelfth Ave (near 53rd St).

⚜ St Patrick's Day Parade   Mar 17

A massive audience, rowdy and wobbly from cups of green beer, lines Fifth Ave on March 17 for this popular parade (www. nycstpatricksparade.org) of bagpipe blowers, sparkly floats and clusters of Irish-lovin' politicians. The parade, which was first held here in 1762, is the city's oldest and largest.

☆ New Directors/ New Films   Late Mar

Hosted by the Film Society of Lincoln Center, this 12-day film fest (www.new directors.org) is a great place to discover emerging directors from around the globe. It's now in its 47th year, so you can count on an impressive lineup.

☉ Macy's Flower Show   Late Mar–Early Apr

For two weeks in the early spring, Macy's becomes a sweet-smelling floral extravaganza. The flagship store on Herald Square hosts elaborate displays of blooms, lush mini-landscapes and clever blends of the natural and human-made environment.

2018

04

April

Spring finally appears: optimistic alfresco joints have a sprinkling of streetside chairs as the city squares overflow with bright tulips and blossom-covered trees.

✿ Easter Parade   Apr 1

Dating back to the 1870s, this parade features a lineup of well-dressed, bonnet-wearing participants who show off their finery along Fifth Ave (from 49th to 57th Sts). Bring your wildest hat, and join in the action. It typically kicks off at 10am.

☆ Tribeca Film Festival   Mid-Apr–Late Apr

Created in response to the tragic events of September 11, Robert De Niro's downtown film festival (www.tribecafilm.com) has quickly become a star in the indie movie circuit. You'll have to make some tough choices: more than 150 films are screened during the 10-day fest.

✿ Cherry Blossom Festival   Apr 28–29

Known in Japanese as Sakura Matsuri (www.bbg.org), this annual tradition celebrates the magnificent flowering of cherry trees in the Brooklyn Botanic Garden. It's complete with entertainment and activities (taiko drumming, folk dancing, origami workshops, ikebana flower displays, samurai sword showmanship), plus refreshments and awe-inspiring beauty.

✦ Earth Day   Apr 22

New York hosts a packed day of events at Union Square, with live music, presentations on sustainability and hands-on activities for kids (www.earthdayinitiative.org). Grand Central Terminal also has displays on green initiatives.

From left: St Patrick's Day Parade; Cherry Blossom Festival

This Year in New York City

GARY718 / SHUTTERSTOCK ©

05

May

April showers bring May flowers in the form of brilliant bursts of blossoms adorning the flowering trees all around the city. The weather is warm and mild without the unpleasant humidity of summer.

⚡ TD Bank Five Boro
Bike Tour   Early May

May is Bike Month, featuring two-wheelin' tours, parties and other events for pedal-pushing New Yorkers. TD Bank Five Boro Bike Tour (www.bikenewyork.org), the main event, sees thousands of cyclists hit the pavement for a 42-mile ride, much of it on roads closed to traffic or on water-front paths through each of the city's five boroughs.

🎉 Memorial Day   May 28

Held on the last Monday of May, this holiday commemorates Americans who've died in combat. The boroughs host parades featuring marching bands, vintage cars and flag-waving seniors; the biggest parade is Queens' Little Neck-Douglaston Memorial Day Parade (www.lndmemorialday.org).

◉ Fleet Week   Late May

For one week (www.fleetweeknewyork.com) at the end of May Manhattan resembles a 1940s movie set as clusters of fresh-faced, uniformed sailors go 'on the town' to look for adventures. For non-swabby visitors, this is a chance to take free tours of ships that have arrived from various corners of the globe. See them docked off Manhattan (around Midtown) and Brooklyn (just south of Brooklyn Bridge Park's Pier 6).

☆ Shakespeare in
the Park   Late May–Aug

The much-loved Shakespeare in the Park (www.publictheater.org) pays tribute to the Bard, with free performances in Central Park. The catch? You'll have to wait hours in line to score tickets, or win them in the online lottery (there's also an in-person lottery on performance days at noon at the Public Theater). Tickets are given out at noon on show days; arrive no later than 10am for a seat.

KAMIRA / SHUTTERSTOCK ©

2018

06

June

Summer's definitely here and locals crawl out of their office cubicles to relax in the city's green spaces. Parades roll down the busiest streets and portable movie screens are strung up in several parks.

☆ River to River Festival Mid-Jun–Late Jun

Over 11 days in June, this arts-loving fest (www.lmcc.net/program/river-to-river) offers a combo of live music, dance and visual art at spaces on the waterfront, on Governors Island and in Lower Manhattan.

☆ Mermaid Parade Late Jun

Celebrating sand, sea and the beginning of summer is this wonderfully quirky after-noon parade (www.coneyisland.com). It's a flash of glitter and glamour, as elaborately costumed folks display their fishy finery along the Coney Island boardwalk. It's even more fun to take part (all in costume are welcome). Usually held on the last Saturday of the month.

☆ NYC Pride Late Jun

Gay Pride Month culminates in a major march down Fifth Ave on the last Sunday

☆ Bryant Park Summer Film Festival Jun–Aug

June through August, Bryant Park (www.bryantpark.org) hosts free Monday-night outdoor screenings of classic Hollywood films, which kick off after sundown. Arrive early (the lawn area opens at 5pm and folks line up by 4pm).

of the month. NYC Pride is a five-hour spec-tacle of dancers, drag queens, gay police officers, leathermen, lesbian soccer-moms and representatives of just about every other queer scene under the rainbow.

☆ SummerStage Jun–Aug

Central Park's SummerStage (www.cityparksfoundation.org/summerstage), which runs from June through August, features an incredible lineup of music and dance throughout the summer. Django Djan-go, Femi Kuti, Shuggie Otis and the Martha Graham Dance Company are among recent standouts. Most events are free.

From left: Fleet Week; Bryant Park Summer Film Festival

Plan Your Trip
This Year in New York City

July

As the city swelters, locals flee to beachside escapes on Long Island. It's a busy month for tourism, however, as holidaying North Americans and Europeans fill the city.

✹ Independence Day   Jul 4
America's Independence Day (www.macys.com) is celebrated on the 4th of July with dramatic fireworks over the East River, starting at 9pm. Good viewing spots include the waterfronts of the Lower East Side and Williamsburg, Brooklyn, or any high rooftop or east-facing Manhattan apartment.

✕ Nathan's Famous
Hot Dog Eating Contest   Jul 4
For rare skills not often celebrated on the sports pages, head to Surf Ave and Stillwell in Coney Island to see competitive eaters down ungodly numbers of hot dogs in just 10 minutes (www.nathansfamous.com/contest). The current record for men is 70 by long-time champ Joey Chestnut. For women, it's 45 – held by the 98lb Sonya Thomas.

☆ Lincoln Center
Festival   Mid-Jul–Late Jul
This summer, skip the beach and take advantage of the stellar lineup of drama, ballet, opera and new music hitting Lincoln Stages over three weeks in July (www.lincolncenterfestival.org). Expect high-quality and highly original fare.

☆ Lincoln Center
Out of Doors   Late Jul–Early Aug
New York City's performing arts power-house stages a festive lineup of concerts and dance parties at outdoor stages in the Lincoln Center complex (www.lcoutofdoors.org). Afrobeat, Latin jazz and country are all part of the lineup, and there are special events for families.

2018

08

August

Thick waves of summer heat slide between skyscrapers as everyone heads to the seashore nearby or gulps cool blasts of air-conditioning when stuck in the city. Myriad outdoor events and attractions add life to the languid urban heat.

☆ FringeNYC   Mid-Aug
The annual mid-August theater festival, FringeNYC (www.fringenyc.org), presents two weeks of performances by companies from all over the world. It's the best way to catch the edgiest, wackiest and most creative up-and-comers around.

☆ Charlie Parker
Jazz Festival   Late Aug
This open-air two-day fest (www.cityparks foundation.org) is a great day out for music fans. Incredible jazz talents take to the stage in Marcus Garvey Park in Harlem and in Tompkins Square Park in the East Village.

☆ Jazz Age
Lawn Party   Late Aug
Don your best 1920s attire and head out to Governors Island for a day of big-band jazz, Charleston dancing and pre-Prohibition-era cocktails (www. jazzagelawnparty.com). Buy tickets as early as possible; this event always sells out. Also happens in June.

☆ US Open   Late Aug–Early Sep
In late August, Flushing Meadows Park in Queens takes center stage in sports as the world's top tennis players compete in the final Grand Slam tournament of the year (www.usopen.org). If you can't make it to the stadium, major sports bars will be showing the matches around town.

From left: Nathan's Famous Hot Dog Eating Contest; Jazz Age Lawn Party

Plan Your Trip
This Year in New York City

09

September

Labor Day officially marks the end of the Hampton's share-house season as the blistering heat of summer fades to more tolerable levels. As locals return to work, the cultural calendar ramps up.

♣ West Indian American Day Carnival
Sep 3

Brooklyn's biggest festival (www.wiadca carnival.org) draws some two million parade-goers to Crown Heights for a day of colorful costumes, steel-pan drumming and calypso bands. Go early to find a spot (and scout out food vendors). The parade starts at 11am.

☆ Electric Zoo
Early Sep

Celebrated over the Labor Day weekend, Electric Zoo (www.electriczoofestival.com) is New York's electronic music festival held in sprawling Randall's Island Park. Past headliners have included Moby, Afrojack, David Guetta, Martin Solveig and The Chemical Brothers.

♣ Atlantic Antic
Late Sep

The best of New York's street festivals brings a medley of live bands, food and drink, and many craft and clothing vendors. You can also climb aboard vintage buses at the New York Transit Museum's display. It usually happens on the fourth Sunday in September and runs along Atlantic Ave (www.atlanticave.org) between Fourth Ave and the waterfront.

☆ BAM's Next Wave Festival
Sep–Dec

Celebrated for more than 30 years, the Brooklyn Academy of Music's Next Wave Festival (www.bam.org), which runs through to December, showcases world-class avant-garde theater, music and dance.

2018

A KATZ / SHUTTERSTOCK ©

October

Brilliant bursts of orange, red and gold fill the trees in Central and Prospect Parks as temperatures cool and alfresco cafes finally shutter their windows. Along with May, October is one of the most pleasant and scenic months to visit NYC.

🏃 Comic Con   Early Oct

Enthusiasts from near and far gather at this annual beacon of nerd-dom (www. newyorkcomiccon.com) to dress up as their favorite characters and cavort with like-minded anime aficionados.

🎊 Blessing of the Animals   Early Oct

In honor of the Feast Day of St Francis, which falls early in the month, pet owners flock to the grand Cathedral Church of St John the Divine for the annual Blessing of the Animals (www.stjohndivine.org) with their sidekicks – poodles, lizards, parrots, llamas, you name it – in tow.

👁 Open House New York   Mid-Oct

The country's largest architecture and design event, Open House New York (www. ohny.org) features special architect-led tours, plus lectures, design workshops, studio visits and site-specific performances all over the city.

🎊 Village Halloween Parade   Oct 31

October 31 brings riotous fun to the city, as New Yorkers don their wildest costumes for a night of revelry. See the most outrageous displays at the Village Halloween Parade (www.halloween-nyc.com) that runs up Sixth Ave in the West Village. It's fun to watch, but even better to join in.

From left: Sankai Juku perform at BAM's Next Wave Festival; Blessing of the Animals

Plan Your Trip
This Year in New York City

November

As the leaves tumble, light jackets are replaced by wool and down. A headliner marathon is tucked into the final days of prehibernation weather, then families gather to give thanks.

☆ New York Comedy Festival
Early Nov

Funny-makers take the city by storm during the New York Comedy Festival (www.nycomedyfestival.com) with stand-up sessions, improv nights and big-ticket shows hosted by the likes of Rosie O'Donnell and Ricky Gervais.

🏃 New York City Marathon
Nov 4

Held in the first week of November, this annual 26-mile run (www.nycmarathon.org) draws thousands of athletes from around the world, and many more excited viewers line the streets to cheer the runners on.

⊙ Rockefeller Center Christmas Tree Lighting Ceremony
Nov 28

The flick of a switch ignites the massive Christmas tree (www.rockefellercenter.com) in Rockefeller Center, officially ushering in the holiday season. Bedecked with more than 25,000 lights, it is NYC's unofficial Yuletide headquarters and a must-see for anyone visiting the city during December.

🎊 Thanksgiving Day Parade
Nov 22

Massive helium-filled balloons soar overhead, high-school marching bands rattle their snares and millions of onlookers bundle up with scarves and coats to celebrate Thanksgiving (the fourth Thursday in November) with Macy's world-famous 2.5-mile-long parade (www.macys.com).

🏃 Ice Skating in New York
Nov–Mar

New Yorkers make the most of the winter by taking advantage of outdoor rinks across the city. These usually open in November and run until late March, with top choices including Central Park, Bryant Park, Prospect Park and Rockefeller Center.

2018

DANIEL W / SHUTTERSTOCK ©

12

December

Winter's definitely here, but there's plenty of holiday cheer to warm the spirit. Fairy lights adorn most buildings and Fifth Ave department stores (as well as Macy's) create elaborate worlds within their storefront windows.

🔒 Holiday Markets   Dec 1–24
In the lead-up to Christmas, New York becomes a wonderland of holiday markets, selling crafts, clothing and accessories, ceramics, toys and more. The big markets are at Union Square, Bryant Park and Grand Central Terminal.

🏃 NYRR
Midnight Run   Dec 31
For a positive start to 2018, go for a 4-mile dash with other running fans through Central Park. The race starts at midnight, though the festivities and fireworks kick off beforehand. Sign up with New York Road Runners (www.nyrr.org).

☆ Radio City Christmas Spectacular   Nov–Dec
Radio City Music Hall stages this extravagant annual show (www. radiocitychristmas.com), featuring high-kicking Rockettes and even a visit from Santa Claus. Always a crowd-pleaser, especially with kids.

🎆 New Year's Eve   Dec 31
The ultimate place to ring in the New Year (www.timessquarenyc.org/nye) in the northern hemisphere, Times Square swarms with millions of gatherers who come to stand squashed together like boxed sardines, swig booze, freeze in subarctic temperatures, witness the annual dropping of the ball made entirely of Waterford Crystal and chant the '10...9...8...' countdown in perfect unison.

From left: Thanksgiving Day Parade; Rockettes perform at Radio City Christmas Spectacular

Plan Your Trip
Need to Know

Daily Costs

Budget
Less than $100

- Dorm bed: $40–70
- Slice of pizza: $4
- Food-truck taco: from $3
- Bus or subway ride: $2.75

Midrange
$100–300

- Double room in a mid-range hotel: around $200
- Brunch for two at a mid-range restaurant: $70
- Dinner for two at a mid-range eatery: $130
- Craft cocktail at a lounge bar: $14–18
- Discount TKTS ticket to a Broadway show: $80
- Brooklyn Academy of Music orchestra seats: from $84

Top End
More than $300

- Luxury stay at the NoMad Hotel: $350–850
- Tasting menu at a top-end restaurant: $90–330
- A 1½-hour massage at the atmospheric Great Jones Spa: $205
- Metropolitan Opera orchestra seats: $100–390

Advance Planning

Two months before Secure hotel reservations as soon as possible – prices increase the closer you get to your arrival date. Snag tickets to your favorite Broadway blockbuster.

Three weeks before If you haven't done so already, score a table at your top-choice high-end restaurant.

One week before Surf the web and scan blogs and Twitter for the latest restaurant and bar openings, plus upcoming art exhibitions.

Useful Websites

- **Lonely Planet** (www.lonelyplanet.com/usa/new-york-city) Destination information, hotel bookings, traveler forum and more.
- **NYC: The Official Guide** (www.nycgo.com) New York City's official tourism portal.
- **Explore Brooklyn** (www.explorebk.com) Brooklyn-specific events and listings.
- **New York Magazine** (www.nymag.com) Comprehensive, current listings for bars, restaurants, entertainment and shopping.
- **New York Times** (www.nytimes.com) Excellent local news coverage and theater listings.

Currency
US dollar (US$)

Language
English

Visas
The US Visa Waiver Program allows nationals of 38 countries to enter the US without a visa.

Money
ATMs widely available; credit cards accepted at most hotels, stores and restaurants.

Cell Phones
Most US cell (mobile) phones, besides the iPhone, operate on CDMA, not the European standard GSM – make sure you check compatibility with your phone service provider. There are many stores (mostly run by T-Mobile, Verizon or AT&T) where you can purchase a cheap phone and load it with prepaid minutes, to avoid a long-term contract.

Time
Eastern Standard Time (GMT/UTC minus five hours)

Tourist Information
There are official NYC Visitor Information Centers throughout the city. The main office is in Midtown (p233).

For more, see the **Survival Guide** (p229)

When to Go

Summers can be scorching hot; winters cold and not without their blizzards. Spring or autumn are the best times to explore.

New York City

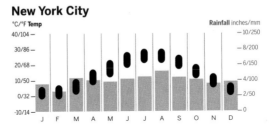

°C/°F **Temp**

Rainfall inches/mm

Arriving in New York

John F Kennedy International Airport (p234) The AirTrain ($5) links to the Metropolitan Transportation Authority's subway ($2.75), which makes the one-hour journey into Manhattan. Express bus to Grand Central or Port Authority costs $18. Shared vans to Manhattan hotels run $20 to $28. Taxis cost a flat rate of $52 excluding tolls and tip.

LaGuardia Airport (p234) This is the closest airport to Manhattan, but the least accessible by public transit: take the Q70 express bus from the airport to the 74th St–Broadway subway station (7 line, or the E, F, M and R lines at the connecting Jackson Heights Roosevelt Ave station). Express bus to Midtown costs $15. Taxis range from $28 to $50 (excluding tolls and tip), depending on traffic.

Newark Liberty International Airport (p235) Take the AirTrain to Newark Airport train station, and board any train bound for New York's Penn Station ($13). Express bus to Port Authority or Grand Central costs $16. Shared shuttle to Midtown costs $20 to $28. Taxis range from $60 to $80 (excluding the unavoidable $13 toll and tip). Allow 45 minutes to one hour of travel time.

Tipping

Tipping is *not* optional; only withhold tips in cases of outrageously bad service.

○ **Airport & hotel porters** $2 per bag, minimum per cart $5.

○ **Bartenders** 15% to 20% per round, minimum $1 per standard drink, and $2 per specialty cocktail.

○ **Hotel maids** $2 to $4 per night, left in an envelope or under the card provided.

○ **Restaurant servers** 18% to 20%, unless a gratuity is already charged on the bill (usually only for groups of five or more).

○ **Taxi drivers** 10% to 15%, rounded up to the next dollar.

Sleeping

In general, accommodation prices in New York City do not abide by any high-season or low-season rules; wavering rates usually reflect availability. With more than 50 million visitors descending upon the city every year, you can expect hotel rooms to fill up quickly – especially in summer. Accommodation options range from boxy cookie-cutter rooms in Midtown high-rises to stylish boutique options downtown. You'll also find a few B&Bs set in residential neighborhoods.

Useful Websites

○ **newyorkhotels.com** (www.newyorkhotels.com)

○ **NYC** (www.nycgo.com/hotels)

○ **Lonely Planet** (lonelyplanet.com/usa/new-york-city/hotels)

Top Days in New York City

EQRDY / SHUTTERSTOCK ©

Midtown & Uptown Icons

Landmarks, highlights, big ticket items: on this itinerary you will experience the NYC of everyone's collective imagination, including the city's most famous museum and park. Take in the mythic landscape of Midtown's concrete and skyscrapers, from the street and from amid the clouds.

Day

01

❶ Breakfast at Café Sabarsky (p137)

Start the morning uptown at the Café Sabarsky, an elegant Viennese-style dining room inside the Neue Galerie. Afterwards, head upstairs into the museum for a look at gorgeous paintings by Gustav Klimt, Paul Klee and other famous Central European artists.

➡ Neue Galerie to Metropolitan Museum of Art

🚶 Travel four blocks south along Fifth Ave.

❷ Metropolitan Museum of Art (p48)

Head over to the big daddy of museums. Delve into the past in the sprawling Ancient Greek and Roman collections. Then check out the Egyptian Wing (including a full-size temple). Afterwards, take in works by European masters on the 2nd floor.

➡ Metropolitan Museum of Art to Central Park

🚶 Walk into Central Park at the 79th St entrance.

DSCITY / SHUTTERSTOCK ©

❸ Central Park (p36)

Get some fresh air in Central Park, the city's spectacular public backyard. Walk south to the Conservatory Pond where toy boats ply the waters.

⊙ Central Park to Times Square

🏃 Exit the park on Fifth Ave however far south you'd like, and grab a cab for Times Square.

❹ Times Square (p62)

Soak up the Vegas-like atmosphere of Times Square from the TKTS Booth and get discounted tickets for that night. Head to the stadium seating at the northern end where you can take in the dazzling tableau.

⊙ Times Square to Rockefeller Center

🏃 For more elbow room, walk up Sixth Ave to 49th St.

❺ Top of the Rock (p84)

Ride to the open-air observation deck at the Top of the Rock in Rockefeller Center for stunning vistas.

⊙ Rockefeller Center to ViceVersa

🏃 It's a half mile walk west along 51st (or the weary can grab a taxi).

❻ Dinner at ViceVersa (p135)

For Broadway-goers, do an early dinner at this polished Italian eatery with a relaxing back patio.

⊙ ViceVersa to Broadway Theater

🏃 Walk east to the theater for which you've already purchased your tickets.

❼ Broadway Theater (p56)

Check out a blockbuster musical for an only-in-New-York spectacle. Afterwards, swig cocktails late into the night at the Edison Hotel's restored piano bar, Rum House (p175).

From left: Neue Galerie (p73); View of Manhattan from the Top of the Rock (p84)

Plan Your Trip
Top Days in New York City

CHRISTOPHE PRENEL / 500PX ©

Lower Manhattan

Surprisingly for this part of downtown dominated by the canyons of Wall St, this day takes in broad horizons and river views, not to mention an iconic historic sight. This itinerary requires a little planning – book your tickets in advance for the Statue of Liberty and Ellis Island.

Day
02

❶ Statue of Liberty & Ellis Island (p40)

Time your arrival with your booked ferry's departure. Ellis Island will likely occupy most of the morning. Food options are poor on the islands, so bring snacks.

⊙ Ellis Island to Hudson Eats

✈ After arriving back in Battery Park, walk about a mile north along the riverfront promenade to the marina.

❷ Lunch at Hudson Eats (p124)

Inside Brookfield Place, you'll find a sprawling food hall, where you can dine on a wide range of delicacies, including sushi, gourmet tacos and French onion soup. Grab a seat by the windows for river views.

⊙ Hudson Eats to One World Trade Center

✈ It's a short stroll up to Vesey St, where you can cross busy West Street on a covered pedestrian overpass. This will put you at the foot of One World Trade Center.

❸ One World Trade Center (p94)

Step into NYC's tallest building and take a futuristic ride up to the One World

Observatory for a magnificent view over the metropolis. Reserve tickets in advance.

⊙ One World Trade Center to the National September 11 Memorial & Museum

🏃 Make the 100-story descent and stroll over to the memorial located next to the building.

❹ National September 11 Memorial & Museum (p90)

One of New York's most powerful sites, this memorial pays moving tribute to the innocent victims of the 2001 terrorist attack. After strolling around the cascades, visit the adjoining museum to learn more about the tragic events that transpired on that day.

⊙ National September 11 Memorial to Brooklyn Bridge

🏃 Walk east on Vesey St Bowery and cut around City Hall Park after crossing Broadway. Walkway access to the bridge is across from the park (and City Hall).

❺ Brooklyn Bridge (p46)

Join the Brooklynites and hordes of other visitors making this magical pilgrimage over one of the city's most beautiful landmarks.

⊙ Brooklyn Bridge to Empire Fulton Ferry State Park

🏃 Walk over the bridge from Manhattan to Brooklyn. Take the stairs and turn left at the bottom. Walk downhill to the waterfront.

❻ Empire Fulton Ferry State Park (p108)

This lovely park has staggering views of Manhattan and the Brooklyn Bridge, and a fully restored 1922 carousel. The atmospheric brick streets behind are sprinkled with cafes, shops and 19th-century warehouses.

⊙ Empire Fulton Ferry State Park to Juliana's

🏃 Walk up Old Fulton St to the corner of Front St.

❼ Dinner at Juliana's (p139)

Don't miss the legendary thin-crust pies by pizza maestro Patsy Grimaldi. The classic margherita is one of New York's best.

From left: Statue of Liberty (p40); One World Observatory (p95)

Top Days in New York City

N.CN STARICHENKO / SHUTTERSTOCK ©

West Side Culture

A famed green way, galleries, market adventures and one spectacular museum set the stage for a fun day's ramble on the West Side. Cap off the day at Lincoln Center, the stunning campus of some of the country's top performance spaces.

❶ The High Line (p52)

Take a taxi to the stroll-worthy High Line, an abandoned railway 30ft above the street, now one of New York's favorite downtown destinations. Enter at 30th St and walk the meandering path for views of the Hudson River and the city streets below.

➲ The High Line to Chelsea Galleries

🏃 Exit at the 26th St stairway and explore the surrounding neighborhood on foot.

❷ Chelsea Galleries (p112)

One of the hubs of the city's art-gallery scene, here you can ogle works by up-and-comers and established artists alike, and maybe even take home an expensive souvenir.

➲ Chelsea Galleries to Chelsea Market

🏃 Walk to Ninth Ave and south to 15th St.

❸ Lunch at Chelsea Market (p130)

This building, a former cookie factory, has a huge concourse packed with food stalls slinging everything from spicy Korean noo-

dle soups to Aussie-style sausage rolls, plus shops selling freshly baked goods, wines, imported cheeses and other temptations.

➡ Chelsea Market to American Museum of Natural History

🚇 Grab an uptown C train at Eighth Ave and 14th St and take it to 86th and Central Park West.

4 American Museum of Natural History (p79)

No matter what your age, you'll experience childlike wonder at the exceptional American Museum of Natural History. Be sure to save time for the Rose Center for Earth & Space, a unique architectural gem.

➡ American Museum of Natural History to Barcibo Enoteca

🚶 Walk west to Amsterdam Ave and turn south; veer left on Broadway at 71st St.

5 Drink at Barcibo Enoteca (p176)

Stop in for a pre-show glass of Italian wine, or go for some grub if you're seeing a full-length show.

➡ Barcibo Enoteca to Lincoln Center

🚶 Walk south on Broadway to 63rd St.

6 Lincoln Center (p76)

Head to the Lincoln Center for opera at the Metropolitan Opera House (p189), the largest in the world, a symphony in Avery Fisher Hall, or a play at one of its two theaters – a promise of a great show in an architecturally mesmerizing setting.

➡ Lincoln Center to Burke & Wills

🚇 Take the No 1 train two stops to 79th St and walk half a block east.

7 Burke & Wills (p138)

After a show, head further uptown to this gastronomic hotspot for a post-performance meal with drinks. Feast on rack of lamb or roasted prawns, while sipping Australian wines or craft brews.

From left: Chelsea Market (p130); Lincoln Center (p76)

Top Days in New York City

EUVENLARGE / GETTY IMAGES ©

Downtown East

Gain insight into immigrant history, grab ethnic eats, check out cutting-edge art and theater (as well as cheap booze and live music), and walk up and down the tiny blocks to peek into stylish boutiques. As a general rule, the further east you go the looser things get.

Day

04

❶ Lower East Side Tenement Museum (p98)

Gain a fantastic insight into the life and shockingly cramped living conditions of immigrants during the 19th and early 20th centuries at this brilliantly curated museum.

⊙ Lower East Side Tenement Museum to Little Italy

🚶 Walk west on Delancey St through Sara D Roosevelt Park to Mulberry St.

❷ Little Italy (p89)

Although it feels more like a theme park than an authentic Italian strip, Mulberry St is still the heart of the hood. Afterwards, stroll further up Mulberry to the boutiques and hip little cafes of Nolita.

⊙ Little Italy to Butcher's Daughter

🚶 Walk two blocks north along Mulberry and turn right onto Kenmare; it's another two blocks further.

❸ Lunch at Butcher's Daughter (p125)

Grab a bite at this delightful earth-friendly eatery in Nolita. The vegan cafe serves up

creative, healthy dishes that also happen to be delicious. Add in craft beer and sidewalk dining, and you may find yourself whiling away the whole afternoon here.

🔵 Butcher's Daughter to New Museum of Contemporary Art

🏃 Walk several blocks east to Bowery and turn north.

❹ New Museum of Contemporary Art (p101)

Symbolic of the once-gritty Bowery's transformation, this ubercontemporary museum has a steady menu of edgy works in new forms. Stop by the bookstore with its eclectic mix of cutting-edge publications.

🔵 New Museum of Contemporary Art to Chinatown

🏃 Turn right on Delancey and then left on Mott St until you reach Canal St.

❺ Chinatown (p86)

Take an afternoon stroll through one of New York's most vibrant districts. The teeming streets of Chinatown are lined with dumpling houses, Chinese bakeries, fish markets, veg-etable stands, massage parlors and colorful shops selling everything under the sun.

🔵 Chinatown to New York Theatre Workshop

🚗 Catch a cab for the 1-mile ride up the Bowery to E 4th St.

❻ New York Theatre Workshop (p185)

A showcase for contemporary and cutting-edge fare, this much-lauded performance space is a great spot to see a show.

🔵 New York Theatre Workshop to Degustation

🏃 It's an easy stroll around the corner to Degustation on E 5th St.

❼ Dinner at Degustation (p128)

An intimate eatery with a strong local following, Degustation is the place for decadent flavors that blend old world recipes with new world creativity. Afterwards, you're well-placed for exploring the bar scene in the East Village.

From left: Lower East Side Tenement Museum (p98); Mulberry Street in Little Italy (p89)

Plan Your Trip
Hotspots For...

CULTURE VULTURES

GLITZ & GLAMOUR

☆ **Broadway** (pictured below) Book seats to an award-winning show starring some of the best actors in show business. (p56)

◉ **Frick Collection** This Gilded Age mansion has Vermeers, El Grecos and Goyas and a stunning courtyard fountain. (p73)

🛍 **Barneys** The fashionista's aspirational closet comes with a hefty price tag. (p156)

✗ **Eleven Madison Park** Arresting, cutting-edge cuisine laced with unexpected whimsy. (p132)

🍷 **Bar SixtyFive** Raise a glass to the glittering views over Manhattan from this elegant spot in Rockefeller Center. (p173)

◉ **MoMA** (pictured above) NYC's darling museum has brilliantly curated spaces boasting the best of the world's modern art. (p48)

◉ **Metropolitan Museum of Art** The most encyclopedic museum in the Americas. (p70)

✗ **Cookshop** Great indoor-outdoor dining spot near the heart of Chelsea's gallery scene. (p129)

🍷 **Barcibo Enoteca** Go-to spot for wine lovers before or after a show at the nearby Lincoln Center. (p176)

☆ **Brooklyn Academy of Music** This hallowed theater hosts cutting-edge works, particularly during its celebrated Next Wave Festival. (p190)

HISTORY BUFFS

◉ **Lower East Side Tenement Museum** Fascinating insight into how the 19th and early-20th century immigrants lived, on a tour of a preserved tenement. (p98)

☆ **Hamilton** An American history lesson set to urban rhythms. (p59)

◉ **Ellis Island** The gateway to freedom and opportunity for so many of America's immigrants. (p41)

✕ **Chumley's** A former speakeasy with Prohibition-era decor and a first-rate seasonal menu. (p131)

♟ **Lantern's Keep** Classic, elegant libations in a historic Midtown hotel. (p173)

CRAFTY CREATIVES

◉ **Chelsea Galleries** (pictured above) Hit a few evening art openings in the epicenter of NYC's art world. (p112)

◉ **MoMA PS1** Former schoolhouse turned art museum with cutting-edge exhibitions and great summer parties. (p116)

✕ **Foragers Table** A triumph of farm-to-table cooking with flavorful sustainable recipes in Chelsea. (p130)

🔒 **Brooklyn Flea** Crafts, clothing, records and other essential gear, plus great food stalls. (p152)

♟ **Apothéke** Apothecary turned cocktail lounge hidden deep in Chinatown. (p167)

ACTIVE OUTDOORS

◉ **The High Line** Wild plants and towering weeds steal the show. (p52)

◉ **Prospect Park** (pictured above) Escape the crowds at Brooklyn's gorgeous park, with trails, hills, a canal, lake and meadows. (p102)

♟ **Pier 66 Maritime** Festive open-air eating and drinking space jutting out over the Hudson. (p171)

🔒 **Union Square Greenmarket** Assemble a picnic from the lovely produce and gourmet goodies at this outdoor market. (p130)

Plan Your Trip
What's New

Whitney Museum of American Art

At the southern end of the High Line the Whitney Museum (p55), inside a new Renzo Piano–designed building, remains the talk of the town. The light-filled galleries bring more space and innovation to downtown's most impressive art center.

Mindful Dining

With increased awareness of the devastation of animal agriculture, growing numbers of New Yorkers are embracing a vegan diet. You'll find outstanding dishes at new hot spots like El Rey (p126) and Dimes (p127).

Market Madness

The love for food markets shows no signs of abating, with sprawling new foodie halls, including Gansevoort Market (p128).

National Sawdust Company

Williamsburg's newest performing arts theater (Map p255; www.nationalsawdust.org; 80 N 6th St, at Wythe Ave, Williamsburg) stages an inspiring mix of genre-bending concerts and artist showcases. The futuristic hall has outstanding acoustics.

St Ann's Warehouse

Speaking of theaters, St Ann's Warehouse (p190) has opened its doors in its first-ever permanent location under the Brooklyn Bridge. Expect to see more cutting-edge programming.

One World Trade Center

The tallest building in New York now looms high above Lower Manhattan. While you can admire its jewel-like facade from afar, the best view is up top from the magnificent observatory (p95) on the 102nd floor.

Uptown Allure

Downtown cool is finally arriving in both the Upper West and Upper East Sides, with a sprinkling of craft brew pubs (West End Hall; p176) and creative cocktail dens (Daisy; p175).

Above: Whitney Museum of American Art (p55)

Plan Your Trip
For Free

DROP OF LIGHT / SHUTTERSTOCK ©

Free New York City

The Big Apple isn't exactly the world's cheapest destination. Nevertheless, there are many ways to kick open the NYC treasure chest without spending a dime – free concerts, theater and film screenings, pay-what-you-wish nights at legendary museums, city festivals, free ferry rides and kayaking, plus loads of green space.

Summertime Events

In summer there are scores of free events around town. From June through early September, SummerStage (p11) features more than 100 free performances at 17 parks around the city, including Central Park. You'll have to be tenacious to get tickets to Shakespeare in the Park (p10), also held in Central Park, but it's well worth the effort. Top actors such as Meryl Streep and Al Pacino have taken the stage in years past. Prospect Park has its own venerable open-air summer concert and events series: **Celebrate Brooklyn** (www.bricarts media.org/performing-arts/ celebrate-brooklyn).

Summertime also brings free film screenings and events to the water's edge during the River to River Festival (p11) at Hudson River Park in Manhattan and at Brooklyn Bridge Park (p106). Another great option for film lovers is the free **Bryant Park** (Map p250; www.bryant park.org) film screenings on Monday nights.

On the Water

The free Staten Island Ferry (p236) provides magical views of the Statue of Liberty, and you can enjoy it with a cold beer (available on the boat). On summer weekends, you can also take a free ferry over to Governors Island (p109), a car-free oasis with priceless views.

For a bit more adventure, take out a free kayak, available in the Hudson River Park (p55), Brooklyn Bridge Park (p106) and Red Hook (p202).

Best Free Museum Days

New Museum of Contemporary Art (p101) 7–9pm Thur

MoMA (p48) 4–8pm Fri

Guggenheim Museum (p80) 5:45–7:45pm Sat

Frick Collection (p73) 11am–1pm Sun

Whitney Museum of American Art (p55) 7-10pm Fri

Above: Staten Island Ferry (p236)

Plan Your Trip
Family Travel

A RUIZ / SHUTTERSTOCK ©

Need to Know

○ **Change Facilities** Not common in bars and restaurants.

○ **Strollers** Not allowed on buses unless folded up.

○ **Transportation** Subway stairs can be challenging with strollers; taxis are exempt from car-seat laws.

○ **Useful Website** Time Out New York Kids (www.timeout.com/new-york-kids) has helpful tips.

Sights & Activities

Museums, especially those geared toward kids, such as the **Children's Museum of the Arts** (www.cmany.org) and the American Museum of Natural History (p79), are always great places, as are children's theaters, movie theaters, book and toy stores, and aquariums. The city is dotted with vintage carousels; rides cost from $2 to $3.

The boat ride to the Statue of Liberty (p40) offers the opportunity to chug around New York Harbor and to get to know an icon that most kids only know from textbooks.

The city has a number of zoos. The best, by far, is the **Bronx Zoo** (www.bronxzoo.com); otherwise, if you're pressed for time, the **Central Park Zoo** (www.centralparkzoo.com) will keep the tots entertained.

Central Park (p36) also has more than 800 acres of green space, a lake that can be navigated by rowboat, a carousel and a massive statue of Alice in Wonderland. Heckscher playground, near Seventh Ave and Central Park South, is the biggest and best of its 21 playgrounds.

With hot dogs, vintage coasters and an open stretch of beach, **Coney Island** (www.coneyisland.com) is just what the doctor ordered if the family is in need of some fun in the sun.

NATTHAWONPHISIT BURARAIRAI / SHUTTERSTOCK ©

Transportation

The biggest pitfalls tend to revolve around public transportation, as a startling lack of subway-station elevators will have you lugging strollers up and down flights of stairs (though you can avoid the turnstile by getting buzzed through an easy-access gate); visit http://web.mta.info/accessibility/stations.htm to find a guide to subway stations with elevators. Regarding fares, anyone over 44 inches is supposed to pay full fare, but the rule is rarely enforced.

Babysitting

While most major hotels (and a handful of boutique-style places) offer on-site baby-sitting services – or can at least provide you with referrals – you could also turn to a local childcare organization. **Baby Sitters' Guild** (www.babysittersguild.com), established in 1940 specifically to serve travelers who are staying in hotels with children, has a stable of sitters who speak a range of 16

 Best Parks for Families

Central Park (p36)

Brooklyn Bridge Park (p106)

Hudson River Park (p55)

The High Line (p52)

languages. All are carefully screened, most are CPR–certified and many have nursing backgrounds; they'll come to your hotel room and even bring games and arts-and-crafts projects. Prices start at $35 per hour.

From left: Central Park (p36); Jane's Carousel, Brooklyn Bridge Park (p108)

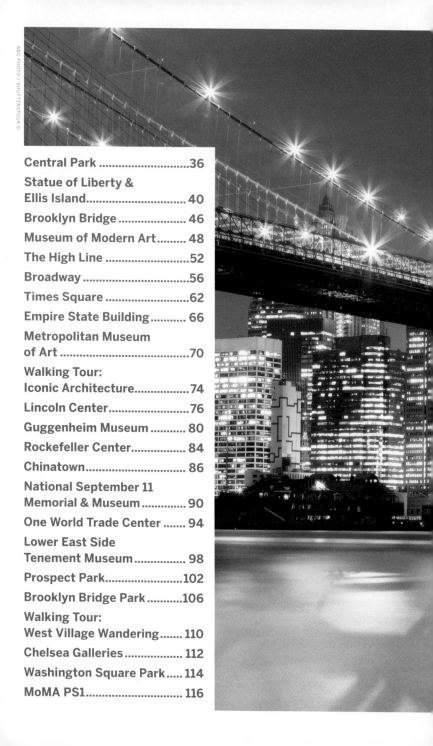

TOP EXPERIENCES

The very best to see and do

Conservatory Water, Central Park

Central Park

Lush lawns, cool forests, flowering gardens, glassy bodies of water and meandering, wooded paths provide a dose of serene nature amid the urban rush of New York City. Today, this 'people's park' is still one of the city's most popular attractions, beckoning throngs of New Yorkers with concerts, events and wildlife.

Great For...

ⓘ Need to Know

(Map p252; www.centralparknyc.org; 59th to 110th Sts, btwn Central Park West & Fifth Ave; ⊘6am-1am; 🚇)

★ **Top Tip**

To escape the crowds, try the North Meadow (north of 97th St) or the Harlem Meer.

Like the city's subway system, the vast and majestic Central Park, an 843-acre rectangle of open space in the middle of Manhattan, is a great class leveler – which is exactly what it was envisioned to be. Created in the 1860s and '70s by Frederick Law Olmsted and Calvert Vaux on the marshy northern fringe of the city, the immense park was designed as a leisure space for all New Yorkers, regardless of color, class or creed.

Olmsted and Vaux (who also created Prospect Park in Brooklyn) were determined to keep foot and road traffic separate and cleverly designed the crosstown transverses under elevated roads to do so.

Throughout the year, visitors find free outdoor concerts at the Great Lawn, precious animals at the Central Park Wildlife Center and top-notch drama at the annual Shakespeare in the Park productions, held

each summer at the open-air Delacorte Theater. Some other recommended stops include the ornate Bethesda Fountain, which edges the Lake, and its Loeb Boathouse, where you can rent rowboats or enjoy lunch at an outdoor cafe; the Shakespeare Garden (west side between 79th & 80th Sts), which has lush plantings and excellent skyline views; and the Ramble (mid-park from 73rd to 79th Sts), a wooded thicket that's popular with birdwatchers. While parts of the park swarm with joggers, in-line skaters, musicians and tourists on warm weekends, it's quieter on weekday afternoons – but especially in less well-trodden spots above 72nd St such as the Harlem Meer and the North Meadow (north of 97th St).

Folks flock to the park even in winter, when snowstorms can inspire cross-

Trio of musicians near Bethesda Fountain

country skiing and sledding or a simple stroll through the white wonderland, and crowds turn out every New Year's Eve for a midnight run. The **Central Park Conservancy** (Map p252; ☎212-310-6600; www.centralparknyc.org/tours; 14 E 60th St, btwn Madison & Fifth Aves; [S]N/R/W to 5th Ave-59th St) offers ever-changing guided tours of the park, including those that focus on public art, wildlife, and places of interest to kids.

Strawberry Fields

This tear-shaped garden serves as a memorial to former Beatle John Lennon. It is composed of a grove of stately elms and a tiled mosaic that reads, simply, 'Imagine.'

☑ Don't Miss

Tours with the Central Park Conservancy; many are free, others cost $15.

T.SLACK / SHUTTERSTOCK ©

Bethesda Terrace & Mall

The arched walkways of Bethesda Terrace, crowned by the magnificent Bethesda Fountain, have long been a gathering area for New Yorkers of all flavors. To the south is the Mall (featured in countless movies), a promenade shrouded in mature North American elms. The southern stretch, known as Literary Walk, is flanked by statues of famous authors.

Conservatory Water & Around

North of the zoo at the level of 74th St is the Conservatory Water, where model sailboats drift lazily and kids scramble about on a toadstool-studded statue of Alice in Wonderland. There are Saturday story hours at the Hans Christian Andersen statue to the west of the water.

Great Lawn & Around

The Great Lawn is a massive emerald carpet at the center of the park – between 79th and 86th Sts – and is surrounded by ball fields and London plane trees. Immediately to the southeast is the Delacorte Theater, home to the annual Shakespeare in the Park festival, as well as Belvedere Castle, a lookout.

What's Nearby?

American Folk Art Museum Museum

(Map p252; ☎212-595-9533; www.folkartmuseum.org; 2 Lincoln Sq, Columbus Ave, at W 66th St; ⏰11:30am-7pm Tue-Thu & Sat, noon-7:30pm Fri, noon-6pm Sun; [S]1 to 66th St-Lincoln Center) [FREE] This tiny institution contains a couple of centuries' worth of folk and outsider art treasures, including pieces by Henry Darger (known for his girl-filled battlescapes) and Martín Ramírez (producer of hallucinatory *caballeros* on horseback). There is also an array of wood carvings, paintings, hand-tinted photographs and decorative objects.

🍴 Take a Break

Class things up with an afternoon martini at the **Loeb Boathouse** (Map p252; ☎212-517-2233; www.thecentralparkboathouse.com).

MICHELE FALZONE / GETTY IMAGES ©

Statue of Liberty & Ellis Island

Stellar skyline views, a scenic ferry ride, a lookout from Lady Liberty's crown, and a moving tribute to America's immigrants at Ellis Island – unmissable is an understatement.

Great For...

☑ **Don't Miss**

The breathtaking views from Lady Liberty's crown (remember to reserve tickets well in advance).

Statue of Liberty

A Powerful Symbol

Lady Liberty has been gazing sternly towards 'unenlightened Europe' since 1886. Dubbed the 'Mother of Exiles,' the statue symbolically admonishes the rigid social structures of the old world. 'Give me your tired, your poor, your huddled masses yearning to breathe free, the wretched refuse of your teeming shore' she declares in Emma Lazarus' famous 1883 poem 'The New Colossus.'

History of the Statue

Conceived as early as 1865 by French intellectual Edouard Laboulaye as a monument to the republican principles shared by France and the USA, the Statue of Liberty is still generally recognized as a symbol for at

OLEGALBINSKY / GETTY IMAGES ©

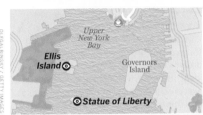

Upper New York Bay

Ellis Island ◎

Governors Island

◎ **Statue of Liberty**

ℹ Need to Know

(☎212-363-3200, tickets 877-523-9849; www.nps.gov/stli; Liberty Island; adult/child incl Ellis Island $18.50/9, incl crown $21.50/12; ⊙8:30am-5:30pm, check website for seasonal changes; ⒮1 to South Ferry or 4/5 to Bowling Green, then ⛴to Liberty Island)

✕ Take a Break

Pack a picnic or chow beforehand at the Hudson Eats (p124) food hall.

★ Top Tip

Pick up a free audioguide when you reach Liberty Island; there's even a kid's version.

least the ideals of opportunity and freedom to many. French sculptor Frédéric-Auguste Bartholdi traveled to New York in 1871 to select the site, then spent more than 10 years in Paris designing and making the 151ft-tall figure Liberty Enlightening the World. It was then shipped to New York, erected on a small island in the harbor and unveiled in 1886. Structurally, it consists of an iron skeleton (designed by Gustave Eiffel) with a copper skin attached to it by stiff but flexible metal bars.

Visiting the Statue

Access to the crown is limited, so reservations are required. Book as far in advance as possible (additional $3). Pedestal access is also limited, so reserve in advance (no additional fee). Keep in mind, there's no elevator and the climb from the base is

equal to a 22-story building. Otherwise, a visit means you can wander the grounds and enjoy the view of Lady Liberty from all sides (plus the great views of Manhattan). A free audioguide (available upon arrival to the island) provides historical details and little-known facts about the statue.

The trip to Liberty Island, via ferry, is usually made in conjunction with nearby Ellis Island. Ferries leave from **Battery Park** (Map p244; www.nycgovparks.org; Broadway, at Battery Pl; ⊙sunrise-1am; ⒮4/5 to Bowling Green, R to Whitehall St, 1 to South Ferry) and tickets include admission to both sights. Reserve in advance to cut down on long wait times.

Ellis Island

Ellis Island (☎212-363-3200, tickets 877-523-9849; www.nps.gov/elis; ferry incl Statue of Liberty adult/child $18.50/9; ⊙9:30am-3:30pm; ⒮1 to South Ferry or 4/5 to Bowling Green, then ⛴to Ellis Island) is America's most famous and historically important gateway – the very spot where old-world despair met new-world promise. Between 1892 and 1924, more than 12 million immigrants passed through this processing station, their dreams in tow. An estimated 40% of Americans today have at least one ancestor who was processed here, confirming the major role this tiny harbor island has played in the making of modern America.

Main Building Architecture

With their Main Building, architects Edward Lippincott Tilton and William A Boring created a suitably impressive and imposing 'prologue' to America. The designing duo won the contract after the original wooden building burnt down in 1897. Having attended the Ecole des Beaux Arts in Paris, it's not surprising that they opted for a beaux-arts aesthetic for the project. The building

evokes a grand train station, with majestic triple-arched entrances, decorative Flemish bond brickwork, and granite quoins (cornerstones) and belvederes.

Inside, it's the 2nd-floor, 338ft-long Registry Room (also known as the Great Hall) that takes the breath away. It was under its beautiful vaulted ceiling that the newly arrived lined up to have their documents checked, and that the polygamists, paupers, criminals and anarchists were turned back. The original plaster ceiling was severely damaged by an explosion of munition barges at nearby Black Tom Wharf. It was a blessing in disguise, the rebuilt version was adorned with striking, herringbone-patterned tiles by Rafael Guastavino. The Catalan-born engineer is also behind the beautiful tiled ceiling at the Grand Central Oyster Bar & Restaurant at Grand Central Terminal.

Ellis Island National Museum of Immigration

Main Building Restoration

After a $160 million restoration, the Main Building was reopened to the public as the Ellis Island National Museum of Immigration in 1990. Now anybody who rides the ferry to the island can experience a cleaned-up, modern version of the historic new-arrival experience, the museum's interactive exhibits paying homage to the hope, jubilation and sometimes bitter disappointment of the millions who came here in search of a new beginning. Among them were Hungarian Erik Weisz (Harry Houdini), Rodolfo Gugliel- mi (Rudolph Valentino) and Brit Archibald Alexander Leach (Cary Grant).

Immigration Museum Exhibits

The museum's exhibits are spread over three levels. To get the most out of your visit, opt for the 50-minute self-guided audio tour (free with ferry ticket, available from the museum lobby). Featuring narratives from a number of sources, including historians, architects and the immigrants themselves, the tour brings to life the museum's hefty collection of personal objects, official documents, photographs and film footage. It's an evocative experience to relive personal memories – both good and bad – in the very halls and corridors in which they occurred.

The collection itself is divided into a number of permanent and temporary exhibitions. If you're very short on time, skip the 'Journeys: The Peopling of America 1550–1890' exhibit on the 1st floor and focus on the 2nd floor. It's here that you'll find the two most fascinating exhibitions. The first, 'Through America's Gate,' examines the step-by-step process faced by the newly arrived, including the chalk-marking of those suspected of illness, a wince-inducing eye examination, and 29 questions in the beautiful, vaulted Registry Room. The second, 'Peak Immigration Years,' explores the motives behind the immigrants' journeys and the challenges they faced once free to begin their new American lives. Particularly interesting is the collection of old photographs, which offers intimate glimpses into the daily lives of these courageous new Americans.

For a history of the rise, fall and resurrection of the building itself, make time for the 'Restoring a Landmark' exhibition on the 3rd floor; its tableaux of trashed desks, chairs and other abandoned possessions are strangely haunting. Best of all, the audio tour offers optional, in-depth coverage for those wanting to delve deeper into the collections and the island's history. If you don't feel like opting for the audio tour, you can always pick up one of the phones in each display area and listen to the recorded, yet affecting memories of real Ellis Island immigrants, taped in the 1980s.

> ### ★ Did You Know?
> The robed statue represents Libertas, the Roman goddess of freedom. The tablet she holds is inscribed with the date of America's declaration of independence (July 4, 1776).

TOOYKRUB / SHUTTERSTOCK ©

Another option is the free, 45-minute guided tour with a park ranger. If booked three weeks in advance by phone, the tour is also available in American sign language.

American Immigrant Wall of Honor & Fort Gibson Ruins

Accessible from the 1st-floor 'Journeys: The Peopling of America 1550–1890' exhibit is the outdoor American Immigrant Wall of Honor, inscribed with the names of more than 700,000 immigrants. Believed to be the world's longest wall of names, it's a fund-raising project, allowing any American to have an immigrant relative's name recorded for the cost of a donation. Construction of the wall in the 1990s uncovered the remains of the island's original structure, Fort Gibson – you can see the ruins at the southwestern corner of the memorial. Built in 1808, the fortification was part of a harbor-defense system against the British that also included Castle Clinton in Battery Park and Castle Williams on Governors Island. During this time, Ellis Island measured a modest 3.3 acres of sand and slush. Between 1892 and 1934, the island expanded dramatically thanks to landfill brought in from the ballast of ships and construction of the city's subway system.

What's Nearby?

Ferries depart from Battery Park. Nearby attractions include the following museums.

Museum of Jewish Heritage   Museum

(Map p244; 646-437-4202; www.mjhnyc. org; 36 Battery Pl; adult/child $12/free, 4-8pm Wed free; 10am-5:45pm Sun-Tue & Thu, to 8pm Wed, to 5pm Fri mid-Mar–mid-Nov, to 3pm Fri rest of year; ; S4/5 to Bowling Green, R to Whitehall St) An evocative waterfront museum, exploring all aspects of modern Jewish identity and culture, from religious traditions to artistic accomplishments. The museum's core exhibition includes a detailed exploration of the Holocaust, with personal artifacts, photographs and documentary films providing a personal,

moving experience. Outdoors is the Garden of Stones installation. Created by artist Andy Goldsworthy and dedicated to those who lost loved ones in the Holocaust, its 18 boulders form a narrow pathway for contemplating the fragility of life.

The building itself consists of six sides and three tiers to symbolize the Star of David and the six million Jews who perished in WWII. Exhibitions aside, the venue also hosts films, music concerts, ongoing lecture series and special holiday performances. Frequent, free workshops for families with children are also on offer, while the on-site, kosher cafe serves light food.

National Museum of the American Indian   Museum

(Map p244; 212-514-3700; www.nmai.si.edu; 1 Bowling Green; 10am-5pm Fri-Wed, to 8pm Thu;

Statues outside the National Museum of the American Indian

S 4/5 to Bowling Green, R to Whitehall St) FREE
An affiliate of the Smithsonian Institution, this elegant tribute to Native American culture is set in Cass Gilbert's spectacular 1907 Custom House, one of NYC's finest beaux-arts buildings. Beyond a vast elliptical rotunda, sleek galleries play host to changing exhibitions documenting Native American art, culture, life and beliefs. The museum's permanent collection includes stunning decorative arts, textiles and ceremonial objects that document the diverse native cultures across the Americas.

The four giant female sculptures outside the building are the work of Daniel Chester French, who would go on to sculpt the seated Abraham Lincoln at Washington, DC's Lincoln Memorial. Representing (from left to right) Asia, North America, Europe and Africa, the figures offer a revealing look at America's world view at the beginning of the 20th century; Asia 'bound' by its religions, America 'youthful and virile,' Europe 'wise yet decaying' and Africa 'asleep and barbaric.' The museum also hosts a range of cultural programs, including dance and music performances, readings for children, craft demonstrations, films and workshops. The museum shop is well-stocked with Native American jewelry, books, CDs and crafts.

★ Mayor in the House

One of NYC's most famous mayors worked at Ellis Island before going into politics. Fluent in Italian, Croatian and Yiddish, Fiorello LaGuardia worked as a translator while attending NYU law school at night.

ANAGLIC/SHUTTERSTOCK ©

GAGLIARDIIMAGES / SHUTTERSTOCK ©

Brooklyn Bridge

Marianne Moore's description of the world's first suspension bridge – which, even before its completion, inspired poets from Walt Whitman to Jack Kerouac – as a 'climactic ornament, a double rainbow' is perhaps most evocative.

Great For...

☑ **Don't Miss**

An early morning stroll over the bridge – a magical time to take in the view.

A New York icon, the Brooklyn Bridge was the world's first steel suspension bridge. Indeed, when it opened in 1883, the 1596ft span between its two support towers was the longest in history. Although its construction was fraught with disaster, the bridge became a magnificent example of urban design, inspiring poets, writers and painters. Today, its pedestrian walkway – which begins just east of City Hall – delivers a soul-stirring view of lower Manhattan.

Construction

Ironically, one man deprived of this view was the bridge's very designer, John Roebling. The Prussian-born engineer was knocked off a pier in Fulton Landing in June 1869, dying of tetanus poisoning before construction of the Brooklyn Bridge even began. Consequently, his son, Washington

Need to Know

(Map p244; [S]4/5/6 to Brooklyn Bridge-City Hall, J/Z to Chambers St, R to City Hall)

🍴 Take a Break

For classic and specialty thin-crust pizzas, head to Juliana's (p139).

★ Top Tip

Crowds can be thick. Don't try riding a bike across unless going in the early morning or at night.

Roebling, supervised its construction, which lasted 14 years and managed to survive budget overruns and the deaths of 20 workers. The younger Roebling himself suffered from the bends while helping to excavate the riverbed for the bridge's western tower and remained bedridden for much of the project; his wife, Emily, oversaw construction in his stead. There was one final tragedy to come in June 1883, when the bridge opened to pedestrian traffic. Someone in the crowd shouted, perhaps as a joke, that the bridge was collapsing into the river, setting off a mad rush in which 12 people were trampled to death.

Crossing the Bridge

Walking across the grand Brooklyn Bridge is a rite of passage for New Yorkers and visitors alike – with this in mind, walk no more than two abreast or else you're in danger of colliding with runners and speeding cyclists. And take care to stay on the side of the walkway marked for folks on foot, and not in the bike lane.

The bridge walk is 1.3 miles (2km), but allow around an hour in either direction to stop and soak up the views.

What's Nearby?

Just north of the Manhattan-side access to the bridge lies Chinatown (p86). On the Brooklyn side, you're a short stroll from Dumbo and Brooklyn Bridge Park (p106).

Dumbo Neighborhood

Dumbo's nickname is an acronym for its location: 'Down Under the Manhattan Bridge Overpass,' and while this north Brooklyn slice of waterfront used to be strictly for industry, it's now the domain of high-end condos, furniture shops and art galleries. Several highly regarded performing-arts spaces are located in the cobblestone streets and the Empire Fulton Ferry State Park (p108) hugs the waterfront and offers picture-postcard Manhattan views.

ANTON_IVANOV / SHUTTERSTOCK ©

Museum of Modern Art

Quite possibly the greatest hoarder of modern masterpieces on earth, the Museum of Modern Art (MoMA) is a cultural promised land. With a vast collection, a scenic sculptural garden, and some of the best temporary shows in New York City, the MoMA is a thrilling crash course in all that is beautiful and addictive about art.

Great For...

☑ Don't Miss

The sculpture garden makes a fine retreat when you have gallery fatigue.

Since its founding in 1929, the museum has amassed almost 200,000 artworks, documenting the emerging creative ideas and movements of the late 19th century through to those that dominate today. For art buffs, it's Valhalla. For the uninitiated, it's a thrilling crash course in all that is beautiful and addictive about art.

Visiting MoMA

It's easy to get lost in MoMA's vast collection. To maximize your time and create a plan of attack, download the museum's free smartphone app from the website beforehand. MoMA's permanent collection spans four levels, with prints, illustrated books and the unmissable Contemporary Galleries on level two; architecture, design, drawings and photography on level three; and painting and sculpture on levels four

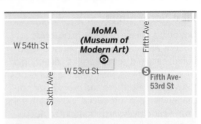

❶ Need to Know

(MoMA; Map p252; ☏212-708-9400; www.
moma.org; 11 W 53rd St, btwn Fifth & Sixth
Aves; adult/child $25/free, 4-8pm Fri free;
⊙10:30am-5:30pm Sat-Thu, to 8pm Fri; 👶;
ⓢE/M to 5th Ave-53rd St)

✕ Take a Break

For a casual vibe, nosh on Italian-
inspired fare at MoMA's **Cafe 2** (☏212-
333-1299; www.momacafes.com; Museum of
Modern Art, 2nd fl; sandwiches & salads $12-
14, mains $19; ⊙11am-5pm, to 7:30pm Fri).

> ### ★ Top Tip
> **Keep your museum ticket handy,
> as it also provides free entry to film
> screenings and MoMA PS1 (p116).**

and five. Many of the big hitters are on
these last two levels, so tackle the museum
from the top down before the fatigue sets
in. Must-sees include Van Gogh's *Starry
Night,* Cézanne's *The Bather,* Picasso's *Les
Demoiselles d'Avignon,* and Henri Rous-
seau's *The Sleeping Gypsy,* not to mention
iconic American works such as Warhol's
Campbell's Soup Cans and *Gold Marilyn
Monroe,* Lichtenstein's equally poptastic
Girl With Ball, and Hopper's haunting *House
by the Railroad.*

Abstract Expressionism

One of the greatest strengths of MoMA's
collections is abstract expressionism, a
radical movement that emerged in New
York in the 1940s and boomed a decade
later. Defined by its penchant for irrev-
erent individualism and monumentally

scaled works, this so-called 'New York
School' helped turn the metropolis into *the*
epicenter of Western contemporary art.
Among the stars are Rothko's *Magenta,
Black, Green on Orange,* Pollock's *One
(Number 31, 1950)* and de Kooning's
Painting.

Lunchtime Talks

To delve a little deeper into MoMA's collection, join one of the museum's lunchtime
talks and readings, which see writers,
artists, curators and designers offering
expert insight into specific works and exhibitions on view. The talks take place daily at
11:30am and 1:30pm. To check upcoming
topics, click the 'Exhibitions & Events' link
on the MoMA website.

Film Screenings

Not only a palace of visual art, MoMA screens an incredibly well-rounded selection of celluloid gems from its collection of over 22,000 films, including the works of the Maysles Brothers and every Pixar animation film ever produced. Expect anything from Academy Award–nominated documentary shorts and Hollywood classics, to experimental works and international retrospectives. Best of all, your museum ticket will get you in for free.

What's Nearby
Radio City
Music Hall   Historic Building
(Map p252; www.radiocity.com; 1260 Sixth Ave, at W 51st St; tours adult/child $27/20; ⊗tours 9:30am-5pm; ⟳; ⟪S⟫ B/D/F/M to 47th-50th

Sts-Rockefeller Center) This spectacular Moderne movie palace was the brainchild of vaudeville producer Samuel Lionel 'Roxy' Rothafel. Never one for understatement, Roxy launched his venue on December 23, 1932 with an over-the-top extravaganza that included camp dance troupe the Roxyettes (mercifully renamed the Rockettes). Guided tours (75 minutes) of the sumptuous interiors include the glorious auditorium, Witold Gordon's classically inspired mural *History of Cosmetics* in the Women's Downstairs Lounge, and the *très* exclusive VIP Roxy Suite.

As far as catching a show here goes, be warned: the vibe doesn't quite match the theater's glamour these days. That said, there are often some fabulous talents in the lineup, with past performers including Rufus Wainwright, Aretha Franklin and Dolly

Radio City Music Hall

Parton. And while the word 'Rockettes' provokes eye rolling from most self-consciously cynical New Yorkers, fans of glitz and kitsch might just get a thrill from the troupe's annual Christmas Spectacular.

Same-day tour tickets are available at the candy store beside the Sixth Ave entrance, though it's worth considering paying the extra $5 to book your ticket online given that tours can sell out quickly, particularly on rainy days.

St Patrick's Cathedral   Cathedral

(Map p252; www.saintpatrickscathedral.org; Fifth Ave, btwn E 50th & 51st Sts; ☺6:30am-8:45pm; ⓢB/D/F/M to 47th-50th Sts-Rockefeller Center, E/M to 5th Ave-53rd St) Fresh from a major restoration, America's largest Catholic cathedral graces Fifth Ave with its Gothic Revival splendor. Built at a cost of nearly $2 million during the Civil War, the building did not originally include the two front spires; those were added in 1888. Step inside to appreciate the Louis Tiffany–designed altar and Charles Connick's stunning Rose Window, the latter gleaming above a 7000-pipe church organ.

A basement crypt behind the altar contains the coffins of every New York cardinal and the remains of Pierre Touissant, a champion of the poor and the first African American up for sainthood.

> ### ★ More Art
> Another 50,000 sq ft of gallery space will be added to MoMA in an expansion and redesign to be completed in 2019.

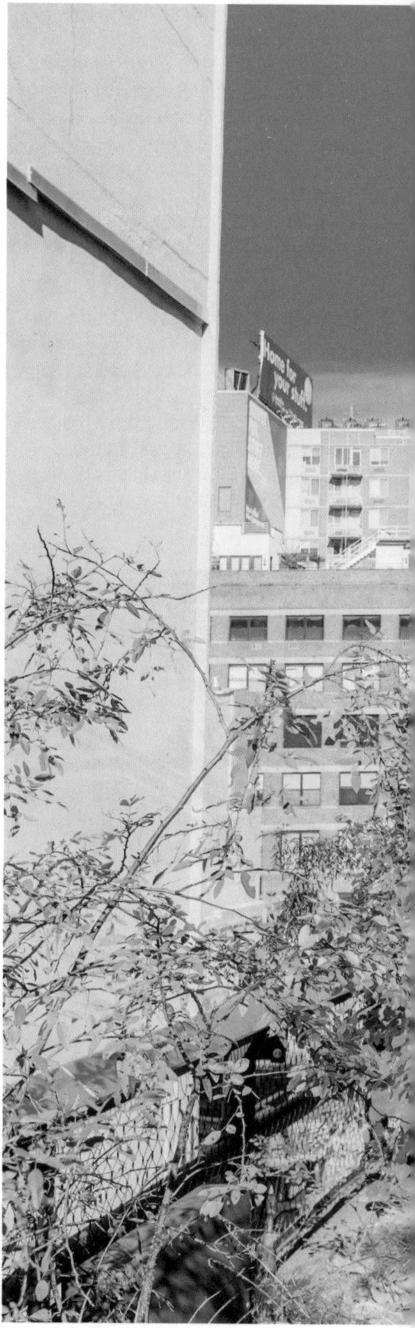

The High Line

A resounding triumph of urban renewal, the High Line is a remarkable linear public park built along a disused elevated rail line. Each year, this aerial greenway attracts millions of visitors who come for stunning vistas of the Hudson River, public art installations, willowy stretches of native-inspired landscaping and a thoroughly unique perspective on the neighborhood streets below.

Great For...

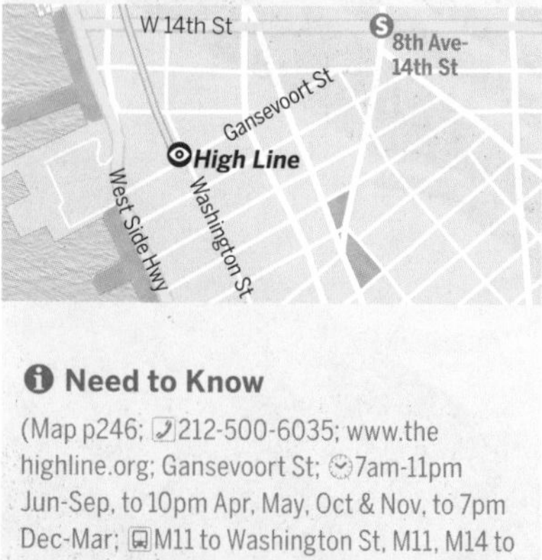

Need to Know

(Map p246; ☎212-500-6035; www.thehighline.org; Gansevoort St; ⏰7am-11pm Jun-Sep, to 10pm Apr, May, Oct & Nov, to 7pm Dec-Mar; 🚌M11 to Washington St, M11, M14 to 9th Ave; M23, M34 to 10th Ave, [S]A/C/E, L to 14th St-8th Ave, C/E to 23rd St-8th Ave)

★ **Top Tip**

Entrances are at Gansevoort, 14th, 16th, 18th, 20th, 23rd, 26th, 30th and 34th Sts.

History

It's hard to believe that the High Line was once a disused railway that anchored a rather unsavory district of ramshackle domestic dwellings and slaughterhouses. The tracks that would one day become the High Line were commissioned in the 1930s when the municipal government decided to raise the street-level tracks after years of deadly accidents.

By the 1980s, the rails became obsolete (thanks to a rise in truck transportation). Petitions were signed by local residents to remove the eyesores, but in 1999 a committee called the Friends of the High Line was formed to save the tracks and to transform them into a public open space. Community support grew and, on June 9, 2009, part one of the celebrated project opened with much ado.

Along the Way

The main things to do on the High Line are stroll, sit and picnic in a park 30ft above the city. Along the park's length you'll pass through willowy stretches of native-inspired landscaping, lounge chairs for soaking up the view and some surprising vantage points over the bustling streets – especially at the cool Gansevoort Overlook, where bleacher-like seating faces a huge pane of glass that allows you to view the traffic, buildings and pedestrians beyond as living works of urban art.

Information, Tours, Events & Eats

As you walk along the High Line you'll find staffers wearing shirts with the signature double-H logo who can point you in the right direction or offer you additional

10th Avenue Square at the High Line

information about the converted rails. There are also myriad staffers behind the scenes organizing public art exhibitions and activity sessions, including warm-weather family events such as story time, science and craft projects.

Free tours take place periodically and explore a variety of topics: history, horticulture, design, art and food. Check the event schedule on the website for the latest details.

To top it all off, the High Line also invites various gastronomic establishments from around the city to set up vending carts and stalls so that strollers can enjoy to-go items on the green. Expect a showing of the finest coffee and ice cream establishments during the warmer months.

☑ Don't Miss

The third and final part of the High Line, which bends by the Hudson River at 34th St.

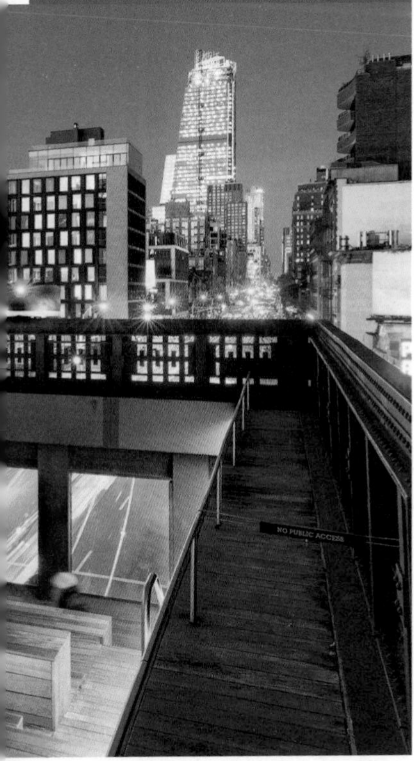

FRANCOIS ROUX / SHUTTERSTOCK ©

What's Nearby?

Whitney Museum of American Art Museum

(Map p246; ☎212-570-3600; www.whitney.org; 99 Gansevoort St, at Washington St; adult/child $22/free; ⏲10:30am-6pm Mon, Wed, Thu & Sun, to 10pm Fri & Sat; [S]A/C/E, L to 14th St-8th Ave) After years of construction, the Whitney's new downtown location opened to much fanfare in 2015. Perched near the foot of the High Line, this architecturally stunning building – designed by Renzo Piano – makes a suitable introduction to the museum's superb collection. Inside the spacious, light-filled galleries, you'll find works by all the great American artists, including Edward Hopper, Jasper Johns, Georgia O'Keeffe and Mark Rothko.

Hudson River Park Park

(Map p246; www.hudsonriverpark.org; 👪) The High Line may be all the rage these days, but one block away from that famous elevated green space, there stretches a five-mile-long ribbon of green that has dramatically transformed the city over the past decade. Covering 550 acres, and running from Battery Park at Manhattan's southern tip to 59th St in Midtown, the Hudson River Park is Manhattan's wondrous backyard. The long riverside path is a great spot for cycling, running and strolling.

Several boathouses (including one in Chelsea near W 26th, and another in the West Village near Houston) offer kayak hire and longer excursions for the more experienced.

🍴 Take a Break

A cache of eateries is stashed within Chelsea Market (p130) at the 14th St exit.

Times Square featuring Broadway theaters and signs

Broadway

Broadway is NYC's dream factory – a place where romance, betrayal, murder and triumph come with dazzling costumes, toe-tapping tunes and stirring scores. The lineup is truly staggering here, with a wide range of musicals, dramas and comedies – and plenty of blurring between genres. Reserve well ahead for top shows, which sell out months in advance.

Great For...

ⓘ Need to Know

Theatermania (www.theatermania.com) provides listings, reviews and ticketing for any form of theater.

★ **Top Tip**

Many shows offer discounted, day-of 'rush' tickets, available each morning when the box office opens; expect queues.

Broadway Beginnings

The neighborhood's first playhouse was the long-gone Empire, opened in 1893 and located on Broadway between 40th and 41st Sts. Two years later, cigar manufacturer and part-time comedy scribe Oscar Hammerstein opened the Olympia, also on Broadway, before opening the Republic (now children's theater New Victory; p189) in 1900. This lead to a string of new venues, among them the still-beating **New Amsterdam Theatre** (Map p250; ☎844-483-9008; www.new-amsterdam-theatre.com; 214 W 42nd St, btwn Seventh & Eighth Aves; ♿; S N/Q/R/W, S, 1/2/3, 7 to Times Sq-42nd St; A/C/E to 42nd St-Port Authority Bus Terminal) and **Lyceum Theatre** (Map p252; www.shubert.nyc/theatres/lyceum; 149 W 45th St, btwn Sixth & Seventh Aves, S N/R/W to 49th St).

The Broadway of the 1920s was well known for its lighthearted musicals, commonly fusing vaudeville and music-hall traditions, and producing classic tunes like Cole Porter's *Let's Misbehave*. At the same time, Midtown's theater district was evolving as a platform for new American dramatists. One of the greatest was Eugene O'Neill. Born in Times Square at the long-gone Barrett Hotel (1500 Broadway) in 1888, the playwright debuted many of his works here, including Pulitzer Prize winners *Beyond the Horizon* and *Anna Christie*. O'Neill's success on Broadway paved the way for other American greats like Tennessee Williams, Arthur Miller and Edward Albee – a surge of serious talent that led to the establishment of the annual Tony Awards in 1947.

Harvey Milk High School perform during the *Kinky Boots* curtain call at Al Hirschfeld Theatre

These days, New York's Theater District covers an area stretching roughly from 40th St to 54th St between Sixth and Eighth Aves, with dozens of Broadway and off-Broadway theaters spanning blockbuster musicals to new and classic drama.

Getting a Ticket

Unless there's a specific show you're after, the best – and cheapest – way to score tickets in the area is at the **TKTS Booth** (www.tdf.org/tkts; Broadway, at W 47th St; 🕒3-8pm Mon, Wed-Sat, 2-8pm Tue, 3-7pm Sun, also 10am-2pm Wed-Sat & 11am-3pm Sun during matinee performances; [S]N/Q/R/W, S, 1/2/3, 7 to Times Sq-42nd St), where you can line up and get same-day discounted tickets for top Broadway and off-Broadway shows. Smartphone users can download the free TKTS app, which offers rundowns of both Broadway and off-Broadway shows, as well as real-time updates of what's available on that day. Always have a back-up choice in case your first preference sells out, and never buy from scalpers on the street.

The TKTS Booth is an attraction in its own right, with its illuminated roof of 27 ruby-red steps rising a panoramic 16ft 1in above the 47th St sidewalk.

★ Did You Know?

The term 'off Broadway' is not a geographical one – it simply refers to theaters that are smaller in size (200 to 500 seats) and usually have less of a glitzy production budget than the Broadway big hitters.

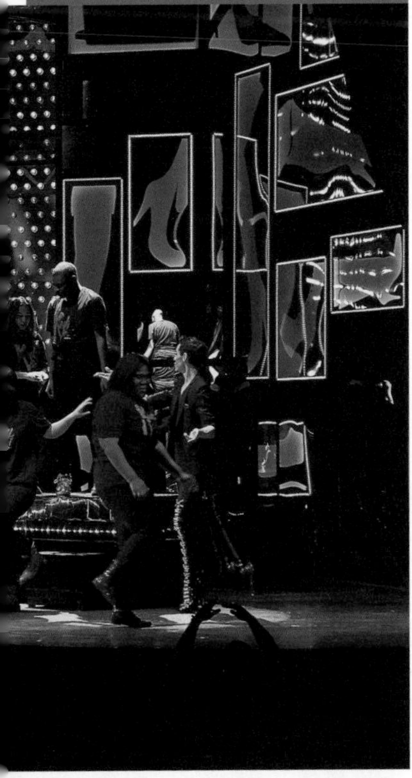

BENNETT RAGLIN / WIREIMAGE / GETTY IMAGES ©

What's On?

Musicals rule the marquees on Broadway, with the hottest shows of the day blending song and dance in lavish, star-studded productions.

Hamilton

Lin-Manuel Miranda's acclaimed new musical is Broadway's hottest ticket, using contemporary hip-hop beats to recount the story of America's founding father, Alexander Hamilton. Inspired by Ron Chernow's biography *Alexander Hamilton*, the musical has won a swath of awards, including Outstanding Musical at the Drama Desk Awards and Best Musical at the New York Drama Critics' Circle Awards.

Book of Mormon

Subversive, obscene and ridiculously hilarious, this cutting musical satire is the work of *South Park* creators Trey Parker and Matt Stone and Avenue Q composer Robert Lopez. Winner of nine Tony Awards, it tells the story of two naive Mormons on a mission to 'save' a Ugandan village.

🍴 Take a Break

Stiff drinks and a whiff of nostalgia await at the no-bull Jimmy's Corner (p175) bar.

Kinky Boots

Adapted from a 2005 British indie film, Harvey Fierstein and Cyndi Lauper's smash hit tells the story of a doomed English shoe factory unexpectedly saved by Lola, a business-savvy drag queen. Its solid characters and electrifying energy have not been lost on critics, the musical has won six Tony Awards, including Best Musical in 2013.

Matilda

Giddily subversive, this multi-award-winning musical is an adaptation of Roald Dahl's classic children's tale. Star of the show is a precocious five-year-old who uses wit, intellect and a little telekinesis to tackle parental neglect, unjust punishment, and even the Russian mafia.

An American in Paris

Adapted from the 1951 film starring Gene Kelly, this elegant, critically acclaimed stage musical tells the story of an American ex-GI in post-war Paris, following his artistic dreams and falling head over heels for an alluring dancer. Packed with toe-tapping Gershwin tunes (including rarer numbers), it's directed by renowned English choreographer Christopher Wheeldon.

Lion King

A top choice for families with kids, Disney's blockbuster musical tells the tale of a lion cub's journey to adulthood and the throne of the animal kingdom. The spectacular sets, costumes and African chants are worth the ticket alone.

Chicago

A little easier to score tickets to than some of the newer Broadway musicals, this beloved Bob Fosse/Kander & Ebb classic tells the story of showgirl Velma Kelly, wannabe Roxie Hart, lawyer Billy Flynn and the fabulously sordid goings-on of the Chicago underworld. Revived by director Walter Bobbie, its sassy, infectious energy more than makes up for the theater's tight-squeeze seating.

Wicked

An extravagant prequel to *The Wizard of Oz*, this long-running, pop-rock musical gives the story's witches a turn to tell the tale. The musical is based on Gregory Maguire's 1995 novel.

Aladdin

This witty dervish of a musical recounts the tale of a street urchin who falls in love with the daughter of a sultan. Based on the 1992 Disney animation, the stage version includes songs from the film, numerous numbers which didn't make the final cut, as well as new material written specifically for the live production.

Model aircraft at the Intrepid Sea, Air & Space Museum

What's Nearby?

Intrepid Sea, Air & Space Museum
Museum

(☎877-957-7447; www.intrepidmuseum.org; Pier 86, Twelfth Ave at W 46th St; Intrepid & Growler submarine adult/child $26/19, incl Space Shuttle Pavilion adult/child $36/29; 🕒10am-5pm Mon-Fri, to 6pm Sat & Sun Apr-Oct, 10am-5pm Mon-Sun Nov-Mar; 👪; 🚌westbound M42, M50 to 12th Ave, [S]A/C/E to 42nd St-Port Authority Bus Terminal) The USS *Intrepid* survived both a WWII bomb and kamikaze attacks. Thankfully, this hulking aircraft carrier is now a lot less stressed, playing host to a multimillion dollar interactive military museum that tells its tale through videos, historical artifacts and frozen-in-time living quarters. The flight deck features fighter planes and military helicopters, which might inspire you to try the museum's high-tech flight simulators.

The rides include the G Force Encounter, allowing you to experience the virtual thrill of flying a supersonic jet plane, and the Transporter FX, a flight simulator promising six full minutes of 'complete sensory overload.' The museum is also home to the guided-missile submarine *Growler,* (not for the claustrophobic), a decommissioned Concorde, and the former NASA space shuttle *Enterprise*.

☑ Don't Miss

The famed Brill Building (1619 Broadway, at W 49th St; bN/R/W to 49th St, 1, C/E to 50th St); Carol King, Neil Diamond and Joni Mitchell are among the musicians who worked here.

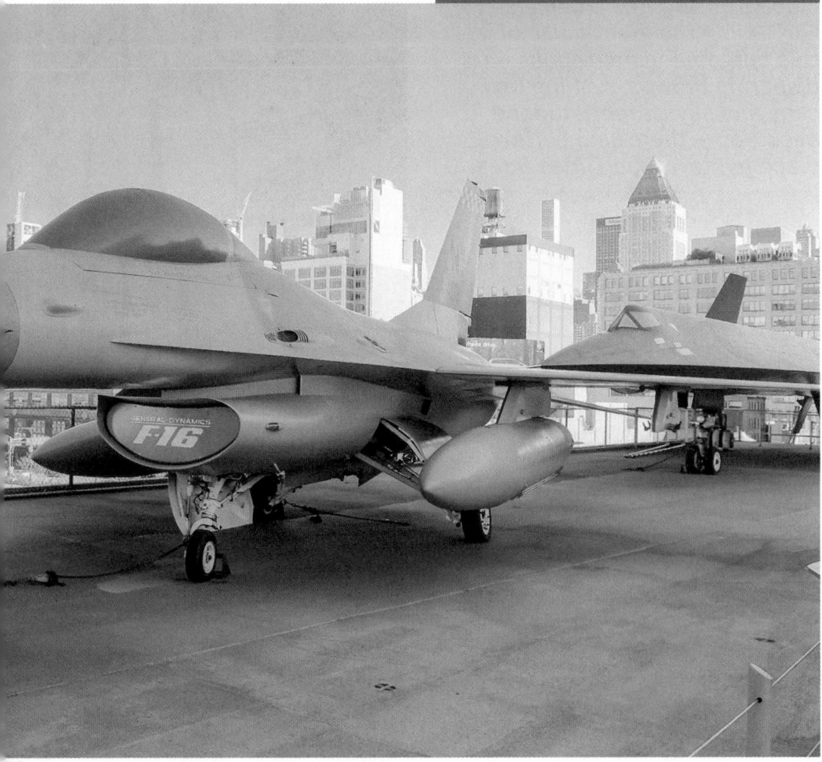

PNPY / SHUTTERSTOCK ©

Times Square

Love it or hate it, the intersection of Broadway and Seventh Ave, better known as Times Square, is New York City's hyperactive heart: a restless, hypnotic torrent of glittering lights, bombastic billboards and raw urban energy. For feeling the great pulse of this burgeoning metropolis – its disparate crowds, rushing taxi cabs and skyscraper-studded backdrop – there's no better place to start than Times Square.

Great For...

❶ Need to Know

(Map p252; www.timessquarenyc.org; Broadway, at Seventh Ave; ⑤ N/Q/R/W, S, 1/2/3, 7 to Times Sq-42nd St)

★ **Top Tip**
In the museum, write your dreams onto a piece of ready-to-flutter New Year's Eve confetti.

NYC Icons

Times Square is not hip, fashionable or in-the-know, and it couldn't care less. It's too busy pumping out iconic, mass-marketed NYC – yellow cabs, golden arches, soaring skyscrapers and razzle-dazzle Broadway marquees. This is the New York of collective fantasies – the place where Al Jolson 'makes it' in the 1927 film *The Jazz Singer*, where photojournalist Alfred Eisenstaedt famously captured a lip-locked sailor and nurse on VJ Day in 1945, and where Alicia Keys and Jay-Z waxed lyrically about this 'concrete jungle where dreams are made.'

For several decades, the dream here was a sordid, wet one. The economic crash of the early 1970s led to a mass exodus of corporations from Times Square. Billboard niches went dark, stores shut and once-grand hotels were converted into SRO (single-room occupancy) dives. While the adjoining Theater District survived, its respectable playhouses shared the streets with porn cinemas and strip clubs. That all changed with tough-talking Mayor Rudolph Giuliani, who, in the 1990s, boosted police numbers and lured a wave of 'respectable' retail chains, restaurants and attractions. By the new millennium, Times Square had gone from 'X-rated' to 'G-rated,' drawing almost 40 million visitors annually.

People-watch

Times Square is often called the 'cross-roads of the world' and you better believe you'll get an eyeful of more than shimmering neon here. All kinds of folks don costumes to make money posing for photographs. Keep an eye out for buffed topless cowboys, *Sesame Street* Elmos and a wide range of superheroes.

Getting a Drink with a View

For a panoramic overview of the square, order a drink at the Renaissance Hotel's **R Lounge** (Map p252; 212-261-5200; www.rloungetimessquare.com; Two Times Square, 714 Seventh Ave, at W 48th St; 5-11pm Mon, to 11:30pm Tue-Thu, to midnight Fri, 7:30am-midnight Sat, to 11pm Sun; **S** N/R/W to 49th St), the floor-to-ceiling windows of which overlook the neon-lit spectacle.

A Subway & A Newspaper

At the turn of last century, Times Square was known as Longacre Sq, an unremark-

> ☑ **Don't Miss**
>
> The view from the bleachers overlooking the frenzy. Take a seat and enjoy some of the finest people-watching on earth.

LUCKY-PHOTOGRAPHER / SHUTTERSTOCK ©

able intersection far from the commercial epicenter of Lower Manhattan. This would change with a deal made between subway pioneer August Belmont and *New York Times* publisher Adolph Ochs.

Belmont approached Ochs, and convinced him that moving the *New York Times* to the intersection of Broadway and 42nd St would be a win-win – an in-house subway station meant faster newspaper distribution and the influx of commuters would also mean more sales right outside its headquarters. Belmont even convinced New York Mayor George B McClellan Jr to rename the square in honor of the broadsheet. It was an irresistible offer and, in the winter of 1904–05, both subway station and the Times' new headquarters at One Times Sq made their debut.

What's Nearby?

Museum of Arts & Design   Museum
(MAD; Map p252; 212-299-7777; www.mad-museum.org; 2 Columbus Circle, btwn Eighth Ave & Broadway; adult/child $16/free, by donation 6-9pm Thu; 10am-6pm Tue, Wed, Fri-Sun, to 9pm Thu; **S** A/C, B/D, 1 to 59th St-Columbus Circle) MAD offers four floors of superlative design and handicrafts, from blown glass and carved wood to elaborate metal jewelry. Its temporary exhibitions are top notch and innovative; one past show explored the art of scent. Usually on the first Sunday of the month, professional artists lead family-friendly explorations of the galleries, followed by hands-on workshops inspired by the current exhibitions. The museum gift shop sells some fantastic contemporary jewelry, while the 9th-floor restaurant/bar **Robert** (Map p252; 212-299-7730; www.robertnyc.com; 11:30am-10pm Mon & Sun, to 11pm Tue, to midnight Wed-Sat) is perfect for panoramic cocktails.

> ✗ **Take a Break**
>
> Grab a legendary cubano sandwich from El Margon (p135), only a minute's walk from the square.

View toward the Empire State Building

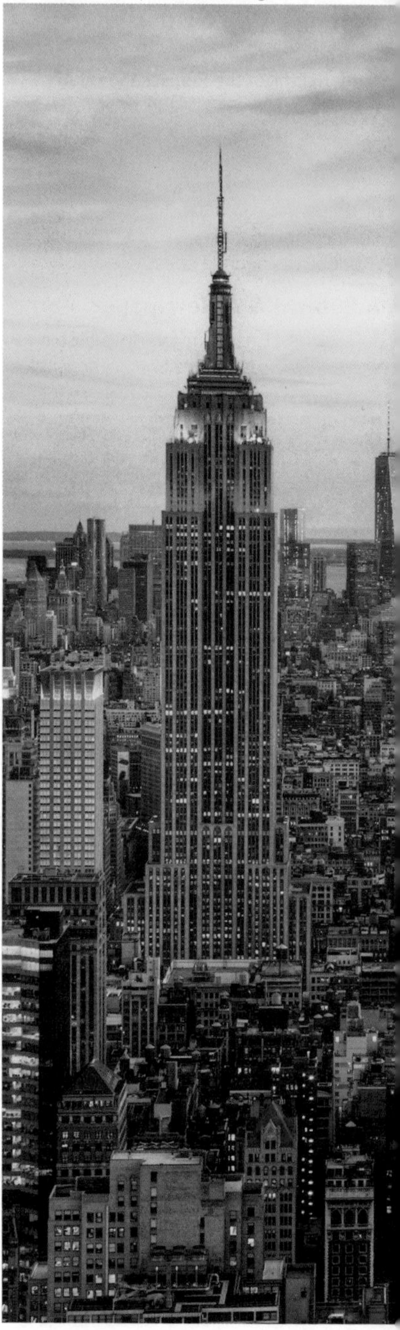

Empire State Building

The striking art-deco skyscraper has appeared in dozens of films and still provides one of the best views in town – particularly around sunset when the twinkling lights of the city switch on. Although the crowds are substantial, no one regrets making the journey to the top. There's no other view quite like it, with the great metropolis spread out before you in all its complicated beauty.

Great For...

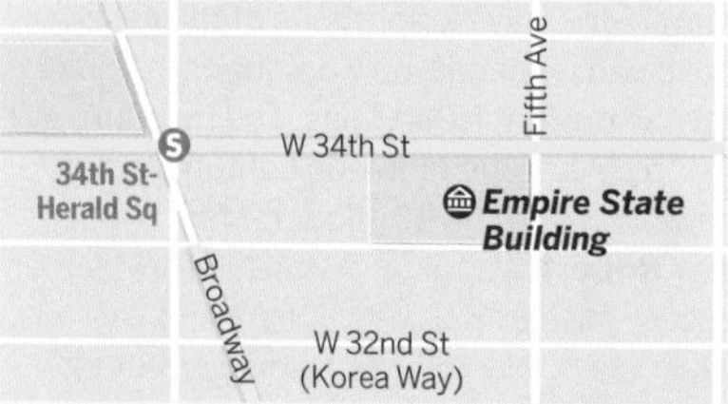

Need to Know

(Map p250; www.esbnyc.com; 350 Fifth Ave, at W 34th St; 86th-fl observation deck adult/child $34/27, incl 102nd-fl observation deck $54/47; ⏰8am-2am, last elevators up 1:15am; [S]B/D/F/M, N/Q/R/W to 34th St-Herald Sq)

★ **Top Tip**
To beat the crowds, buy tickets online (well worth the extra $2 convenience fee).

The Chrysler Building may be prettier and One World Trade Center and 432 Park Avenue may be taller, but the Queen Bee of the New York skyline remains the Empire State Building. NYC's tallest star, it has enjoyed close-ups in around 100 films, from *King Kong* to *Independence Day*. Heading up to the top is a quintessential NYC experience.

Observation Decks

There are two observation decks. The open-air 86th-floor deck offers an alfresco experience, with coin-operated telescopes for close-up glimpses of the metropolis in action. Further up, the enclosed 102nd-floor deck is New York's second-highest observation deck, trumped only by the observation deck at One World Trade Center. Needless to say, the views over the city's five boroughs (and five neighboring states, weather permitting) are spectacular. Particularly memorable are the views at sunset, when the city dons its nighttime cloak in dusk's afterglow. For a little of that Burt Bacharach magic, head to the 86th floor between 9pm and 1am from Thursday to Saturday, when the twinkling sea of lights is accompanied by a soundtrack of live sax (yes, requests are taken). Alas, the passage to heaven will involve a trip through purgatory: the queues to the top are notorious. Getting here very early or very late will help you avoid delays – as will buying your tickets online, ahead of time.

By the Numbers

The statistics are astonishing: 10 million bricks, 60,000 tons of steel, 6400 windows

Shake Shack (p131) in Madison Square Park

and 328,000 sq ft of marble. Built on the original site of the Waldorf-Astoria, construction took a record-setting 410 days, using seven million hours of labor and costing a mere $41 million. It might sound like a lot, but it fell well below its $50 million budget (just as well, given it went up during the Great Depression). Coming in at 102 stories and 1472ft from bottom to top, the limestone monolith opened for business on May 1, 1931.

Language of Light

Since 1976, the building's top 30 floors have been floodlit in a spectrum of colors each night, reflecting seasonal and holiday hues. Famous combos include orange, white and green for St Patrick's Day; blue and white for Chanukah; white, red and green for Christmas; and the rainbow colors for Gay Pride weekend in June. For a full rundown of the color schemes, check the website.

What's Nearby?

Madison Square Park   Park

(Map p250; ☎212-520-7600; www.madison squarepark.org; E 23rd to 26th Sts, btwn Fifth & Madison Aves; ⊙6am-midnight; 🚻; ⓢR/W, F/M, 6 to 23rd St) This park defined the northern reaches of Manhattan until the island's population exploded after the Civil War. These days it's a much-welcome oasis from Manhattan's relentless pace, with a popular children's playground, dog-run area and Shake Shack (p131) burger joint. It's also one of the city's most cultured parks, with specially commissioned art installations and (in the warmer months) activities ranging from literary discussions to live music gigs. See the website for more information.

The park is also the perfect spot from which to gaze up at the landmarks that surround it, including the Flatiron Building to the southwest, the moderne Metropolitan Life Tower to the southeast and the New York Life Insurance Building, topped with a gilded spire, to the northeast.

Between 1876 and 1882 the torch-bearing arm of the Statue of Liberty was on display here, and in 1879 the first Madison Square Garden arena was constructed at Madison Ave and 26th St. At the southeastern corner of the park, you'll find one of the city's few self-cleaning, coin-operated toilets.

> ☑ **Don't Miss**
> Live jazz held on Thursday to Saturday nights from 9pm to 1am.

DW LABS INCORPORATED / SHUTTERSTOCK ©

> ✕ **Take a Break**
> Feast on dumplings, barbecue and kimchi in nearby restaurant-lined Koreatown (32nd St between Fifth & Sixth Aves).

KOTSOVOLOS PANAGIOTIS/SHUTTERSTOCK ©

Metropolitan Museum of Art

This museum of encyclopedic proportions has more than two million objects in its permanent collection, and many of its treasures are showcased in no less than 17 acres' worth of galleries. You could spend weeks exploring the Met and still not see it all.

Great For...

☑ Don't Miss

The hieroglyphic-covered Temple of Dendur, complete with reflecting pond and Central Park views.

This sprawling museum, founded in 1870, houses one of the biggest art collections in the world. Its permanent collection has everything from Egyptian temples to American paintings. Known colloquially as 'The Met,' the museum draws over six million visitors a year to its galleries – making it the largest single-site attraction in New York City. In other words, plan on spending some time here.

Egyptian Art

The museum has an unrivaled collection of ancient Egyptian art, some of which dates back to the Paleolithic era. Located to the north of the Great Hall, the 39 Egyptian galleries open dramatically with one of the Met's prized pieces: the Mastaba Tomb of Perneb (c 2300 BC), an Old Kingdom burial chamber crafted from limestone. From

Ancient Roman sculpture

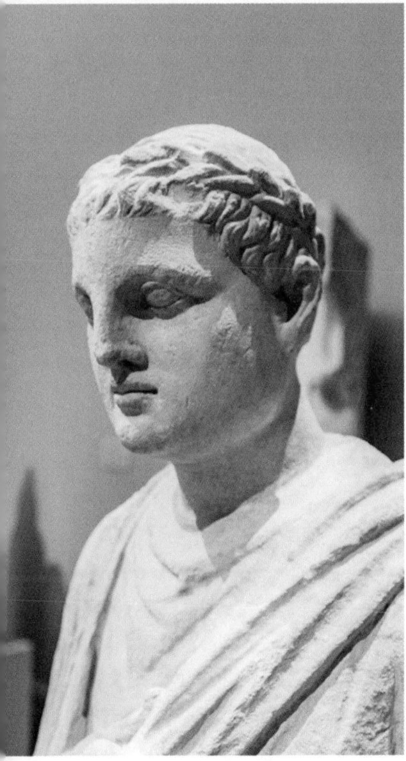

GORAN BOGICEVIC / SHUTTERSTOCK ©

here, a web of rooms is cluttered with funerary stelae, carved reliefs and fragments of pyramids. (Don't miss the intriguing Models of Meketre, clay figurines meant to help in the afterlife, in Gallery 105.) These eventually lead to the Temple of Dendur (Gallery 131), a sandstone temple to the goddess Isis that resides in a sunny atrium gallery with a reflecting pool.

Greek & Roman Art

The 27 galleries devoted to classical antiquity are another Met doozy. From the Great Hall, a passageway takes viewers through a barrel vaulted room flanked by the chiseled torsos of Greek figures. This spills right into one of the Met's loveliest spaces: the airy Roman sculpture court (Gallery 162), full of marble carvings of gods and historical figures. The statue of a bearded Hercules

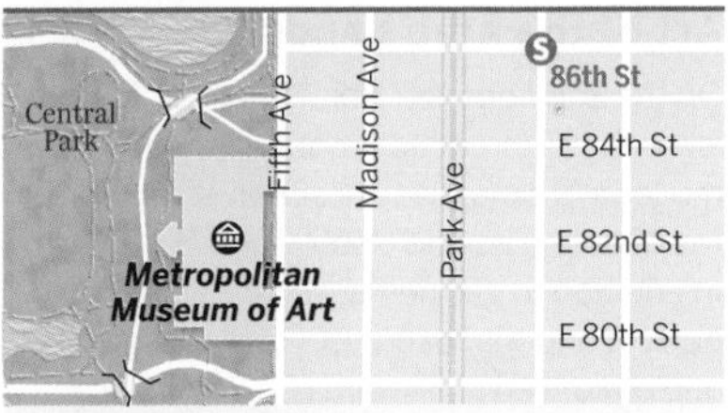

Need to Know

(Map p252; ☎212-535-7710; www.metmuseum.org; 1000 Fifth Ave, at E 82nd St; suggested donation adult/child $25/free; 🕐10am-5:30pm Sun-Thu, to 9pm Fri & Sat; 👪; [S]4/5/6 to 86th St)

Take a Break

The casual Petrie Court cafe serves good lunch and drink options in a pretty setting.

★ Top Tip

Docents offer free guided tours of specific galleries. Check the website or information desk for details.

from AD 68–98, with a lion's skin draped about him, is particularly awe-inspiring.

European Paintings

Want Renaissance? The Met's got it. On the museum's 2nd floor, the European Paintings' galleries display a stunning collection of masterworks. This includes more than 1700 canvases from the roughly 500-year-period starting in the 13th century, with works by every important painter from Duccio to Rembrandt. In fact, everything here is, literally, a masterpiece. In Gallery 621 are several Caravaggios, including the masterfully painted *The Denial of St Peter.* Gallery 611, to the west, is packed with Spanish treasures, including El Greco's famed *View of Toledo*. Continue south to Gallery 632 to see various Vermeers, including the *Young Woman with a Water Pitcher*. Nearby, in Gallery 634, gaze at several Rembrandts, including a 1660 *Self-Portrait*.

Art of the Arab Lands

On the 2nd floor you'll find the Islamic galleries with 15 incredible rooms showcasing the museum's extensive collection of art from the Middle East and Central and South Asia. In addition to garments, secular decorative objects and manuscripts, you'll find gilded and enameled glassware (Gallery 452) and a magnificent 14th-century *mihrab* (prayer niche) lined with elaborately patterned polychrome tile-work (Gallery 455).

American Wing

In the northwestern corner, the American galleries showcase a wide variety of decorative and fine art from throughout US history. These include everything from colonial portraiture to Hudson River School masterpieces to John Singer Sargent's unbearably sexy *Madame X* (Gallery 771) – not to mention Emanuel Leutze's massive canvas of *Washington Crossing the Delaware* (Gallery 760).

The Roof Garden

One of the best spots in the entire museum is the roof garden, which features rotating sculpture installations by contemporary and 20th-century artists (Jeff Koons, Andy Goldsworthy and Imran Qureshi have all shown here). But its best feature is the view it offers of the city and Central Park. It's also home to the **Roof Garden Café & Martini Bar** (Map p252; 212-570-3711; www. metmuseum.org; 10am-4:30pm Sun-Thu, to 8:15pm Fri & Sat May-Oct;), an ideal spot for a drink – especially at sunset. The roof garden is open from May to October.

Tours

A desk inside the Great Hall has audio tours in several languages ($7), though you can access audio tours for free if you have a smartphone. Docents also offer guided tours of specific galleries (free with admission). Check the website or information desk for details. If you can't stand crowds, avoid weekends.

What's Nearby?

Frick Collection Gallery

(Map p252; ☎212-288-0700; www.frick.org; 1 E 70th St, at Fifth Ave; $22, by donation 11am-1pm

N.ENE / SHUTTERSTOCK ©

> ★ **Kids at the Met**
>
> The Met hosts plenty of kid-centric happenings (check the website) and distributes a special brochure and map created specifically for the tykes.

Sun; ⊘10am-6pm Tue-Sat, 11am-5pm Sun; Ⓢ6 to 68th St-Hunter College) This spectacular art collection sits in a mansion built by prickly steel magnate Henry Clay Frick, one of the many such residences that made up Millionaires' Row. The museum has over a dozen splendid rooms that display masterpieces by Titian, Vermeer, Gilbert Stuart, El Greco and Goya.

The museum is a treat for a number of reasons. One, it resides in a lovely, rambling beaux-arts structure built from 1913 to 1914 by Carrère and Hastings. Two, it's generally not crowded (one exception being during popular shows). And, three, it feels refreshingly intimate, with a trickling indoor courtyard fountain and gardens that can be explored on warmer days. A demure Portico Gallery displays decorative works and sculpture.

A worthwhile audio tour (available in several languages) is included in the price of admission. Classical music fans will enjoy the frequent piano and violin concerts that take place on Sunday.

Neue Galerie Museum

(Map p252; ☎212-628-6200; www.neuegalerie. org; 1048 Fifth Ave, cnr E 86th St; $20, 6-8pm 1st Fri of the month free; ⊘11am-6pm Thu-Mon; Ⓢ4/5/6 to 86th St) This restored Carrère and Hastings mansion from 1914 is a resplendent showcase for German and Austrian art, featuring works by Paul Klee, Ernst Ludwig Kirchner and Egon Schiele. In pride of place on the 2nd floor is Gustav Klimt's golden 1907 portrait of Adele Bloch-Bauer I – which was acquired for the museum by cosmetics magnate Ronald Lauder for a whopping $135 million.

This is a small but beautiful place with winding staircases and wrought-iron banisters. It also boasts a lovely, street-level eatery, Café Sabarsky (p137). Avoid weekends (and the free first Friday of the month) if you don't want to deal with gallery-clogging crowds.

Iconic Architecture

Midtown is home to some of New York's grandest monuments, with artful works of architecture soaring above. This walk provides a mix of perspectives – with godlike views from up high and street-side exploring amid the raw energy of the whirling city.

Start Grand Central Terminal
Finish Rockefeller Center
Distance 2 miles; **Duration** 3 hours

7 Nearby is the **Rockefeller Center** (p84), a magnificent complex of art-deco skyscrapers and sculptures.

8 Head to the Rockefeller Center's 70th-floor for an unforgettable vista at the **Top of the Rock** (p84).

W 51st St

Rockefeller Plaza

W 50th St

W 49th St

8 **7**

FINISH

Fifth Ave

Madison Ave

6

5 Between Sixth and Fifth Aves is the **Diamond District** (W 47th St) where more than 2600 businesses sell gems and jewelry.

47th-50th Sts-Rockefeller Center

5

W 46th St

4 The **Bank of America Tower** (Map p252) is NYC's fourth-tallest building and one of its most ecofriendly.

Sixth Ave (Avenue of the Americas)

W 45th St

W 44th St

W 43rd St

42nd St-Times Sq

W 42nd St

4

42nd St-Bryant Park

5th Ave

Take a Break...

In Bryant Park, stop in for a tasty snack or meal at **Bryant Park Grill** (www.arkrestaurants.com/bryant_park; mains $19.50-45; ⊙11:30am-11pm)

Bryant Park
W 40th St

3

3 Step inside the **New York Public Library** (www.nypl.org; Fifth Ave, at W 42nd St) to peek at its spectacular Rose Reading Room.

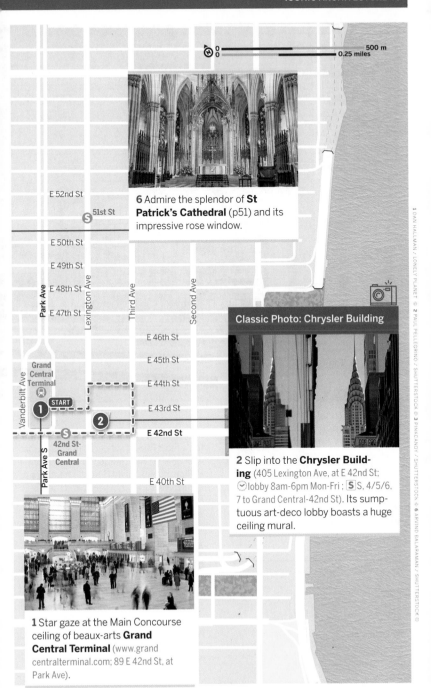

500 m
0.25 miles

E 52nd St

Ⓢ 51st St

E 50th St

E 49th St

E 48th St

E 47th St

Park Ave

Lexington Ave

Third Ave

Second Ave

6 Admire the splendor of **St Patrick's Cathedral** (p51) and its impressive rose window.

E 46th St

E 45th St

E 44th St

Grand Central Terminal

Vanderbilt Ave

❶ START

E 43rd St

❷

Ⓢ

E 42nd St

42nd St-Grand Central

Park Ave S

E 40th St

Classic Photo: Chrysler Building

2 Slip into the **Chrysler Building** (405 Lexington Ave, at E 42nd St; ⊙lobby 8am-6pm Mon-Fri ; Ⓢ S, 4/5/6, 7 to Grand Central-42nd St). Its sumptuous art-deco lobby boasts a huge ceiling mural.

1 Star gaze at the Main Concourse ceiling of beaux-arts **Grand Central Terminal** (www.grand centralterminal.com; 89 E 42nd St, at Park Ave).

1 DAN HALLMAN / LONELY PLANET © 2 PAUL PELLEGRINO / SHUTTERSTOCK © 3 PINKCANDY / SHUTTERSTOCK © 6 ARVIND BALARAMAN / SHUTTERSTOCK ©

ATLANTIDE PHOTOTRAVEL / GETTY IMAGES ©

Lincoln Center

This vast cultural complex is the epicenter of high art in Manhattan. Famed venues spread around the 16-acre campus include concert halls, an opera house, film screening centers and the renowned Julliard School. The big draw here is seeing one of the Met's lavish opera productions.

Great For...

☑ **Don't Miss**

A lush production at the world-famous Metropolitan Opera House.

This stark arrangement of gleaming modernist temples contains some of Manhattan's most important performance spaces: Avery Fisher Hall (home to the New York Philharmonic), David H Koch Theater (site of the New York City ballet), and the iconic Metropolitan Opera House, the interior walls of which are dressed with brightly saturated murals by painter Marc Chagall.

A History of Building & Rebuilding

Built in the 1960s, this imposing campus replaced a group of tenements called San Juan Hill, a predominantly African American neighborhood where the exterior shots for the movie *West Side Story* were filmed. In addition to being a controversial urban planning move, Lincoln Center wasn't exactly well received at an architectural level – it

❶ Need to Know

(Map p252; 📞212-875-5456, tours 212-875-5350; www.lincolncenter.org; Columbus Ave btwn W 62nd & 66th Sts; tours adult/student $25/20; 👶; Ⓢ1 to 66th St-Lincoln Center) **FREE**

✕ Take a Break

Across the street from the Lincoln Center, **Smith** (Map p252; 📞212-496-5700; www.thesmithrestaurant.com; 1900 Broadway, btwn 63rd & 64th Sts; mains $23-43; ⏱7:30am-midnight Mon-Fri, from 9am Sat & Sun; Ⓢ1, A/C, B/D to 59th-St-Columbus Circle) serves high-end comfort fare.

★ Top Tip

Daily tours are a great way to get acquainted with the many facets of Lincoln Center.

was relentlessly criticized for its conservative design, fortress-like aspect and poor acoustics. For the center's 50th anniversary (2009–10), Diller Scofidio + Renfro and other architects gave the complex a much-needed and critically acclaimed freshening up.

Highlights

A survey of the three classic buildings surrounding Revson Fountain is a must. These include the Metropolitan Opera, Avery Fisher Hall and the David H Koch Theater, the latter designed by Philip Johnson. (These are all located on the main plaza at Columbus Ave, between 62nd and 65th Sts.) The fountain is spectacular in the evenings when it puts on Las Vegas–like light shows.

Of the refurbished structures, there are a number that are worth examining, including Alice Tully Hall, now displaying a very contemporary translucent, angled facade, and the David Rubenstein Atrium, a public space offering a lounge area, a cafe, an information desk and a ticket vendor plying day-of discount tickets to Lincoln Center performances. Free events are held here on Thursday evenings, with a wide-ranging roster including eclectic global sounds (such as Indian classical music or Afro-Cuban jazz), prog rock, chamber music, opera and ballet.

Performances & Screenings

On any given night, there are at least 10 performances happening throughout Lincoln Center – and even more in summer, when Lincoln Center Out of Doors (a series of dance and music concerts) and Midsummer Night Swing (ballroom dancing under the stars) lure those who love parks and culture. For details on seasons, tickets and programming – which runs the gamut from opera to dance to theater to ballet – check the website.

Metropolitan Opera House

New York's premier opera company, the Metropolitan Opera is the place to see classics such as *Carmen, Madame Butterfly* and *Macbeth,* not to mention Wagner's *Ring Cycle.* The Opera also hosts premieres and revivals of more contemporary works, such as Peter Sellars' *Nixon in China.* The season runs from September to April.

Ticket prices start around $35 and can get close to $500. Note that the box seats can be a bargain, but unless you're in boxes right over the stage, the views are dreadful. Seeing the stage requires sitting with your head cocked over a handrail – a literal pain in the neck.

New York City Ballet

This prestigious ballet company was first directed by renowned Russian-born choreographer George Balanchine back in the 1940s. Today, the company has 90 dancers and is the largest ballet organization in the US, performing 23 weeks a year at Lincoln Center's David H Koch Theater. During the holidays the troop is best known for its annual production of *The Nutcracker*.

New York Philharmonic

The oldest professional orchestra in the US (dating back to 1842) holds its season every year at Avery Fisher Hall. Directed by

Visitors at the planetarium, American Museum of Natural History

Alan Gilbert, the son of two Philharmonic musicians, the orchestra plays a mix of classics (Tchaikovsky, Mahler, Haydn) and contemporary works, as well as concerts geared towards children.

What's Nearby?

American Museum of Natural History

Museum

(Map p252; ☎212-769-5100; www.amnh.org; Central Park West, at W 79th St; suggested donation adult/child $22/12.50; 🕐10am-5:45pm, Rose Center to 8:45pm Fri; 👪; [S] B, C to 81st St-Museum of Natural History, 1 to 79th St)

Founded in 1869 this classic museum contains a veritable wonderland of more than 30 million artifacts, including lots of menacing dinosaur skeletons, as well as the Rose Center for Earth & Space, with its cutting-edge planetarium. From September through May, the museum is home to the Butterfly Conservatory, a glass-house featuring 500-plus butterflies from all over the world.

On the natural history side, the museum is perhaps best known for its Fossil Halls containing nearly 600 specimens, including the skeletons of a massive mammoth and a fearsome Tyrannosaurus Rex.

There are also plentiful animal exhibits (the stuffed Alaskan brown bears are popular), galleries devoted to gems and an IMAX theater. The Milstein Hall of Ocean Life contains dioramas devoted to ecologies, weather and conservation, as well as a beloved 94ft replica of a blue whale. At the 77th St Lobby Gallery, visitors are greeted by a 63ft canoe carved by the Haida people of British Columbia in the middle of the 19th century.

For the space set, it's the Rose Center that is the star of the show. Its mesmerizing glass-box facade – home to space-show theaters and the planetarium – is indeed an otherworldly setting. Every half-hour between 10:30am and 4:30pm you can drop yourself into a cushy seat to view *Dark Universe,* narrated by famed astrophysicist Neil deGrasse Tyson, which explores the mysteries and wonders of the cosmos.

Celebrities provide narration for some of the other films: Meryl Streep gives us the evolutionary lowdown on vertebrates on the fourth floor, while Liam Neeson narrates the four-minute *Big Bang,* which provides a fine introduction to exploring the rest of the Rose Center.

☑ Don't Miss

The gift shop is full of operatic bric-a-brac, including Met curtain cuff links and Rhinemaidens soap. (Seriously.)

ANDREA IZZOTTI / SHUTTERSTOCK ©

★ Behind the Scenes

For a behind-the-scenes look at the Opera House, tours ($25) are offered weekdays at 3pm and Sundays at 10:30am and 1:30pm during the performance season.

Guggenheim Museum

A sculpture in its own right, architect Frank Lloyd Wright's swirling white building is one of New York's most photogenic museums. Although the permanent collection on display is small, the Guggenheim stages some exceptional shows, with critically acclaimed retrospectives and thought-provoking site-specific installations by some of the greatest artists of the 20th and 21st centuries.

Great For...

Jacqueline Kennedy Onassis Reservoir — E 90th St — Lexington Ave

Guggenheim Museum — Fifth Ave — Madison Ave — Park Ave

Central Park — E 86th St — 86th St S

ℹ️ Need to Know

(Map p252; ☎212-423-3500; www.guggenheim.org; 1071 Fifth Ave, at E 89th St; adult/child $25/free, by donation 5:45-7:45pm Sat; ⏰10am-5:45pm Sun-Wed & Fri, to 7:45pm Sat, closed Thu; ♿; S4/5/6 to 86th St)

★ Top Tip

Entrance lines can be brutal; save time by purchasing tickets online in advance.

THE SOLOMON R GUGGENHEIM M

Architect Frank Lloyd Wright's elegant curvilinear building almost overshadows the collection of 20th-century art that it houses. Completed in 1959, the inverted ziggurat structure was derided by some critics but hailed by others, who welcomed it as a beloved architectural icon. Since it first opened, this unusual structure has appeared on countless postcards, TV programs and films.

Abstract Roots

The Guggenheim came out of the collection of Solomon R Guggenheim, a New York mining magnate who began acquiring abstract art in his sixties at the behest of his art adviser, an eccentric German baroness named Hilla Rebay. In 1939, with Rebay serving as director, Guggenheim opened a temporary museum on 54th St titled the Museum of Non-Objective Painting. (Incredibly, it had grey velour walls, piped-in classical music and burning incense.) Four years later, the pair commissioned Wright to construct a permanent home for the collection.

Years in the Making

Like any development in New York City, the project took forever to come to fruition. Construction was delayed for almost 13 years due to budget constraints, the outbreak of WWII and outraged neighbors who weren't all that excited to see an architectural spaceship land in their midst. Construction was completed in 1959, after both Wright and Guggenheim had passed away.

When the Guggenheim finally opened its doors in October 1959, the ticket price

The Guggenheim's ascending ramps

was 50¢ and the works on view included pieces by Kandinsky, Alexander Calder and abstract expressionists Franz Kline and Willem de Kooning.

Visiting Today

A renovation in the early 1990s added an eight-story tower to the east, which provided an extra 50,000 sq ft of exhibition space. These galleries show the permanent collection and other exhibits, while the museum's ascending ramps are occupied by rotating exhibitions of modern and contemporary art. Though Wright intended visitors to go to the top and wind their way down, the cramped, single elevator doesn't allow for this. Exhibitions, therefore, are installed from bottom to top.

Alongside works by Picasso and Jackson Pollock, the museum's permanent holdings include paintings by Monet, Van Gogh and Degas, photographs by Robert Mapplethorpe, and key surrealist works donated by Guggenheim's niece Peggy.

☑ Don't Miss

The view of the instantly recognizable facade from Fifth Ave and 88th St.

INTERIOR OF THE SOLOMON R. GUGGENHEIM MUSEUM, NEW YORK. © SRGF, NY. USED WITH PERMISSION. / MARCO BRIVIO / ALAMY STOCK PHOTO ©

What's Nearby?

Cooper-Hewitt National Design Museum Museum

(Map p252; ☎212-849-8351; www.cooperhewitt.org; 2 E 91st St, at Fifth Ave; adult/student/child $18/9/free, by donation 6-9pm Sat; 🕒10am-6pm Sun-Fri, to 9pm Sat; [S]4/5/6 to 86th St) Part of the Smithsonian Institution in Washington, DC, this house of culture is the only museum in the country that's dedicated to both historic and contemporary design. The collection, which spans 3000 years, is housed in the 64-room mansion built by billionaire Andrew Carnegie in 1901.

Jewish Museum Museum

(Map p252; ☎212-423-3200; www.thejewishmuseum.org; 1109 Fifth Ave, btwn E 92nd & 93rd Sts; adult/child $15/free, Sat free, by donation 5-8pm Thu; 🕒11am-6pm Sat-Tue, to 4pm Thu & Fri, closed Wed; 👪; [S]6 to 96th St) This New York City gem is tucked into a French-Gothic mansion from 1908, housing 30,000 items of Judaica, as well as sculpture, painting and decorative arts. It hosts excellent temporary exhibits, featuring retrospectives on influential figures such as Art Spiegelman, as well as world-class shows on the likes of Marc Chagall, Édouard Vuillard and Man Ray among other past luminaries.

🍴 Take a Break

The **Wright** (☎212-427-5690; www.thewrightrestaurant.com; Guggenheim Museum; mains $22-28; 🕒11:30am-3:30pm Mon-Wed & Fri, from 11am Sat & Sun; [S]4/5/6 to 86th St), at ground level, is a space-age eatery serving modern American brunch and lunch dishes.

Rockefeller Center

Always a hive of activity, Rockefeller Center has wide-ranging appeal, with art-deco towers, a sky-high viewing platform and a famed ice rink in winter.

Great For...

☑ **Don't Miss**

Drinks with panoramic views at Sixty-Five (p173).

This 22-acre 'city within a city' debuted at the height of the Great Depression. Taking nine years to build, it was America's first multiuse retail, entertainment and office space – a modernist sprawl of 19 buildings (14 of which are the original art-deco structures), outdoor plazas and big-name tenants. Developer John D Rockefeller Jr may have sweated over the cost (a mere $100 million), but it was all worth it; the Center was declared a National Landmark in 1987.

Top of the Rock

There are views, and then there's *the* view from the **Top of the Rock** (Map p252; ☏212-698-2000; www.topoftherocknyc.com; 30 Rockefeller Plaza, entrance on W 50th St btwn Fifth & Sixth Aves; adult/child $39/33, sunrise/sunset combo $54/48; ☺8am-midnight, last

Atlas by Lee Lawrie and Rene Paul Chambellan

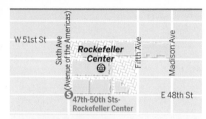

❶ Need to Know

(Map p252; www.rockefellercenter.com; Fifth to Sixth Aves btwn W 48th & 51st Sts; [S]B/D/F/M to 47th-50th Sts-Rockefeller Center)

✕ Take a Break

Grab a bite at Burger Joint (p134), well concealed inside Le Parker Meridien Hotel.

★ Top Tip

To beat the wintertime ice-skating crowds, come at the first skating period (8:30am) to avoid a long wait.

elevator at 11pm). Crowning the GE Building, 70 stories above Midtown, its blockbuster vista includes one icon that you won't see from atop the Empire State Building – *the* Empire State Building. If possible, head up just before sunset to see the city transform from day to glittering night (if you're already in the area and the queues aren't long, purchase your tickets in advance to avoid the late-afternoon rush). Alternatively, if you don't have under-21s in tow, ditch Top of the Rock for the 65th-floor cocktail bar (p173), where the same spectacular views come with well-mixed drinks... at a cheaper price than the Top of the Rock admission.

Public Artworks

Rockefeller Center features the work of 30 great artists, commissioned around the theme 'Man at the Crossroads Looks Uncertainly But Hopefully at the Future.' Paul Manship contributed *Prometheus*, overlooking the sunken plaza, and *Atlas*, in front of the International Building (630 Fifth Ave). Isamu Noguchi's *News* sits above the entrance to the Associated Press Building (50 Rockefeller Plaza), while José Maria Sert's oil *American Progress* awaits in the lobby of the GE Building. The latter work replaced Mexican artist Diego Rivera's original painting, rejected by the Rockefellers for containing 'communist imagery.'

Rockefeller Plaza

Come the festive season, Rockefeller Plaza is where you'll find New York's most famous Christmas tree. Ceremoniously lit just after Thanksgiving, it's a tradition that dates back to the 1930s, when construction workers set up a small tree on the site. In its shadow, Rink at Rockefeller Center (p201) is the city's most famous (and infamously crowded) ice-skating rink.

Chinatown

Take a trip to Asia without leaving the US mainland on a wander through the narrow lanes of Chinatown. It's pure sensory overload amid fast-talking street vendors, neon-lit noodle parlors and colorful storefronts packed with eye candy from the Far East.

Great For...

ⓘ Need to Know

(Map p246; www.explorechinatown.com; south of Broome St & east of Broadway; SN/Q/R/W, J/Z, 6 to Canal St, B/D to Grand St, F to East Broadway)

★ **Top Tip**

Don't forget to wander down the back alleys for a Technicolor assortment of spices and herbs to perfect your own Eastern dishes.

Endless exotic moments await in New York City's most colorfully cramped community, where a walk through the neighborhood is never the same, no matter how many times you pass through. Catch the whiff of fresh fish and ripe persimmons, hear the clacking of mah-jongg tiles on makeshift tables, and shop for everything imaginable, from rice-paper lanterns and embroidered slippers to a pound of pressed nutmeg.

Museum of Chinese in America

In a space designed by architect Maya Lin, the **Museum of Chinese in America** (Map p246; ☎212-619-4785; www.mocanyc.org; 215 Centre St, btwn Grand & Howard Sts; adult/child $10/5, first Thu of month free; 🕒11am-6pm Tue, Wed & Fri-Sun, to 9pm Thu; [S]N/Q/R/W, J/Z, 6 to Canal St) is a multifaceted space whose engaging permanent and temporary exhibitions shed light on Chinese American life, both past and present. Browse through interactive multimedia exhibits, maps, timelines, photos, letters, films and artifacts. The museum's anchor exhibit, 'With a Single Step: Stories in the Making of America,' provides an often intimate glimpse into topics including immigration, cultural identity and racial stereotyping.

Food Glorious Food

The most rewarding experience for Chinatown neophytes is to access this wild and wonderful world through their taste buds. More than any other area of Manhattan, Chinatown's menus sport wonderfully low prices, uninflated by ambience, hype or reputation. But more than cheap eats, the neighborhood is rife with family recipes passed across generations and continents.

Pedestrian street in Little Italy

Food displays and preparation remain unchanged and untempered by American norms, and steaming street stalls clutter the sidewalk serving pork buns and other finger-friendly food.

Buddhist Temples

Chinatown is home to Buddhist temples large and small, public and obscure. They are easily stumbled upon during a full-on stroll of the neighborhood, and at least two such temples are considered landmarks. The **Eastern States Buddhist Temple** (Map p246; ☎212-966-6229; 64 Mott St, btwn Bayard & Canal Sts; ☺8:30am-6pm; ⓢN/Q/R/W, J/Z, 6 to Canal St) is filled with hundreds of Buddhas,

☑ **Don't Miss**

A family-style meal at a bustling, back-alley dive.

ANDRIY BLOKHIN / SHUTTERSTOCK ©

while the **Mahayana Temple** (Map p246; ☎212-925-8787; http://en.mahayana. us; 133 Canal St, at Manhattan Bridge Plaza; ☺8:30am-6pm; ⓢB/D to Grand St, J/Z to Bowery, 6 to Canal St) holds one golden, 16ft-high Buddha, sitting on a lotus and edged with offerings of fresh oranges, apples and flowers. Mahayana is the largest Buddhist temple in Chinatown, and its entrance, which overlooks the frenzied vehicle entrance to the Manhattan Bridge, is guarded by two proud and handsome golden lions. Step inside and you'll find a simple interior of wooden floor and red paper lanterns, dramatically upstaged by the temple's magnificent Buddha.

Canal Street

Walking down Canal St is like a game of Frogger played on the streets of Shanghai. This is Chinatown's spine, where you'll dodge oncoming human traffic as you scurry into side streets to scout treasures from the Far East. You'll pass stinky seafood stalls hawking slippery fish; mysterious herb shops peddling a witch's cauldron's worth of roots and potions; storefront bakeries with steamy windows and the tastiest 80¢ pork buns you've ever had; restaurants with whole, roasted ducks hanging by their skinny necks in the windows; and produce markets piled high with fresh lychee, bok choy and Asian pears.

What's Nearby?

Little Italy   Area

(Map p246; ⓢN/Q/R/W, J/Z, 6 to Canal St, B/D to Grand St) This once-strong Italian neighborhood saw an exodus in the mid-20th century when many of its residents moved to more suburban neighborhoods in Brooklyn and beyond. Today, it's mostly concentrated on Mulberry St between Broome and Canal Sts, a stretch packed with checkerboard tablecloths and (mainly mediocre) Italian fare.

✖ **Take a Break**

Nyonya (p125) is a bustling temple to Chinese-Malay cuisine.

CATE_89 / SHUTTERSTOCK ©

National September 11 Memorial & Museum

An evocative museum and North America's largest artificial waterfalls are as much a symbol of hope and renewal as they are a tribute to the victims of terrorism.

Great For...

☑ Don't Miss

The museum houses the last steel column removed during the clean-up, adorned with the messages and mementos of recovery workers, responders and loved ones of the victims.

The National September 11 Memorial & Museum is a dignified tribute to the victims of the worst terrorist attack on American soil. Titled *Reflecting Absence*, the memorial's two massive reflecting pools are a symbol of renewal and commemorate the thousands who lost their lives. Beside them stands the Memorial Museum, a striking, solemn space documenting that horrific fall day in 2001.

Reflecting Pools

Surrounded by a plaza planted with 400 swamp white oak trees, the 9/11 Memorial's reflecting pools occupy the very footprints of the ill-fated twin towers. From their rim, a steady cascade of water pours 30ft down towards a central void. The flow of the water is richly symbolic, beginning as hundreds of smaller streams, merging into

Reflecting Pool

ⓘ Need to Know

(Map p244; www.911memorial.org; 180 Greenwich St; ⏰7:30am-9pm; Ⓢ E to World Trade Center, R to Cortlandt St, 2/3 to Park Pl) FREE

✕ Take a Break

Head up to Tribeca for great dining options such as Locanda Verde (p124).

★ Top Tip

It was the image of a child releasing a dove that inspired Santiago Calatrava's dramatic WTC Transportation Hub, located next to the museum.

a massive torrent of collective confusion, and ending with a slow journey towards an abyss. Bronze panels frame the pools, inscribed with the names of those who died in the terrorist attacks of September 11, 2001, and in the World Trade Center car bombing on February 26, 1993. Designed by Michael Arad and Peter Walker, the pools are both striking and deeply poignant.

Memorial Museum

The contemplative energy of the memorial is further enhanced by the **National September 11 Memorial Museum** (Map p244; www.911memorial.org/museum; museum adult/child $24/15, 5-8pm Tue free; ⏰9am-8pm Sun-Thu, to 9pm Fri & Sat, last entry 2hr before close). Standing between the reflective pools, the museum's glass entrance pavilion eerily evokes a toppled tower. Inside the

entrance, an escalator leads down to the museum's main subterranean lobby. On the descent, visitors stand in the shadow of two steel tridents, originally embedded in the bedrock at the base of the North Tower. Each standing over 80ft tall and weighing 50 tons, they once provided the structural support that allowed the towers to soar over 1360ft into the sky. In the subsequent sea of rubble, they remained standing, becoming immediate symbols of resilience.

The tridents are two of more than 10,300 objects in the museum's collection. Among these are the Vesey Street Stairs, dubbed the 'survivors staircase,' they allowed hundreds of workers to flee the WTC site on the morning of 9/11. At the bottom of these stairs is the moving In Memoriam gallery, its walls lined with the photographs and names of those who perished. Interactive touch screens and a central reflection room shed light on the victims' lives. Their humanity is further fleshed out by the numerous personal effects on display. Among these is a dust-covered wallet belonging to Robert Joseph Gschaar, an insurance underwriter working on level 92 of the South Tower. The wallet's contents include a photograph of Gschaar's wife, Myrta, and a $2 bill, twin to the one given to Myrta by Gschaar as a symbol of their second chance at happiness.

Around the corner from the In Memoriam gallery is the New York City Fire Department's Engine Company 21. One of the largest artifacts on display, its burnt-out cab is testament to the inferno faced by those at the scene. The fire engine stands at the entrance to the museum's main Historical Exhibition. Divided into three sections – Events of the Day, Before 9/11 and After 9/11 – its collection of videos, real-time audio recordings, images, objects and testimonies provide a rich, meditative exploration of the tragedy, the events that preceded it (including the WTC bombing of 1993), and the stories of grief, resilience and hope that followed.

The Historical Exhibition spills into the monumental Foundation Hall, flanked by a massive section of the original slurry wall, built to hold back the waters of the Hudson River during the towers' construction. It's also home to the last steel column removed during the clean-up, adorned with the messages and mementos of recovery workers, responders and loved ones of the victims.

What's Nearby?

Trinity Church   Church
(Map p244; ☏212-602-0800; www.trinity wallstreet.org; 75 Broadway, at Wall St; ☺church 7am-6pm Mon-Fri, 8am-4pm Sat, 7am-4pm

Foundation Hall, Memorial Museum

Sun, churchyard 7am-4pm Mon-Fri, 8am-3pm Sat, 7am-3pm Sun; S R to Rector St, 2/3, 4/5 to Wall St) New York City's tallest building upon completion in 1846, Trinity Church features a 280ft-high bell tower and a richly colored stained-glass window over the altar. Famous residents of its serene cemetery include Founding Father Alexander Hamilton, while its excellent music series includes Concerts at One (1pm Thursdays) and magnificent choir concerts, including

an annual December rendition of Handel's *Messiah.*

The original Anglican parish church was founded by King William III in 1697 and once presided over several constituent chapels, including St Paul's Chapel at the corner of Fulton St and Broadway. Its huge landholdings in Lower Manhattan made it the country's wealthiest and most influential church throughout the 18th century. Burnt down in 1776, its second incarnation was demolished in 1839. The third and current church, designed by English architect Richard Upjohn, helped launch the picturesque neo-Gothic movement in America.

St Paul's Chapel — Church

(Map p244; ☎212-602-0800; www.trinitywall street.org; 209 Broadway, at Fulton St; ◷10am-6pm Mon-Sat, 7am-6pm Sun; S A/C, J/Z, 2/3, 4/5 to Fulton St, R to Cortlandt St, E to World Trade Center) After his inauguration in 1789, George Washington worshipped at this classic revival brownstone chapel, which found new fame in the aftermath of September 11. With the World Trade Center destruction occurring just a block away, the mighty structure became a spiritual support and volunteer center, movingly documented in its exhibition 'Unwavering Spirit: Hope & Healing at Ground Zero.'

Through photographs, personal objects and messages of support, the exhibition honors both the victims and the volunteers who worked round the clock, serving meals, setting up beds, doling out massages and counseling rescue workers.

☑ Don't Miss

In the museum, look out for the so-called 'Angel of 9/11', the eerie outline of a woman's anguished face on a twisted girder believed to originate from the point where American Airlines Flight 11 slammed into the North Tower.

KOTSOVOLOS PANAGIOTIS / SHUTTERSTOCK ©

One World Trade Center

Soaring above the city skyline is this shimmering tower, a symbol of Lower Manhattan's rebirth. Its observation decks offer mesmerizing views over the vast metropolis (and surrounding states).

Filling what was a sore and glaring gap in the Lower Manhattan skyline, One World Trade Center symbolizes rebirth, determination and a city's resilience. More than just another super-tall building, this tower is a richly symbolic giant, well aware of the past yet firmly focused on the future. For lovers of New York, it's also the hot new stop for dizzying, unforgettable urban views.

The Building

Leaping up from the northwest corner of the World Trade Center site, the 104-floor tower is architect David M Childs' redesign of Daniel Libeskind's original 2002 concept. Not only the loftiest building in America, this tapered giant is currently the tallest building in the Western Hemisphere, not to mention the fourth tallest in the world by pinnacle height. The tower soars skywards

Great For...

☑ **Don't Miss**

The staggering view from the base of the tower looking skyward.

ⓘ Need to Know

(One WTC; Map p244; cnr West & Vesey Sts; Ⓢ E to World Trade Center, 2/3 to Park Pl; A/C, J/Z, 4/5 to Fulton St, R to Cortlandt St)

✕ Take a Break

Inside Brookfield Place (p124), you'll find a string of chef-driven dining spots and a French food emporium.

★ Top Tip

You can save a bit of time in line by pre-purchasing your tickets online (oneworldobservatory.com/tickets).

with chamfered edges. The result is a series of isosceles triangles that, seen from the building's base, reach to infinity.

Crowning the structure is a 408ft cabled-stayed spire. Co-designed by sculptor Kenneth Snelson, it brings the building's total height to 1776ft, a symbolic reference to the year of American independence. Indeed, symbolism feeds several aspects of the building: the tower's footprint is equal to those of the twin towers, while the observation decks match the heights of those in the old complex. Unlike the original towers, however, One WTC was built with a whole new level of safety in mind, its precautionary features including a 200ft-high blast-resistant base (clad in over 2000 pieces of glimmering prismatic glass) and 1m-thick concrete walls encasing all elevators, stairwells, and communication and safety systems.

One thing that wasn't foreseen by the architects and engineers was the antenna's noisy disposition; the strong winds that race through its lattice design produce a haunting, howling sound known to keep some locals up at night.

One World Observatory

Not one to downplay its assets, the sky-scraper is home to **One World Observatory** (Map p244; ☎844-696-1776; www.oneworld observatory.com; adult/child $34/28; ⊙9am-8pm, last ticket sold at 7:15pm; Ⓢ E to World Trade Center, 2/3 to Park Pl, A/C, J/Z, 4/5 to Fulton St, R to Cortlandt St), the city's loftiest observation deck. While the observatory spans levels 100 to 102, the experience begins at the ground-floor Global Welcome Center, where an electronic world map highlights the homeland of visitors (data relayed from tick-et scans). The bitter bickering that plagued much of the project's development is all but forgotten in the adjoining Voices exhibition, where architects and construction workers wax lyrically about the tower's formation on 144 video screens.

After a quick rundown of the site's geology, the real thrills begin as you step inside one of five Sky Pod elevators, among the fastest in the world. As the elevators begin their 1250ft skyward journey, LED wall panels kick into action. Suddenly, you're in a veritable time machine, watching Manhattan's evolution from forested island to teeming concrete jungle. Forty-seven seconds (and 500 years) later, you're on level 102, where another short presentation ends with a spectacular reveal.

Skip the overpriced eateries on level 101 and continue down to the real highlight: level 100. Waiting for you is an epic, 360-degree panorama guaranteed to keep your index finger busy pointing out landmarks, from the Brooklyn and Manhattan Bridges, to Lady Liberty and the Woolworth, Empire State and Chrysler Buildings. If you need a

hand, interactive mobile tablets are available for hire ($15). As expected, the view is extraordinary (choose a clear day!), taking in all five boroughs and adjoining states.

What's Nearby?

Woolworth Building
Notable Building

(Map p244; ☎203-966-9663; www.woolworth tours.com; 233 Broadway, at Park Pl; 30/60/90min tours $20/30/45; **S**R to City Hall, 2/3 to Park Pl, 4/5/6 to Brooklyn Bridge-City Hall) The world's tallest building upon completion in 1913, Cass Gilbert's 60-story, 792ft-tall Woolworth Building is a neo-Gothic marvel, elegantly clad in masonry and terracotta. Surpassed in height by the Chrysler Building in 1930, its landmarked lobby is a breathtaking spectacle of dazzling, Byzantine-like mosaics. The lobby is only

One World Observatory

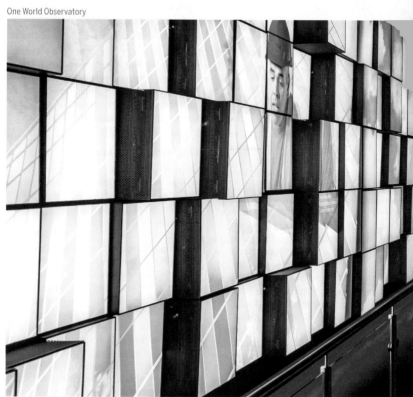

accessible on prebooked guided tours, which also offer insight into the building's more curious original features, among them a dedicated subway entrance and a secret swimming pool.

At its dedication, the building was described as a 'cathedral of commerce'; though meant as an insult, FW Woolworth, head of the five-and-dime chain-store empire headquartered there, took the comment as a compliment and began throwing the term around himself.

★ Did You Know?

One World Trade Center has green credentials, including a gray water system that collects and uses rainwater and building materials made substantially of post-industrial recycled content.

Federal Reserve
Bank of New York   Notable Building

(Map p244; ☎212-720-6130; www.newyorkfed. org; 33 Liberty St, at Nassau St, entrance at 44 Maiden Lane; reservation required; ⊗guided tours 1pm & 2pm Mon-Fri; Ⓢ A/C, J/Z, 2/3, 4/5 to Fulton St) **FREE** The best reason to visit the Federal Reserve Bank is the chance to (briefly) ogle at its high-security vault – more than 10,000 tons of gold reserves reside here, 80ft below ground. You'll only see a small part of that fortune, but signing on to a free tour (the only way down; book several months ahead) is worth the effort.

While you don't need to join a guided tour to browse the bank's interactive museum, which delves into the bank's history and research, you will still need to book a time online. Bring your passport or other official ID.

Lower East Side Tenement Museum

In a neighborhood once teeming with immigrants, this museum opens a window to the past on guided tours through meticulously preserved tenements. You'll learn all about real people who lived on these densely packed streets.

Great For...

Sara D Roosevelt Park
Delancey St
Delancey-Essex Sts
🏛 *Lower East Side Tenement Museum*
Broome St
Chrystie St
Forsyth St
Orchard St
Essex St
Ⓢ Grand St

ℹ Need to Know

(Map p246; 📞877-975-3786; www.tenement. org; 103 Orchard St, btwn Broome & Delancey Sts; tours adult/student & senior $25/20; ⊙10am-6:30pm Fri-Wed, to 8:30pm Thu; Ⓢ B/D to Grand St, J/M/Z to Essex St, F to Delancey St)

★ **Top Tip**
Watch the free 30-minute film shown in the visitor center that gives an overview of immigrant life in NYC.

There's no museum in New York that humanizes the city's colorful past quite like the Lower East Side Tenement Museum, which puts the neighborhood's heartbreaking but inspiring heritage on full display in several re-creations of former tenements. Always evolving and expanding, the museum has a variety of tours and talks beyond the museum's walls – a must for anyone interested in old New York.

Inside the Tenement

A wide range of tenement tours lead visitors into the building where hundreds of immigrants lived and worked over the years. Hard Times, one of the most popular tours, visits apartments from two different time periods – the 1870s and the 1930s. There you'll see the squalid conditions tenants faced – in the early days there was a wretched communal outhouse, and no electricity or running water – and what life was like for the families who lived there. Other tours focus on Irish immigrants and the harsh discrimination they faced, sweatshop workers and 'shop life' (with a tour through a re-created 1870s German beer hall).

103 Orchard St

The visitor center at 103 Orchard St has a museum shop and a small screening room that plays an original film. Several evenings a month, the museum hosts talks here, often relating to the present immigrant experience in America. The building itself was, naturally, a tenement, too – ask the staff about the interesting families of East European and Italian descent that once dwelled here.

Tenement Museum guided tour

Meet Victoria

Travel back to 1916 and meet Victoria Confino, a 14-year-old girl from a Greek Sephardic family. Played by a costumed interpreter, Victoria interacts with visitors answering questions about what her life was like in those days. It's especially recommended for kids, as visitors are free to handle household objects. This one-hour tour is held on weekends year-round, and daily during the summer.

Neighborhood Tours

A great way to understand the immigrant experience is on a walking tour around the

> ☑ **Don't Miss**
>
> A peek into the 1870s and the 1930s on the Hard Times tour.

PATTI MCCONVILLE / ALAMY STOCK PHOTO ©

neighborhood. These tours, ranging from 75 minutes to two hours, explore a variety of topics. Foods of the Lower East Side looks at the ways traditional foods have shaped American cuisine; Then & Now explores the way the neighborhood has changed over the decades; and Outside the Home looks at life beyond the apartment – where immigrants stored (and lost) their life savings, the churches and synagogues so integral to community life, and the meeting halls where poorly paid workers gathered to fight for better conditions.

What's Nearby?

New Museum of Contemporary Art   Museum

(Map p246; ☏ 212-219-1222; www.newmuseum. org; 235 Bowery, btwn Stanton & Rivington Sts; adult/child $18/free, 7-9pm Thu by donation; ⊙11am-6pm Tue & Wed & Fri-Sun, to 9pm Thu; ⓢ R/W to Prince St, F to 2nd Ave, J/Z to Bowery, 6 to Spring St) Rising above the neighborhood, the New Museum of Contemporary Art is a sight to behold: a seven-story stack of off-kilter, white, ethereal boxes designed by Tokyo-based architects Kazuyo Sejima and Ryue Nishizawa of SANAA and the New York–based firm Gensler. It was a long-awaited breath of fresh air along what was a completely gritty Bowery strip when it arrived back in 2007 – though since its opening, many glossy new constructions have joined it, quickly transforming this once down-and-out avenue.

Founded in 1977 by Marcia Tucker and housed in five different locations over the years, the museum's mission statement is simple: 'New art, new ideas.' The institution gave gallery space to artists Keith Haring, Jeff Koons, Joan Jonas, Mary Kelly and Andres Serrano at the beginning of their careers, and continues to show contemporary heavy hitters.

> ✖ **Take a Break**
>
> Take a bite out of history at famed Jewish deli Russ & Daughters (p126), in business since 1914.

Prospect Park

Brooklyn's favorite green space is a grassy wonderland of rolling meadows, babbling brooks, hillside overlooks, flower strewn trails and an open lake. It's a fantastic place for running, walking, picnicking, skating or just getting a dose of the great outdoors.

Great For...

❶ Need to Know

(Map p254; ☎718-965-8951; www.prospect-park.org; Grand Army Plaza; ⏰5am-1am; Ⓢ2/3 to Grand Army Plaza, F to 15th St-Prospect Park)

★ Top Tip
One of the prettiest places for a park stroll is alongside the Lullwater, near the Boathouse.

DAVID GROSSMAN / ALAMY STOCK PHOTO ©

The creators of the 585-acre Prospect Park, Calvert Vaux and Frederick Olmsted, considered this an improvement on their other New York project, Central Park. Created in 1866, Prospect Park has many of the same features: a gorgeous meadow, a scenic lake, forested pathways and rambling hills that are straddled with leafy walkways. It receives roughly 10 million visitors a year.

Grand Army Plaza

A large, landscaped traffic circle with a massive ceremonial arch sits at the intersection of Flatbush Ave and Prospect Park West. This marks the beginning of Eastern Parkway and the entrance to Prospect Park. The arch, which was built in the 1890s, is a memorial to Union soldiers who fought in the Civil War.

Long Meadow

The 90-acre Long Meadow, which is bigger than Central Park's Great Lawn, lies to the south of the park's formal entrance at Grand Army Plaza. It's a super strolling and lounging spot, filled with pick-up ball games and families flying kites. On the south end is the Picnic House, with a snack stand and public bathrooms.

Children's Corner

Near Flatbush Ave, the Children's Corner contains a terrific 1912 carousel, originally from Coney Island, and the **Prospect Park Zoo** (Map p254; ☑718-399-7339; www.prospect-parkzoo.com; 450 Flatbush Ave; adult/child $8/5; ☺10am-5:30pm Apr-Oct, to 4:30pm Nov-Mar; 🚼; ⓢ2/3 to Grand Army Plaza), featuring sea lions, baboons, wallabies and a small petting zoo. To the northeast of the carousel is the

Audubon Center boathouse

18th-century **Lefferts Historic House** (Map p254; ☎718-789-2822; www.prospectpark.org; Prospect Park; suggested donation $3; 🕑noon-5pm Thu-Sun Apr-Nov; [S]B, Q to Prospect Park), which has plenty of old-fashioned toys to goof around with.

Audubon Center Boathouse

Sitting on a northern finger of Prospect Park Lake, the photogenic boathouse (aka Prospect Park Audubon Center) hosts a range of activities throughout the year (guided bird-watching sessions, free yoga classes, nature-themed art exhibitions, hands-on craft activities for kids). From here, there is a trailhead for 2.5 miles of woodsy nature trails.

LITTLENY / SHUTTERSTOCK ©

Lakeside

Prospect Park's newest attraction continues to turn heads. The 26-acre Lakeside (p200) complex features rinks for ice skating and roller skating, as well as a cafe, new walking trails and a small concert space.

What's Nearby?

Brooklyn Botanic Garden Gardens

(Map p254; www.bbg.org; 150 Eastern Pkwy, Prospect Park; adult/child $12/free, Tue & 10am-noon Sat free; 🕑8am-6pm Tue-Fri, 10am-6pm Sat & Sun, hours vary in winter; 👪; [S]2/3 to Eastern Pkwy-Brooklyn Museum) One of Brooklyn's most picturesque attractions, this 52-acre garden is home to thousands of plants and trees, as well as a Japanese garden where river turtles swim alongside a Shinto shrine. The best time to visit is late April or early May, when the blooming cherry trees (a gift from Japan) are celebrated in Sakura Matsuri, the Cherry Blossom Festival.

Brooklyn Museum Museum

(Map p254; ☎718-638-5000; www.brooklynmuseum.org; 200 Eastern Pkwy, Prospect Park; suggested donation $16, 19 & under free; 🕑11am-6pm Wed & Fri-Sun, to 10pm Thu; 👪; [S]2/3 to Eastern Pkwy-Brooklyn Museum) This encyclopedic museum is housed in a five-story, 560,000-sq-ft beaux-arts building designed by McKim, Mead & White. Today, the building houses more than 1.5 million objects, including ancient artifacts, 19th-century period rooms, and sculptures and paintings from across several centuries. The museum offers a great alternative to the packed-to-the-gills institutions in Manhattan, and it often features thought-provoking temporary exhibitions.

🍴 Take a Break

Near the park's north entrance, friendly **Cheryl's Global Soul** (☎347-529-2855; www.cherylsglobalsoul.com; 236 Underhill Ave, Prospect Heights; sandwiches $8-14, mains $15-25; 🕑8am-4pm Mon, to 10pm Tue-Sun; 🌿👪; [S]2/3 to Eastern Pkwy-Brooklyn Museum) is a neighborhood favorite.

Jane's Carousel

Brooklyn Bridge Park

The pride and joy of Brooklyn, this revitalized waterfront park offers loads of amusement, with playgrounds, walkways, and lawns with plenty of summertime outdoor entertainment, including live music and open-air cinema, not to mention grand views of Manhattan skyscrapers across the river.

Great For...

❶ Need to Know

(Map p254; ☎718-222-9939; www.brooklyn bridgepark.org; East River Waterfront, btwn Atlantic Ave & Adams St; ☺6am-1am; 👷; 🚇A/C to High St, 2/3 to Clark St, F to York St) FREE

★ **Top Tip**
Be sure to check out what's on when you're in town: the website lists outdoor yoga and dance classes, theater and cinema, family activities and more.

This 85-acre park, nearing completion, is one of Brooklyn's most talked-about new sights. Wrapping around a bend on the East River, it runs for 1.3 miles from Jay St in Dumbo to the west end of Atlantic Ave in Cobble Hill. It has revitalized a once-barren stretch of shoreline, turning a series of abandoned piers into public park land.

Empire Fulton Ferry

Just east of the Brooklyn Bridge, in the northern section of Dumbo, you'll find a state park with a grassy lawn that faces the East River. Near the water is **Jane's Carousel** (Map p254; www.janescarousel.com; Brooklyn Bridge Park, Empire Fulton Ferry, Dumbo; tickets $2; ⏰11am-7pm Wed-Mon mid-May–mid-Sep, to 6pm Thu-Sun mid-Sep–mid-May; 👪; [S]F to York St), a lovingly restored 1922 carousel set inside a glass pavilion designed by Pritzker Prize–winning architect Jean Nouvel. The park is bordered on one side by the **Empire Stores & Tobacco Warehouse** (Map p254; Water St, near Main St, [S]F to York St, A/C to High St), a series of Civil War–era structures that house restaurants, shops and a theater. Keep heading up to the Manhattan Bridge to find a new bouldering wall. There's also a much-loved playground, which resembles a pirate ship.

Pier 1

A 9-acre pier just south of the Empire Fulton Ferry is home to a stretch of park featuring a playground, walkways and the Harbor View and Bridge View Lawns, both of which overlook the river. On the Bridge View Lawn, you'll find artist Mark di Suvero's 30ft kinetic sculpture *Yoga* (1991). From July through August, free outdoor

View of Pier 1 pilings and the Manhattan skyline from Brooklyn Bridge Park

films are screened on the Harbor View Lawn against a stunning backdrop of Manhattan. Other free open-air events (outdoor dance parties, group yoga classes, history tours) happen throughout the summer. The seasonal Brooklyn Bridge Garden Bar (brooklynbridgegardenbar.com) can be found on the pier's north end. You can also catch the East River Ferry (www.eastriverferry.com) from the north end of the pier.

Pier 2 & Pier 4

At Pier 2, you'll find courts for basketball, handball and boccie, plus a skating rink. Nearby, there's a tiny beach at Pier 4.

☑ Don't Miss

The views of Manhattan and the East River from Empire Fulton Ferry at sunset.

WINSTON TAN / SHUTTERSTOCK ©

Though swimming is not allowed, you can hire stand-up paddleboards here. If you want to head up to Brooklyn Heights, you can take a bouncy pedestrian bridge (access near Pier 2).

Pier 5 & Pier 6

At the southern end of the park, off Atlantic Ave, Pier 6 has a fantastic playground and a small water play area for tots (if you're bringing kids, pack swimsuits and towels). Neighboring Pier 5, just north, has walkways, sand volleyball courts, soccer fields and barbecue grills. There's also a few seasonal concessions (May to October), including wood-fired pizza, beer and Italian treats at **Fornino** (Map p254; ☎718-422-1107; www.fornino.com; Pier 6, Brooklyn Bridge Park, Brooklyn Heights; pizzas $12-25; 🕙10am-10pm Apr-Oct; 🚌B45 to Brooklyn Bridge Park/Pier 6, [S]2/3, 4/5 to Borough Hall), which has a rooftop deck. A free seasonal ferry runs on weekends from Pier 6 to **Governors Island** (☎212-825-3045; www.govisland.com; 🕙10am-6pm Mon-Fri, to 7pm Sat & Sun May-Oct; [S]4/5 to Bowling Green, 1 to South Ferry) [FREE].

Still in the works are plans to transform the west end of Pier 6 with meadows, trees and a triangular platform with unrivaled views of Lower Manhattan.

What's Nearby?

Brooklyn Heights Promenade — Viewpoint

(Map p254; btwn Orange & Remsen Sts; 🕙24hr; 👪; [S]2/3 to Clark St) All of the east–west lanes of Brooklyn Heights (such as Clark and Pineapple Sts) lead to the neighborhood's number-one attraction: a narrow park with breathtaking views of Lower Manhattan and New York Harbor. Though it hangs over the busy Brooklyn–Queens Expressway (BQE), this little slice of urban beauty is a great spot for a sunset walk.

🍴 Take a Break

In the park at Pier 6, Fornino (see above) has wood-fired pizzas and rooftop dining at picnic tables with panoramic views.

West Village Wandering

Of all the neighborhoods in New York City, the West Village is easily the most walkable, its cobbled corners straying from the signature gridiron that unfurls across the rest of the island. An afternoon stroll is not to be missed; hidden landmarks and quaint cafes abound.

Start Cherry Lane Theater
Finish Washington Sq Park
Distance 1 mile; **Duration** 1 hour

4 To the north of **Christopher Park** is the **Stonewall Inn** (www. thestonewallinnnyc.com) the starting place of the gay revolution.

3 For another TV landmark, head to **66 Perry St**, Carrie Bradshaw's apartment in *Sex and the City*.

2 The apartment block at **90 Bedford** was the fictitious home of the cast of *Friends*.

1 Established in 1924, **Cherry Lane Theater** (p187) is the city's longest continuously running off-Broadway establishment.

5 The **Jefferson Market Library** building once served as a court-house and a fire-lookout tower.

Take a Break...

Near Washington Square, **Stumptown Coffee Roasters** (☏855-711-3385; www.stumptowncoffee.com; 30 W 8th St, at MacDougal St; ◷7am-8pm) serves some of NYC's best coffee.

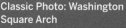

Classic Photo: Washington Square Arch

7 Washington Square Park (p115) is the beating heart of the Village and hosts a dynamic cross-section of the city, from students and buskers, to canoodling couples and chess hustlers.

6 Swing by **Cafe Wha?** (www.cafewha.com), where many musicians and comedians – including Bob Dylan and Richard Pryor – got their start.

0   400 m
0   0.2 miles

Frieze Art Fair exhibition by Gagosian gallery

Chelsea Galleries

Chelsea is home to the highest concentration of art galleries in the entire city. Here you'll find works by some of the world's top living artists – as well as a few retrospectives from past greats. While there are scores of galleries to choose from, a few heavy hitters should not be missed.

Great For...

☑ **Don't Miss**

A stroll along the High Line after getting an eyeful of art.

Pace Gallery

In a dramatically transformed garage, the **Pace Gallery** (Map p250; ☎212-929-7000; www.pacegallery.com; 510 W 25th St; ⊘10am-6pm Tue-Sat; ⓢC/E to 23rd St) has worked with some of the leading artists of recent years including Sol LeWitt, David Hockney, Chuck Close and Robert Rauschenberg. It has two locations in Chelsea (the other is around the corner at 537 W 24th St) and one in Midtown (at 32 E 57th St).

Cheim & Read

Sculptures of every shape, size and material abound at **Cheim & Read** (Map p250; ☎212-242-7727; www.cheimread.com; 547 W 25th St, btwn Tenth & Eleventh Aves; ⊘10am-6pm Tue-Sat; ⓢC/E to 23rd St) and monthly rotations keep the exhibits fresh – expect blazing light installations and inspired photography displays.

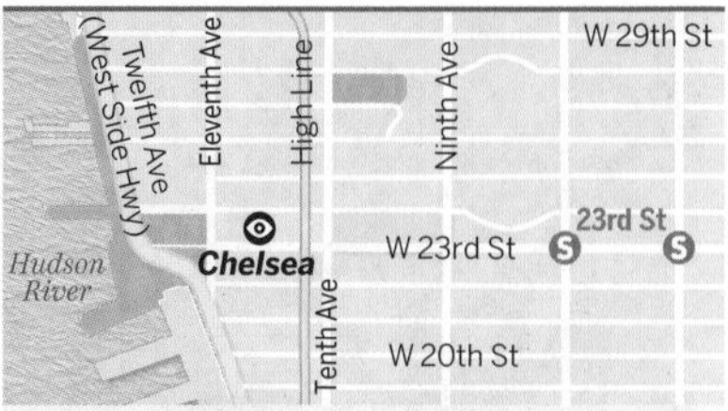

ℹ Need to Know

Most of the galleries lie in the West 20s, between Tenth and Eleventh Aves. By subway, take the C or E line to 23rd St.

🍴 Take a Break

Refuel on mouthwatering tapas and Spanish wines at the cozy **Tía Pol** (Map p250; ☎212-675-8805; www.tiapol.com; 205 Tenth Ave, btwn 22nd & 23rd Sts; small plates $5-14; 🕒noon-11pm Tue-Sun, from 5:30pm Mon; [S]C/E to 23rd St).

★ Top Tip

Openings for new shows typically take place on Thursday evenings, with wine and a festive art-minded crowd.

Gagosian

Gagosian (Map p250; ☎212-741-1111; www.gagosian.com; 555 W 24th St; 🕒10am-6pm Tue-Sat; [S]C/E to 23rd St) offers a different vibe than most of the one-off galleries, as it's part of a constellation of showrooms that spreads well across the globe. Also check out the other Chelsea location (522 W 21st St), which easily rivals some of the city's museums with its large-scale installations.

Mary Boone

Check out **Mary Boone Gallery** (Map p250; ☎212-752-2929; www.maryboonegallery.com; 541 W 24th St; 🕒10am-6pm Tue-Sat; [S]C/E, 1 to 23rd St), whose owner found fame in the '80s with her eye for Jean-Michel Basquiat and Julian Schnabel. It's considered one of the main 'blue-chip' galleries in the area.

Barbara Gladstone

The curator of the eponymous **Barbara Gladstone Gallery** (Map p250; ☎212-206-9300; www.gladstonegallery.com; 515 W 24th St, btwn Tenth & Eleventh Aves; 🕒10am-6pm Tue-Sat; [S]C/E, 1 to 23rd St) has learned a thing or two in her 30 years in the Manhattan art world. Ms Gladstone consistently puts together the most talked-about and well-critiqued displays around.

Paula Cooper

An icon of the art world, **Paula Cooper Gallery** (Map p250; ☎212-255-1105; www.paulacoopergallery.com; 534 W 21st St, btwn Tenth & Eleventh Aves; 🕒10am-6pm Tue-Sat; [S]C/E to 23rd St) was one of the first to move from SoHo to Chelsea. She continues to push boundaries and draw crowds, as she did for her 2011 exhibition *The Clock* when the gallery stayed open 24 hours a day on weekends.

Washington Square Park

The unofficial town square of the Village is Washington Square Park, a photogenic quadrangle of park space that's bursting with energy – impromptu music jams, spirited political debate and giddy student chatter.

Great For...

☑ Don't Miss

The chance to cool off in the fountain. Dip your toes – or your torso – on hot days.

What was once a potter's field and a square for public executions is now the epicenter of life in Greenwich Village. Encased in perfectly manicured brownstones and gorgeous twists of modern architecture (all owned by NYU), Washington Square Park is one of the most striking garden spaces in the city – especially as you are welcomed by the iconic Stanford White Arch on the north side of the green.

History

Although quite ravishing today, the park had a long and sordid history before finally blossoming into the paradigm of public space we see today (thanks largely to a $30 million renovation completed in 2014).

When the Dutch settled Manhattan to run the Dutch East India Company, they gave what is now the park to their freed black slaves. The land was squarely between the

A breakdancer performs for a park audience

❶ Need to Know

(Map p246; Fifth Ave at Washington Sq N; 🚻; Ⓢ A/C/E, B/D/F/M to W 4th St-Washington Sq, R/W to 8th St-NYU)

✖ Take a Break

You'll find loads of good street food down on MacDougal Street, including falafel legend **Mamoun's** (Map p246; www.mamouns.com; 119 Macdougal St; sandwiches from $3, plates from $6; ⊘11am-5am; Ⓢ F, M, B, D, A, C, or E train to West 4th Street).

★ Top Tip

Come on a weekend spring or summer afternoon to see the park at its liveliest.

Dutch and Native settlements, so, in a way, the area acted as a buffer between enemies. Though fairly marshy, it was arable land and farming took place for around 60 years.

At the start of the 19th century, the municipality of New York purchased the land for use as a burial ground straddling the city's limit. At first the cemetery was mainly for indigent workers, but the space quickly reached capacity during an outbreak of yellow fever. Over 20,000 bodies remain buried under the park today.

By 1830 the grounds were used for military parades, and then quickly transformed into a park for the wealthy elite who were constructing lavish townhouses along the surrounding streets.

Stanford White Arch

The Stanford White Arch, colloquially known as the Washington Square Arch, dominates the park with its 72ft of beaming white Dover marble. Originally designed in wood to celebrate the centennial of George Washington's inauguration in 1889, the arch proved so popular that it was replaced with stone six years later and adorned with statues of the general in war and peace. In 1916 artist Marcel Duchamp famously climbed to the top of the arch by its internal stairway and declared the park the 'Free and Independent Republic of Washington Square.'

Changes

In 1935 the Parks Department sought to change the shape and usage of the space but met with fierce local resistance. Many amended proposals and protests later, in 1958 the residents were victorious. As a result of their efforts, the square's shape has remained largely unchanged since the 1800s.

MoMA PS1

The smaller, hipper sibling of Manhattan's Museum of Modern Art, MoMA PS1 hunts down razor-sharp art and serves it up in a former school.

Great For...

☑ **Don't Miss**

Hidden art and secret chambers – including a basement door leading to a gilded furnace.

Forget about lily ponds in gilded frames. Here you'll be peering at videos through floorboards and debating the meaning of nonstatic structures while staring through a hole in the wall. Nothing is predictable.

Roots, Radicals & PS1 Classics

PS1 first hit the scene in the 1970s. This was the age of Dia, Artists' Space and the New Museum – new-gen projects showcasing the city's thriving experimental, multimedia art scene. In 1976, Alanna Heiss – a supporter of art in alternative spaces – took possession of an abandoned school building in Queens and invited artists like Richard Serra, James Turrell and Keith Sonnier to create site-specific works. The end result was PS1's inaugural exhibition, *Rooms*. Surviving remnants include Richard Artschwager's oval-shaped wall 'blimps' and

ⓘ Need to Know

(☎718-784-2084; www.momaps1.org; 22-25 Jackson Ave, Long Island City; suggested donation adult/child $10/free, free with MoMA ticket; 🕒noon-6pm Thu-Mon, Warm Up parties 3-9pm Sat Jul & Aug; [S]E, M to Court Sq-23rd St, G, 7 to Court Sq)

🍴 Take a Break

Set with desk-like tables, **M Wells Dinette** (☎718-786-1800; www.magasinwells.com; 22-25 Jackson Ave, Long Island City; mains $9-29; 🕒noon-6pm Thu-Mon) is just like being back at school, but with much better grub.

★ Top Tip

Come on Friday nights (from 4pm to 8pm) for free admission.

Alan Saret's light-channeling *The Hole at P.S.1, Fifth Solar Chthonic Wall Temple,* on the north wing's 3rd floor. These works are part of the gallery's long-term installations, which also include Pipilotti Rist's video *Selbstlos im Lavabad* (Selfless in the Bath of Lava) – viewable through the lobby floorboards – and James Turrell's awe-inspiring *Meeting,* where the sky is the masterpiece.

Summer 'Warm Up' Parties

On Saturday afternoon from July to early September, rock on at one of New York's coolest weekly music/culture events, Warm Up. It's a hit with everyone from verified hipsters to plugged-in music geeks, who spill into the MoMA PS1 courtyard to eat, drink and catch a stellar line-up of top bands, experimental music and DJs. Featured artists have included acid-house deity DJ Pierre and techno pioneer Juan Atkins. It's like one big block party, albeit with better music and art than your usual neighborhood slap-up. Linked to it is the annual YAP (Young Architects Program) competition, in which one design team is selected to transform the museum courtyard with a large-scale structure that provides shade and creative party space.

Sunday Sessions

Another cultural treat is the Sunday Sessions, on Sunday from September to May. Spanning lectures, film screenings, music performances, even architectural projects, the lineup has included experimental comedy, postindustrial noise jams and Latin art-house dance. One week you might catch a symphony debut, the next an architectural performance from Madrid. Upcoming events are listed on the MoMA PS1 website.

DINING OUT

Pizza, high-end cuisine
and cheap eats

Dining Out

From inspired iterations of world cuisine to quintessentially local nibbles, New York City's dining scene is infinite, all-consuming and a proud testament to the kaleidoscope of citizens that call the city home.

The great variety of the restaurant scene can be staggering. Ask for some 'New York food' and you'll wind up with anything from a hot dog to a Gallic-inspired tasting menu at Le Bernardin. Cuisine in the multicultural town is global by definition, a testament to the immigrants who have unpacked their bags and recipes on its streets. And just like the city itself, it's a scene that's constantly evolving, driven by insatiable ambition.

So go ahead, take a bite out of the Big Apple – we promise you won't be sorry.

In This Section

Price Ranges & Tipping

The following price ranges refer to a main dish, exclusive of tax and tip:

$ less than $15

$$ $15–25

$$$ more than $25

New Yorkers tip between 18% and 20% of the final price of the meal. For takeaway, it's polite to drop a few dollars in the tip jar.

Harlem & Upper Manhattan
Comfort cuisine meets global flavors (p138)

Upper West Side & Central Park
A few top eats tucked between
apartment blocks (p137)

Upper East Side
Ladies-who-lunch meet
cafe culture (p137)

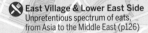
Midtown
Fine dining, cocktail-literate
bistros and old-school delis (p134)

**West Village, Chelsea &
Meatpacking District**
See-and-be-seen brunch spots, wine
bars and New American darlings (p128)

Union Square, Flatiron District & Gramercy
Everything from Michelin-starred
meccas to parkside burgers (p131)

SoHo & Chinatown
Dirt-cheap noodles, hip cafes and
fashionable foodie hangouts (p124)

East Village & Lower East Side
Unpretentious spectrum of eats,
from Asia to the Middle East (p126)

**Financial District &
Lower Manhattan**
Celebrity-chef hot spots and a gourmet
French marketplace (p124)

Brooklyn
Plenty of pizza and ethnic joints that
offer pleasantly simple eats (p138)

Best Blogs & Websites

Open Table (www.opentable.com)
Click-and-book reservation service for
many restaurants.

Eater (www.ny.eater.com) Food news
and restaurant round-ups.

Grub Street (www.grubstreet.com)
In-the-know articles on NYC dining.

Restaurant Girl (www.restaurantgirl.
com) Blogger and restaurant critic
eating her way around the city.

Must Try NYC Foods

Bagel A great start to the day, best
served with cream cheese.

Pizza The perfect anytime snack,
served up at ubiquitous pizza parlors.

Egg Creams Frothy, old-school bever-
age of milk, seltzer water and chocolate
syrup.

New York–Style Cheesecake Iconic
dessert with cream cheese and a cookie
crust.

The Best...

Experience New York City's finest eating establishments

By Budget

$

Taïm (p128) Outstanding falafel sandwiches at downtown locations.

El Rey (p126) Daring combinations at a locavore haunt in the Lower East Side.

Moustache (p128) Tiny West Village gem serving satisfying Middle Eastern dishes.

$$

Upstate (p128) A seafood feast awaits in the East Village.

Jeffrey's Grocery (p130) Much-loved West Village neighborhood spot.

ViceVersa (p135) Elegant Italian in the shadow of the Theater District.

$$$

Blue Hill (p130) A West Village classic using ingredients sourced straight from the associated farm upstate.

Degustation (p128) A tiny East Village eatery where you can watch the chefs create edible works of art.

Gramercy Tavern (p132) Prime produce, culinary finesse and the choice of bustling tavern or fine-dining den.

For Brunch

Estela (p125) Brilliant seasonal plates in a buzzing Nolita wine bar.

Rabbit Hole (p139) Excellent brunch plates served daily till 5pm at this Williamsburg gem.

Cookshop (pictured above; p129) Great indoor-outdoor dining spot in west Chelsea.

Cafe Mogador (p128) An icon of the East Village brunch scene.

For Upscale Groceries

Eataly (p132) A mecca for lovers of Italian food.

Union Square Greenmarket (pictured above; p130) Delicious veggies and bakery items from upstate producers.

Le District (p124) A sprawling food emporium on the Hudson packed with Gallic larder essentials.

For Old-School NYC

Barney Greengrass (p137) Perfect plates of smoked salmon and sturgeon for over 100 years in the Upper West Side.

Russ & Daughters (pictured above; p126) A celebrated Jewish deli in the Lower East Side.

El Margon (p135) Unfussy, unchanged Cuban lunch counter in Midtown.

By Cuisine

Asian

Uncle Boons (p124) Zesty, Michelin-starred Thai with a generous serve of fun in Nolita.

Zenkichi (p139) Candlelit culinary temple of exquisite sushi in Williamsburg.

Italian

Rosemary's (p129) A beautifully designed West Village spot with memorable cooking.

Morandi (p129) A West Village gem that invites lingering.

Vegetarian

Butcher's Daughter (p125) Inventive vegetarian menu in Nolita.

Hangawi (p135) Meat-free (and shoe-free) Korean restaurant in Koreatown.

Champs Diner (p138) Comfort-food diner in East Williamsburg with outstanding vegan plates.

★ Lonely Planet's Top Choices

Eleven Madison Park (p132) Arresting, cutting-edge cuisine laced with unexpected whimsy.

RedFarm (p130) Savvy Sino-fusion dishes boast bold flavors, but it doesn't take itself too seriously.

Dovetail (p137) Simplicity is key at this Upper West Side stunner – vegetarians unite on Monday for a divine tasting menu.

Foragers Table (p130) A triumph of farm-to-table cooking with flavorful sustainable recipes in Chelsea.

Pye Boat Noodle (p139) Outstanding Thai cooking in a quaint country-house setting in Astoria.

🍴 Financial District & Lower Manhattan

Seaport Smorgasburg Market $

(Map p244; www.seaport.smorgasburg.com; Fulton St, btwn Front & South Sts; dishes $6-19; ⏲11am-9pm May-Dec; [S]A/C, J/Z, 2/3, 4/5 to Fulton St) Brooklyn's hipster food market has jumped the East River, injecting touristy **South Street Seaport** with some much-needed local cred. Cooking up a storm from May to late September, its offerings include anything from lobster rolls, ramen and pizza to slow-smoked Texan-style brisket sandwiches. Add a splash of historic architecture and you have one of downtown's coolest cheap feeds.

Hudson Eats Fast Food $

(Map p244; ☎212-417-2445; www.brookfieldplaceny.com/directory/food; Brookfield Place, 230 Vesey St, at West St; dishes from $7; ⏲10am-9pm Mon-Sat, noon-7pm Sun; 📶; [S]E to World Trade Center; 2/3 to Park Place; R to Cortlandt St; A/C, 4/5, J/Z to Fulton St) Renovated office and retail complex **Brookfield Place** (Map p244; ☎212-978-1698; www.brookfieldplaceny.com) is home to Hudson Eats, a sleek, fashionable, new-school food hall. Decked out in terrazzo floors, marble counter tops and floor-to-ceiling windows with views of Jersey City and the Hudson River, its string of respected, chef-driven eateries includes Blue Ribbon Sushi, Umami Burger and Dos Toros Taqueria.

Le District French $$

(Map p244; ☎212-981-8588; www.ledistrict.com; Brookfield Place, 230 Vesey St, at West St; sandwiches $6-15, market mains $16-24, Beauborg dinner mains $18-45; ⏲6:30am-11pm Mon-Fri, 8:30am-11pm Sat, to 10pm Sun; 📶; [S]E to World Trade Center, 2/3 to Park Place, R to Cortlandt St; A/C, 4/5, J/Z to Fulton St) Paris on the Hudson is what you get at Le District, a sprawling French food emporium selling everything from high-gloss pastries and pretty *tartines* to stinky cheese and gritty steak *frites*. For a sit-down feed, skip the main restaurant Beaubourg for the two central bar counters.

Locanda Verde Italian $$$

(Map p246; ☎212-925-3797; www.locandaverdenyc.com; 377 Greenwich St, at N Moore St; mains lunch $19-29, dinner $25-40; ⏲7am-11pm Mon-Thu, to 11:30pm Fri, 8am-11:30pm Sat, to 11pm Sun; [S]A/C/E to Canal St, 1 to Franklin St) Step through the velvet curtains into a scene of loosened button-downs, black dresses and slick barmen behind a long, crowded bar. This celebrated brasserie showcases modern, Italo-inspired fare like house-made pappardelle with lamb Bolognese, mint-and-sheep's-milk ricotta and Sicilian-style halibut with heirloom squash and almonds. Weekend brunch is no less creative: try scampi and grits or lemon ricotta pancakes with blueberries.

🍴 SoHo & Chinatown

Xi'an Famous Foods Chinese $

(Map p246; www.xianfoods.com; 45 Bayard St, btwn Elizabeth St & Bowery; dishes $3-12; ⏲11:30am-9pm Sun-Thu, to 9:30pm Fri & Sat; [S]N/Q/R/W, J/Z, 6 to Canal St) Food bloggers hyperventilate at the mere mention of this small chain's hand-pulled noodles. It moved recently from its original Chinatown location a block away (now a dumpling spot) to this more comfortable storefront. Another star menu item is the spicy cumin lamb burger – tender lamb sautéed with ground cumin, toasted chili seeds, peppers, red onions and scallions.

Uncle Boons Thai $$

(Map p246; ☎646-370-6650; www.uncleboons.com; 7 Spring St, btwn Elizabeth St & Bowery; small plates $12-16, large plates $21-29; ⏲5:30-11pm Mon-Thu, to midnight Fri & Sat, to 10pm Sun; 📶; [S]J/Z to Bowery, 6 to Spring St) Michelin-star Thai served up in a fun, tongue-in-cheek combo of retro wood-paneled dining room with Thai film posters and old family snaps. Spanning the old and the new, zesty, tangy dishes include fantastically crunchy *mieng kum* (betel-leaf wrap with ginger, lime, toasted coconut, dried shrimp, peanuts and chili), *kao pat puu* (crab fried rice) and banana blossom salad.

Butcher's Daughter Vegetarian $$

(Map p246; 212-219-3434; www.thebutchersdaughter.com; 19 Kenmare St, at Elizabeth St; salads & sandwiches $12-14, dinner mains $16-18; 8am-11pm; ; J to Bowery, 6 to Spring St) The butcher's daughter certainly has rebelled, peddling nothing but fresh herbivorous fare in her white-washed cafe. While healthy it is, boring it's not: everything from the soaked organic muesli to the spicy kale Caesar salad with almond Parmesan or the dinnertime Butcher's burger (vegetable and black-bean patty with cashew cheddar cheese) is devilishly delish.

Nyonya Malaysian $$

(Map p246; 212-334-3669; www.ilovenyonya.com; 199 Grand St, btwn Mott & Mulberry Sts; mains $8-26; 11am-11:30pm Mon-Thu & Sun, to midnight Fri & Sat; N/Q/R/W, J/Z, 6 to Canal Street, B/D to Grand St) Take your palate to steamy Melaka at this bustling temple to Chinese-Malay cuisine. Savor the sweet, the sour and the spicy in classics such as tangy Assam fish-head casserole, rich beef *rendang* (spicy dry curry) and refreshing *rojak* (savory fruit salad tossed in a piquant tamarind dressing). Vegetarians, be warned: there's not much on the menu for you. Cash only.

Amazing 66 Chinese $$

(Map p246; 212-334-0099; www.amazing66.com; 66 Mott St, btwn Canal & Bayard Sts; mains $10-27; 11am-11pm; N/Q/R/W, J/Z, 6 to Canal St) One of the best places to chomp on Cantonese cuisine, bright, bustling Amazing 66 draws waves of local Chinese immigrants pining for a taste of home. Join them for standout dishes such as barbecued honey spare ribs, shrimp with black-bean sauce and salt-and-pepper chicken wings. Lunch prices are significantly cheaper than dinner.

Estela Modern American $$$

(Map p246; 212-219-7693; www.estelanyc.com; 47 E Houston St, btwn Mulberry & Mott Sts; dishes $15-38; 5:30-11pm Sun-Thu, to 11:30pm

The butcher's daughter certainly has rebelled, peddling nothing but fresh herbivorous fare...

Lunching alfresco at the Butcher's Daughter

SIVAN ASKAYO / LONELY PLANET ©

ROBERT CICCHETTI / SHUTTERSTOCK ©

From left: Pastrami on rye at Katz's Deli; Juliana's (p139); Momofuku Noodle Bar

Fri & Sat; [S]B/D/F/M to Broadway-Lafayette St, 6 to Bleecker St) Estela might be hopeless at hide-and-seek (its location up some nondescript stairs hardly tricks savvy gourmands), but this busy, skinny wine-bar slays on the food and vino front. Graze from a string of market-driven sharing plates, from phenomenal beef tartare (spiked with beef heart for added complexity) to moreish mussels *escabeche* on toast, or an impossibly sexy endive salad with walnuts and anchovy.

Dutch Modern American **$$$**
(Map p246; ☎212-677-6200; www.thedutchnyc.com; 131 Sullivan St, at Prince St; mains lunch $18-35, dinner $25-58; ⏰11:30am-11pm Mon-Thu, to 11:30pm Fri, 10am-11:30pm Sat, to 11pm Sun; [S]C/E to Spring St; R/W to Prince St, 1 to Houston St) Whether perched at the bar or dining snugly in the back room, you can always expect smart, farm-to-table comfort grub at this see-and-be-seen stalwart. Flavors traverse the globe, from sweet potato tempura with Thai basil and fermented chili sauce to ricotta ravioli with Swiss chard and walnut pesto. Reservations are recommended, especially for dinner and all day on weekends.

🍴 East Village & Lower East Side

El Rey Cafe, Vegetarian **$**
(Map p246; ☎212-260-3950; www.elreynyc.com; 100 Stanton St, btwn Orchard & Ludlow; small plates $8-15; ⏰7am-7pm Mon-Fri, from 8am Sat & Sun; 🌿; [S]F to 2nd Ave) This white, minimalist space on Stanton feels more SoCal than LES, and has a devoted following for its delectably inventive (and fairly priced) farm-to-table vegetarian plates. Stop by any time of day for chia pudding with winter berries and agave, and after 11am for a grain bowl or an inventive beet dish with leeks, sunflower and a sieved egg.

Russ & Daughters Deli **$**
(Map p246; ☎212-475-4800; www.russanddaughters.com; 179 E Houston St, btwn Orchard & Allen Sts; mains $10-14; ⏰8am-8pm Mon-Fri, to 7pm Sat, to 5:30pm Sun; [S]F to 2nd Ave) In business since 1914, this landmark establishment serves up Eastern European Jewish delicacies such as caviar, herring and lox, and, of course, a smear of cream cheese on a bagel. There's nowhere to sit, so grab

THE WASHINGTON POST / GETTY IMAGES ©

a number when you come in, order your salmon-topped bagel and other goodies, then retreat to a park bench around the corner.

Momofuku Noodle Bar Noodles $$

(Map p246; ☎212-777-7773; www.noodlebar-ny.momofuku.com; 171 First Ave, btwn E 10th & 11th Sts; mains $16; 🕒noon-11pm Sun-Thu, to 1am Fri & Sat; [S]L to 1st Ave; 6 to Astor Pl) With just 30 stools and a no-reservations policy, you'll always have to wait to cram into this bustling phenomenon. Queue up for the namesake special: homemade ramen noodles in broth, served with poached egg and pork belly or some other interesting combos. The menu changes daily and includes buns (such as brisket and horseradish), snacks (smoked chicken wings) and desserts.

Katz's Delicatessen Deli $$

(Map p246; ☎212-254-2246; www.katzsdelicatessen.com; 205 E Houston St, at Ludlow St; sandwiches $15-22; 🕒8am-10:45pm Mon-Wed, Sun, to 2:45am Thu, from 8am Fri, 24hr Sat; [S]F to 2nd Ave) Though visitors won't find many remnants of the classic, old-world Jewish LES dining scene, there are a few stellar holdouts, among them Katz's Delicatessen, where Meg Ryan faked her famous orgasm in the 1989 movie *When Harry Met Sally*. If you love classic deli grub like pastrami and salami on rye, it just might have the same effect on you.

Dimes Cafe $$

(Map p246; ☎212-925-1300; www.dimesnyc.com; 49 Canal St, btwn Orchard & Ludlow Sts; mains breakfast $8-13, dinner $15-24; 🕒8am-11pm Mon-Fri, from 9am Sat & Sun; 🌱) This tiny, sun-drenched eatery has a strong local following for its friendly service and healthy, good-value dishes. A design-minded group crowds in for spicy breakfast tacos (served til 4pm), bowls of granola with açaí berries, creative salads (with sunchokes, anchovies, goat cheese) and heartier dishes for dinner (striped bass with green curry, pulled pork with jasmine rice).

Luzzo's Pizza $$

(Map p246; ☎212-473-7447; www.luzzosgroup.com; 211 First Ave, btwn E 12th & 13th Sts; pizzas $18-25; 🕒noon-11pm Sun-Thu, to midnight Fri & Sat; [S]L to 1st Ave) Fan-favorite Luzzo's occupies a thin, rustically designed sliver of real estate in the East Village, which gets stuffed to the gills each evening as discerning diners feast on thin-crust pies, kissed with ripe tomatoes and cooked in a coal-fired stove. Cash only.

Upstate Seafood $$

(Map p246; ☑212-460-5293; www.upstatenyc. com; 95 First Ave, btwn E 5th & 6th Sts; mains $15-30; ☺5-11pm; Ⓢ F to 2nd Ave) Upstate serves outstanding seafood dishes and craft beers. The small, always-changing menu features the likes of beer-steamed mussels, seafood stew, scallops over mushroom risotto, softshell crab and wondrous oyster selections. There's no freezer – seafood comes from the market each day, so you know you'll be getting only the freshest ingredients. Lines can be long, so go early.

Cafe Mogador Moroccan $$

(Map p246; ☑212-677-2226; www.cafemogador. com; 101 St Marks Pl; mains lunch $8-15, dinner $16-21; ☺9am-11pm Sun-Thu, to midnight Fri & Sat; Ⓢ6 to Astor Pl) Family-run Mogador is a long-running NYC classic, serving fluffy piles of couscous, chargrilled lamb and *merguez* sausage over basmati rice, as well as satisfying mixed platters of hummus and baba ghanoush. The standouts, however, are the tagines – traditionally spiced, long-simmered chicken or lamb dishes served up five different ways.

Degustation Modern European $$$

(Map p246; ☑212-979-1012; www.degustation-nyc.com; 239 E 5th St, btwn Second & Third Aves; small plates $12-22, tasting menu $85; ☺6pm-11:30pm Mon-Sat, to 10pm Sun; Ⓢ6 to Astor Pl) Blending Iberian, French and new-world recipes, Degustation does a beautiful array of tapas-style plates at this narrow, 19-seat eatery. It's an intimate setting, with guests seated around a long wooden counter while chef Oscar Islas Díaz and his team are center stage, firing up crisp octopus, lamb belly with soft poached egg and paella with blue prawns and chorizo.

Fung Tu Fusion $$$

(Map p246; ☑212-219-8785; www.fungtu.com; 22 Orchard St, btwn Hester & Canal Sts; small plates $12-15, mains $22-32; ☺6-11pm Tue-Thu, to midnight Fri & Sat, to 10pm Sun; Ⓢ F to East Broadway) Celebrated chef Jonathan Wu brilliantly blends Chinese cooking with global accents at this elegant little eatery on the edge of Chinatown. The complex sharing plates are as delicious and interesting (try scallion pancakes with steamed clams and bacon) as the mains (General Tso's lobster with leeks) and pair nicely with cocktails.

⊗ West Village, Chelsea & Meatpacking District

Gansevoort Market Market $

(Map p246; www.gansmarket.com; 353 W 14th St, at Ninth Ave; mains $5-20; ☺8am-8pm; Ⓢ A/C/E, L to 14th St-8th Ave) Inside a brick building in the heart of the Meatpacking District, this sprawling market is the latest and greatest food emporium to land in NYC. A raw, industrial space lit by skylights, it features several dozen gourmet vendors slinging tapas, arepas, tacos, pizzas, meat pies, ice cream, pastries and more.

Moustache Middle Eastern $

(Map p246; ☑212-229-2220; www.moustache pitzawest.com; 90 Bedford St, btwn Grove & Barrow Sts; mains $10-17; ☺noon-11pm Sun-Thu, to midnight Fri & Sat; Ⓢ1 to Christopher St-Sheridan Sq) In its warm, earthy space, small and delightful Moustache serves up rich, flavorful sandwiches (leg of lamb, *merguez* sausage, falafel), thin-crust pizzas, tangy salads and hearty specialties such as *ouzi* (phyllo stuffed with chicken, rice and spices) and moussaka. The best start to a meal: a platter of hummus or baba ghanoush served with fluffy, piping-hot pita bread.

Taïm Israeli $

(Map p246; ☑212-691-1287; www.taimfalafel. com; 222 Waverly Pl, btwn Perry & W 11th Sts; sandwiches $7-8; ☺11am-10pm; Ⓢ1/2/3, A/C/E to 14th St, L to 6th Ave) This tiny joint whips up some of the best falafel in the city. You can order it Green (traditional style), Harissa (with Tunisian spices) or Red (with roasted peppers) – whichever you choose, you'll get it stuffed into pita bread with creamy tahini sauce and a generous dose of Israeli salad.

Rosemary's   Italian $$

(Map p246; ☏212-647-1818; www.rosemarysnyc. com; 18 Greenwich Ave, at W 10th St; mains $15-32; ⊗8am-midnight Mon-Fri, from 10am Sat & Sun; ⓢ1 to Christopher St-Sheridan Sq) One of the West Village's hottest restaurants, Rosemary's serves high-end Italian fare that more than lives up to the hype. In a vaguely farmhouse-like setting, diners tuck into generous portions of house-made pastas, rich salads, and cheese and *salumi* (cured meat) boards. Current favorites include the *acqua pazza* (seafood stew) and smoked lamb with roasted vegetables.

Cookshop   Modern American $$

(Map p250; ☏212-924-4440; www.cookshop ny.com; 156 Tenth Ave, btwn W 19th & 20th Sts; mains brunch $14-20, lunch $16-24, dinner $22-48; ⊗8am-11:30pm Mon-Fri, from 10am Sat, 10am-10pm Sun; ⓢL to 8th Ave, A/C/E to 23rd St) A brilliant brunching pit stop before (or after) tackling the verdant High Line (p52) across the street, Cookshop is a lively place that knows its niche and does it oh so well. Excellent service, eye-opening cocktails (good morning, bacon-infused BLT Mary!), a perfectly baked breadbasket and a selection of inventive egg mains make this a Chelsea favorite on a Sunday afternoon.

Morandi   Italian $$

(Map p246; ☏212-627-7575; www.morandiny. com; 211 Waverly Place, btwn Seventh Ave & Charles St; mains $18-38; ⊗8am-midnight Mon-Fri, from 10am Sat & Sun; ⓢ1 to Christopher St-Sheridan Sq) Run by celebrated restaurateur Keith McNally, Morandi is a warmly lit space where the hubbub of garrulous diners resounds amid brick walls, wide plank floors and rustic chandeliers. Squeeze into a table for the full-meal experience – hand-rolled spaghetti with lemon and Parmesan, meatballs with pine nuts and raisins, and grilled whole sea bream.

🍽 Urban Farm to Table

Whether it's upstate triple-cream Kunik at **Bedford Cheese Shop** (p156) or Montauk Pearls oysters at fine-dining **Craft** (Map p250; ☏212-780-0880; www. craftrestaurant.com; 43 E 19th St, btwn Broadway & Park Ave S; lunch $29-36, dinner mains $28-45; ⊗noon-10pm Mon-Thu, to 11pm Fri, 5:30pm-11pm Sat, to 10pm Sun; ☎; ⓢ4/5/6, N/Q/R/W, L to 14th St-Union Sq) ✔, New York City's passion for all things local and artisanal continues unabated. The city itself has become an unlikely food bowl, with an ever-growing number of rooftops, backyards and community gardens finding new purpose as urban.

While you can expect to find anything from organic tomatoes atop Upper East Side delis to beehives on East Village tenement rooftops, the current queen of the crop is **Brooklyn Grange** (www. brooklyngrangefarm.com), an organic farm covering two rooftops in Long Island City and the Brooklyn Navy Yards. At 2.5 acres, it's purportedly the world's biggest rooftop farm, producing over 50,000lb of organically cultivated goodness annually, from eggs to carrots, chard and heirloom tomatoes. The project is the brainchild of young farmer Ben Flanner. Obsessed with farm-to-table eating, he kick-started NYC's rooftop revolution in 2009 with the opening of its first rooftop soil farm – Eagle Street Rooftop Farm – in nearby Greenpoint. Flanner's collaborators include some of the city's top eateries, among them **Marlow & Sons** (p138) and **Roberta's** (p139) in Brooklyn, and **Dutch** (p126) in Manhattan.

Fresh oysters with lemon
MALIUTINA ANNA / SHUTTERSTOCK ©

🍴 To Market, to Market

Don't let the concrete streets and buildings fool you – New York City has a thriving greens scene that comes in many shapes and sizes. At the top of your list should be the **Chelsea Market** (Map p250; ☎212-652-2121; www.chelsea-market.com; 75 9th Ave, btwn 15th & 16th Sts; 🕐7am-9pm Mon-Sat, 8am-8pm Sun), which is packed with gourmet goodies of all kinds – both shops (where you can assemble picnics) and food stands (where you can eat on-site). Many other food halls have opened in recent years, including **Gansevoort Market** (p128) in the Meatpacking District and a trio of food halls at **Brookfield Place** (p124), in Lower Manhattan.

Many neighborhoods in NYC have their own greenmarket. One of the biggest is the **Union Square Greenmarket** (Map p250; www.grownyc.org; Union Square, 17th St, btwn Broadway & Park Ave S; 🕐8am-6pm Mon, Wed, Fri & Sat), open four days a week throughout the year. Check **Grow NYC** (www.grownyc.org/greenmarket) for a list of the other 50-plus markets around the city.

Out in Brooklyn, the best weekend markets for noshers are **Smorgasburg** (www.smorgasburg.com; 🕐11am-6pm Sat & Sun), with over 100 craft food vendors, and the **Brooklyn Flea** (Map p255; www.brooklynflea.com; 90 Kent Ave, btwn N 7th & N 10th Sts, Williamsburg; 🕐10am-5pm Sat Apr-Oct), which has tons of stalls.

Also popular are high-end market-cum-grocers such as **Eataly** (p132) and **Dean & DeLuca** (Map p246; ☎212-226-6800; www.deananddeluca.com; 560 Broadway, at Prince St; 🕐7am-8pm Mon-Fri, 8am-8pm Sat & Sun), where fresh produce and ready-made fare are given the five-star treatment. **Whole Foods** is another big draw, particularly its ecofriendly, locavore-focused **Brooklyn outpost** (Map p254; ☎718-907-3622; www.wholefoodsmarket.com; 214 3rd St, btwn Third Ave & Bond St; 🕐8am-11pm; 📶) 🍃.

Blue Hill American $$$

(Map p246; ☎212-539-1776; www.bluehillfarm.com; 75 Washington Pl, btwn Sixth Ave & Washington Sq W; prix-fixe menu $88-98; 🕐5-11pm Mon-Sat, to 10pm Sun; [S]A/C/E, B/D/F/M to W 4th St-Washington Sq) A place for slow-food junkies with deep pockets, Blue Hill was an early crusader in the 'Local is Better' movement. Gifted chef Dan Barber, who hails from a farm family in the Berkshires, Massachusetts, uses harvests from that land and from farms in upstate New York to create his widely praised fare.

Jeffrey's Grocery Modern American $$$

(Map p246; ☎646-398-7630; www.jeffreysgrocery.com; 172 Waverly Pl, at Christopher St; mains $25-39; 🕐8am-11pm Mon-Fri, from 9:30am Sat & Sun; [S]1 to Christopher St-Sheridan Sq) This West Village classic is a lively eating and drinking spot that hits all the right notes. Seafood is the focus: there's an oyster bar and beautifully executed selections such as razor clams with caviar and dill, whole roasted dourade with curry, and sharing platters. Meat dishes include roasted chicken with Jerusalem artichoke and a humble but juicy pastrami burger.

Foragers Table Modern American $$$

(Map p250; ☎212-243-8888; www.foragersmarket.com/restaurant; 300 W 22nd St, at Eighth Ave; mains $23-36; 🕐5:30-10pm, plus 10:30am-2:30pm Sat & Sun; 🌿; [S]C/E, 1 to 23rd St) Owners of this outstanding restaurant run a 28-acre farm in the Hudson Valley, from which much of their seasonal menu is sourced. It changes frequently, but recent temptations include Long Island duck breast with roasted acorn squash, apples, chanterelle mushrooms and figs, grilled skate with red quinoa, creamed kale and *cippolini* onion and deviled farm eggs with Dijon mustard.

RedFarm Fusion $$$

(Map p246; ☎212-792-9700; www.redfarmnyc.com; 529 Hudson St, btwn W 10th & Charles Sts; mains $22-46, dim sum $10-16; 🕐5-11pm, plus 11am-2:30pm Sat & Sun; [S]A/C/E, B/D/F/M

Food vendors at Gansevoort Market (p128)

to W 4th St-Washington Sq, 1 to Christopher St-Sheridan Sq) RedFarm transforms Chinese cooking into pure, delectable artistry at this small, buzzing space on Hudson St. Fresh crab and eggplant bruschetta, juicy rib steak (marinated overnight in papaya, ginger and soy) and pastrami egg rolls are among the many creative dishes that brilliantly blend cuisines. Other hits include spicy crispy beef, pan-fried lamb dumplings and the grilled jumbo-shrimp red curry.

Chumley's Modern American **$$$**
(Map p246; ☎212-675-2081; www.chumleysnewyork.com; 86 Bedford St, btwn Grove & Barrow Sts; mains $25-33; 🕒5:30-10:30pm Tue-Thu & Sun, to 11pm Fri & Sat) Occupying the same space as the legendary West Village speakeasy, this new incarnation maintains its historic air while upgrading everything else. The ambitious, seasonal menu includes aged rib-eye and arctic char, but the highlight might be the burger – constructed from two 4oz patties. Walls are lined with portraits and book jackets of Prohibition-era writers, many of them once bar patrons.

this sprawling market is the latest and greatest food emporium to land in NYC

🍴 Union Square, Flatiron District & Gramercy

Eisenberg's Sandwich Shop Sandwiches **$**
(Map p250; ☎212-675-5096; www.eisenbergsnyc.com; 174 Fifth Ave, btwn W 22nd & 23rd St; sandwiches $4-13; 🕒6:30am-8pm Mon-Fri, 9am-6pm Sat, to 5pm Sun; [S]R/W to 23rd St) This old-school diner – an anomaly on this mostly upscale stretch of real estate – is filled from morning to close with regulars in for traditional Jewish diner fare such as chopped liver, pastrami and whitefish salad. Grab a stool at the long bar and rub elbows with an eclectic mix of customers who know meatloaf isn't a joke dish.

Shake Shack Burgers **$**
(Map p250; ☎646-889-6600; www.shakeshack.com; Madison Square Park, cnr E 23rd St & Madison Ave; burgers $4.20-9.50; 🕒11am-10:30pm;

S R/W, F/M, 6 to 23rd St) The flagship of chef
Danny Meyer's gourmet burger chain,
Shake Shack whips up hyper-fresh burgers,
hand-cut fries and a rotating line-up of
frozen custards. Veg-heads can dip into the
crisp portobello burger. Lines are long –
but worth it – and you can digest the filling
meal while people-watching at tables and
benches in the park.

Eataly Food Hall $$

(Map p250; 212-229-2560; www.eataly.com;
200 Fifth Ave, at W 23rd St; 7am-11pm; ;
S R/W, F/M, 6 to 23rd St) Mario Batali's sleek,
sprawling temple to Italian gastronomy is a
veritable wonderland. Feast on everything
from vibrant *crudo* (raw fish) and *fritto mis-
to* (tempura-style vegetables) to steamy
pasta and pizza at the emporium's string
of sit-down eateries. Alternatively, guzzle
espresso at the bar and scour the countless counters and shelves for a DIY picnic
hamper *nonna* would approve of.

Eleven Madison Park Modern American $$$

(Map p250; 212-889-0905; www.eleven
madisonpark.com; 11 Madison Ave, btwn 24th &
25th Sts; tasting menu $295; 5:30-10pm Mon-
Thu & noon-1pm Fri-Sun; S N/R, 6 to 23rd St) In
2017, Eleven Madison Park was named the
number one restaurant in the world on a list
compiled by the World's 50 Best Restaurants organization. Frankly, they deserve
it: this revamped poster child of modern,
sustainable American cooking is also one
of only six NYC restaurants sporting three
Michelin stars.

Driving the buzz is young-gun co-owner
and chef Daniel Humm, whose insane
attention to detail is matched by intense
creativity and whimsy. Reserve a table
weeks in advance and dress to impress.

Gramercy Tavern Modern American $$$

(Map p250; 212-477-0777; www.gramercy
tavern.com; 42 E 20th St, btwn Broadway & Park
Ave S; tavern mains $29-36, dining room 3-course
menu $125, tasting menus $140-165; tavern
noon-11pm Sun-Thu, to midnight Fri & Sat, dining

🍽 NYC Restaurant Week

Bargain-savvy gastronomes love the biannual NYC Restaurant Week. Taking place in January to February and July to August, it sees many of the city's restaurants, including some of its very best, serve up three-course lunches for $29, or three-course dinners for $42. Check www.nycgo.com/restaurantweek for details and reservations.

Clockwise from top left: Parmigiano Reggiano for sale at Eataly; Eleven Madison Park; New York street-style hotdogs; Shake Shack (p131) in Madison Square Park

room noon-2pm & 5:30-10pm Mon-Thu, to 11pm Fri, noon-1:30pm & 5.30-11pm Sat, 5:30-10pm Sun; 📶✎; [S] R/W, 6 to 23rd St) 🌿 Seasonal, local ingredients drive this perennial favorite, a vibrant, country-chic institution aglow with copper sconces, murals and dramatic floral arrangements. Choose from two spaces: the walk-in-only tavern and its à la carte menu, or the swankier dining room and its fancier prix-fixe and degustation feasts. Tavern highlights include a show-stopping duck meatloaf with mushrooms, chestnuts and brussels sprouts.

🍴 Midtown

Totto Ramen Japanese $

(Map p252; ☎212-582-0052; www.tottoramen.com; 366 W 52nd St, btwn Eighth & Ninth Aves; ramen from $11; ⏱noon-4:30pm & 5:30pm-midnight Mon-Sat, 4-11pm Sun; [S] C/E to 50th St) There might be another two branches in Midtown, but purists know that neither beats the tiny, 20-seat original. Write your name and number of guests on the clipboard and wait your turn. Your reward: extraordinary ramen. Go for the pork, which sings in dishes such as miso ramen (with fermented soybean paste, egg, scallion, bean sprouts, onion and homemade chili paste).

Burger Joint Burgers $

(Map p252; ☎212-708-7414; www.burgerjointny.com; Le Parker Meridien, 119 W 56th St, btwn Sixth & Seventh Aves; burgers from $9.50; ⏱11am-11:30pm Sun-Thu, to midnight Fri & Sat; [S] F to 57th St) With only a small neon burger as your clue, this speakeasy-style burger hut lurks behind the lobby curtain in the Le Parker Meridien hotel. Though it might not be as 'hip' or as 'secret' as it once was, it still delivers the same winning formula of graffiti-strewn walls, retro booths and attitude-loaded staff slapping up beef 'n' patty brilliance.

ViceVersa is quintessential Italian: suave and sophisticated, affable and scrumptious

Dining outside at ViceVersa

ROSAIRENEBETANCOURT 4 / ALAMY ©

El Margon   Cuban $

(Map p252; 212-354-5013; 136 W 46th St, btwn
Sixth & Seventh Aves; sandwiches $4-8, mains
from $9; ⏰6am-5pm Mon-Fri, from 7am Sat;
Ⓢ B/D/F/M to 47th-50th Sts-Rockefeller Center)
It's still 1973 at this ever-packed Cuban
lunch counter, where orange Laminex and
greasy goodness never went out of style.
Go for gold with its legendary *cubano* sand-
wich (a pressed panino jammed with rich
roast pork, salami, cheese, pickles, *mojo*
sauce and mayo). It's obscenely good.

Hangawi   Korean, Vegan $$

(Map p250; 212-213-0077; www.hangawi
restaurant.com; 12 E 32nd St, btwn Fifth &
Madison Aves; mains lunch $11-30, dinner $19-
30; ⏰noon-2:30pm & 5:30-10:15pm Mon-Fri,
1-10:30pm Sat, 5-9:30pm Sun; ✎; Ⓢ B/D/F/M,
N/Q/R/W to 34th St-Herald Sq) Meat-free
Korean is the draw at high-achieving
Hangawi. Leave your shoes at the entrance
and slip into a soothing, Zen-like space
of meditative music, soft low seating and
clean, complex dishes. Show-stoppers
include the leek pancakes and a seductively
smooth tofu claypot in ginger sauce.

ViceVersa   Italian $$$

(Map p252; 212-399-9291; www.viceversa
nyc.com; 325 W 51st St, btwn Eighth & Ninth
Aves; 3-course lunch $29, dinner mains $24-33;
⏰noon-2:30pm & 4:30-11pm Mon-Fri, 4:30-11pm
Sat, 11:30am-3pm & 4:30-10pm Sun; Ⓢ C/E to
50th St) ViceVersa is quintessential Italian:
suave and sophisticated, affable and
scrumptious. The menu features refined,
cross-regional dishes such as arancini
with black truffle and fontina cheese. For a
celebrated classic, order the *casoncelli alla
bergamasca* (ravioli-like pasta filled with
minced veal, raisins and amaretto cookies
and seasoned with sage, butter, pancetta
and Grana Padano), a nod to chef Stefano
Terzi's Lombard heritage.

Le Bernardin   Seafood $$$

(Map p252; 212-554-1515; www.le-bernardin.
com; 155 W 51st St, btwn Sixth & Seventh Aves;
prix fixe lunch/dinner $87/150, tasting menus
$180-270; ⏰noon-2:30pm & 5:15-10:30pm

🍽️ Vegetarians & Vegans

Though the city's herbivore scene has
long lagged behind that of West Coast
cities, and was for years mocked by
serious foodies, many former nay-
sayers are beginning to come around.
That's thanks in part to the local-food
movement, which has hit NYC like a ton
of potatoes, as well as a slow but steady
trickle of new eateries that have enticed
skeptics by injecting big doses of cool
ambience – and top-notch wine, liquor
and dessert options – into the mix. But
herbivore oases also dot the entire landscape, and even the most meat-heavy
four-star restaurants are figuring out
the lure of legume; the market-inspired
le potager section on the menu at **Café
Boulud** (Map p252; 212-772-2600; www.
cafeboulud.com/nyc; 20 E 76th St, btwn Fifth
& Madison Aves; mains around $45; ⏰7am-
10:30am, noon-2:30pm & 5:30-10:30pm
Mon-Fri, from 8am Sat & Sun; ✎; Ⓢ 6 to 77th
St) offers highbrow veggie dishes, while
on Monday night **Dovetail** (p137) hosts
a decadent prix-fixe vegetarian feast.

Veganists have much to celebrate
with the arrival of excellent eateries
serving up guilt-free goodness all around
town. Top choices include **Champs
Diner** (p138), which serves up comfort
fare out in Williamsburg, and elegant
Blossom (Map p250; 212-627-1144; www.
blossomnyc.com; 187 Ninth Ave, btwn 21st &
22nd Sts; mains lunch $15-19, dinner $20-25;
⏰noon-2:45pm & 5-9:30pm; ✎; Ⓢ C/E to
23rd St), with locations in Chelsea and
elsewhere.

Couscous with vegetables
SVARIOPHOTO / SHUTTERSTOCK ©

New York City on a Plate

For perfection, put your lox and cream cheese on a plain or 'everything' bagel.
NYC's world-class bagels are made by boiling then baking.
'Lox' usually means smoked salmon.
The 'shmear' (cream cheese) has more tang than store-bought versions.
The best salmon has a rich, lightly smoky taste.
The Best Bagel & Lox

A New York 'Classic' Breakfast

One of the best ways to start the day in NYC is by noshing on a bagel with lox and cream cheese in a classic Jewish deli. Here, you can join regulars at the counter as lightning fast prep staff whip up those delicacies in a hurry. One bite and you're hooked for life: the crunch of bagel crust, lush-textured lox and smooth cream cheese creating a holy trinity of perfection.

Bagel with cream cheese, lox, capers and red onion

★ Top Five Bagel & Lox Joints

Barney Greengrass (p137)

Russ & Daughters (p126)

Mile End (☎718-852-7510; www.mileenddeli.com; 97A Hoyt St, Boerum Hill; sandwiches $12-16; 🕒8am-4pm & 5-10pm Mon-Fri, from 10am Sat & Sun; [S] A/C, G to Hoyt Schermerhorn Sts)

Marlow & Sons (p138)

Zabar's (Map p252; ☎212-787-2000; www.zabars.com; 2245 Broadway, at W 80th St; 🕒8am-7:30pm Mon-Fri, to 8pm Sat, 9am-6pm Sun; [S] 1 to 79th St)

Mon-Thu, to 11pm Fri, 5:15-11pm Sat; [S] 1 to 50th St, B/D, E to 7th Ave) The interiors may have been subtly sexed-up for a 'younger clientele' (the stunning storm-themed triptych is by Brooklyn artist Ran Ortner), but triple-Michelin-starred Le Bernardin remains a luxe, fine-dining holy grail. At the helm is French-born celebrity chef Éric Ripert, whose deceptively simple-looking seafood often borders on the transcendental.

🍴 Upper East Side

Boqueria Spanish $$

(Map p252; ☎212-343-2227; www.boquerianyc.com; 1460 Second Ave, btwn E 76th & 77th Sts; tapas $6-16, paella for two $38-46; 🕒noon-10:30pm Sun-Thu, 11am-11:30pm Fri & Sat; [S] 6 to 77th St, Q to 72nd St) This lively, much-loved tapas place brings a bit of downtown cool to the Upper East Side, with nicely spiced *patatas bravas*, tender slices of *jamon ibérico* and rich *pulpo a gallega* (grilled octopus). Head chef Marc Vidal, who hails from Barcelona, also creates an exquisite seafood paella.

Beyoglu Turkish $$

(Map p252; ☎212-650-0850; 1431 Third Ave, at E 81st St; mains $16-18, sharing plates $6-8; 🕒noon-10:30pm Sun-Thu, to 11pm Fri & Sat; 🌿; [S] 6 to 77th St, 4/5/6, Q to 86th St) A long-time favorite of Mediterranean-craving Upper East Siders, Beyoglu whips up meze (appetizers) platters that are ideal for sharing. Creamy rich hummus, juicy lamb kebabs, tender grape leaves and lemon-scented chargrilled octopus. It has an airy and comfy interior, though on sunny days you can head to one of the sidewalk tables in front.

Café Sabarsky Austrian $$

(Map p252; ☎212-288-0665; www.neuegalerie.org/cafes/sabarsky; 1048 Fifth Ave, cnr E 86th St; mains $18-30; 🕒9am-6pm Mon & Wed, to 9pm Thu-Sun; 🌿👪; [S] 4/5/6 to 86th St) The lines get long at this popular cafe, which evokes opulent turn-of-the-century Vienna. But the well-rendered Austrian specialties make the wait worth it. Expect crêpes with smoked trout, goulash soup and roasted bratwurst.

Tanoshi Sushi $$$

(☎917-265-8254; www.tanoshisushinyc.com; 1372 York Ave, btwn E 73rd & 74th Sts; chef's sushi selection $80-100; 🕒6-10:30pm Mon-Sat; [S] Q to 72nd St) It's not easy to snag one of the 20 stools at Tanoshi, a wildly popular sushi spot. The setting may be humble, but the flavors are simply magnificent, which might include Hokkaido scallops, Atlantic shad or mouthwatering *uni* (sea urchin). Only sushi is on offer and only *omakase* (chef's selection). BYO beer, sake or whatnot.

🍴 Upper West Side & Central Park

Barney Greengrass Deli $$

(Map p252; ☎212-724-4707; www.barneygreengrass.com; 541 Amsterdam Ave, at W 86th St; mains $12-22; 🕒8:30am-4pm Tue-Fri, to 5pm Sat & Sun; [S] 1 to 86th St) The self-proclaimed 'King of Sturgeon' Barney Greengrass serves up the same heaping dishes of eggs and salty lox, luxuriant caviar, and melt-in-your-mouth chocolate babkas that first made it famous when it opened over a century ago. Pop in to fuel up in the morning or for a quick lunch.

Dovetail Modern American $$$

(Map p252; ☎212-362-3800; www.dovetailnyc.com; 103 W 77th St, cnr Columbus Ave; prix fixe $68-88, tasting menu $145; 🕒5:30-10pm Mon-Thu, to 11pm Fri & Sat, 5-10pm Sun; 🌿; [S] B, C to 81st St-Museum of Natural History, 1 to 79th St) This Michelin-starred restaurant showcases its Zen-like beauty in both its decor (exposed brick, bare tables) and its delectable, seasonal menus – think striped bass with sunchokes and burgundy truffle, and venison with bacon, golden beets and foraged greens. Each evening there are two seven-course tasting menus: one for omnivores ($145) and one for vegetarians ($125).

Burke & Wills Modern Australian $$$

(Map p252; ☎646-823-9251; www.burkeandwillsny.com; 226 W 79th St, btwn Broadway & Amsterdam Ave; mains lunch $19-30, dinner $19-39; 🕐noon-3pm & 5:30pm-late Mon-Fri, from 11am Sat & Sun; [S]1 to 79th St) This ruggedly attractive bistro and bar brings a touch of the outback to the Upper West Side. The menu leans toward Modern Australian pub grub: juicy kangaroo burgers with triple-fried chips, grilled prawns, kale Cobb salad, braised pork belly with apple-and-celery slaw, and seafood platters with oysters, clams and crab claws.

🍴 Harlem & Upper Manhattan

Red Rooster Modern American $$

(☎212-792-9001; www.redroosterharlem.com; 310 Malcolm X Blvd, btwn W 125th & 126th Sts, Harlem; mains $18-30; 🕐11:30am-10:30pm Mon-Thu, to 11:30pm Fri, 10am-11:30pm Sat, 10am-10pm Sun; [S]2/3 to 125th St) Transatlantic super-chef Marcus Samuelsson laces upscale comfort food with a world of flavors at his effortlessly cool, swinging brasserie. Like the work of the contemporary New York–based artists displayed on the walls, dishes are up to date: mac 'n' cheese joins forces with lobster, blackened catfish pairs with pickled mango, and spectacular Swedish meatballs salute Samuelsson's home country.

Dinosaur Bar-B-Que Barbecue $$

(☎212-694-1777; www.dinosaurbarbque.com; 700 W 125th St, at Twelfth Ave, Harlem; mains $12.50-25; 🕐11:30am-11pm Mon-Thu, to midnight Fri & Sat, noon-10pm Sun; [S]1 to 125th St) Jocks, hipsters, moms and pops: everyone dives into this honky-tonk rib bar for a rockin' feed. Get messy with dry-rubbed, slow-pit-smoked ribs, slabs of juicy steak and succulent burgers, or watch the waist with the lightly seasoned grilled-chicken options. The (very) few vegetarian options include a fantastic version of Creole-spiced deviled eggs.

🍴 Brooklyn

Champs Diner Vegan $

(Map p255; ☎718-599-2743; www.champsdiner.com; 197 Meserole St, btwn Humboldt St & Bushwick Ave, East Williamsburg; sandwiches & salads $9-13; 🕐9am-midnight; 📶🌱; [S]L to Montrose) This airy little diner whips up delicious plates of comfort food – all made with vegan ingredients. The reasonable prices and all-day breakfasts keep things busy. Try the French toast slam (with tofu scramble and tempeh bacon), the chocolate chip and banana pancakes, mac 'n' cheese or a 'bacon cheeseburger' (a black-bean burger with tempeh bacon and veggie cheese).

Lincoln Station Cafe

(Map p254; ☎718-399-2211; www.stationfoods.com; 409 Lincoln Pl, at Washington Ave; 🕐7am-9pm Mon-Fri, from 8am Sat & Sun; 👪; [S]2/3 to Eastern Pkwy-Brooklyn Museum) Whatever time of day, there's no better place in the neighborhood for a casual drink with friends. Join the laptop-toting hordes who occupy every seat at the long center table for top-notch espresso drinks, or grab a beer (all drafts $4.50 from 8pm to 9pm) in the evening, when candles set a romantic mood.

Marlow & Sons Modern American $$

(Map p255; ☎718-384-1441; www.marlowandsons.com; 81 Broadway, btwn Berry St & Wythe Ave, Williamsburg; mains lunch $15, dinner $28; 🕐8am-midnight; [S]J/M/Z to Marcy Ave, L to Bedford Ave) The dimly lit, wood-lined space feels like an old farmhouse cafe, and hosts a buzzing nighttime scene as diners and drinkers crowd in for oysters, tip-top cocktails and a changing daily menu of locavore specialties (smoked pork loin, crunchy-crust pizzas, caramelized turnips, fluffy Spanish-style tortillas). Brunch is also a big draw, though prepare for lines.

Pok Pok Thai $$

(Map p254; ☎718-923-9322; www.pokpokny.com; 117 Columbia St, cnr Kane St, Columbia Street Waterfront District; sharing plates $12-20; 🕐5:30-10pm Mon-Fri, from noon Sat & Sun; [S]F to Bergen St) Andy Ricker's NYC outpost is a smashing success, wowing diners with a rich and complex menu inspired by Northern Thailand street food. Fiery, fish-sauce-slathered chicken wings; spicy green-papaya salad with salted black crab; smoky grilled eggplant salad and sweet pork belly with ginger, turmeric and tamarind are among the many unique dishes. The setting is fun and ramshackle. Reserve ahead.

Juliana's   Pizza $$

(Map p254; ☏718-596-6700; www.julianaspizza. com; 19 Old Fulton St, btwn Water & Front Sts, Dumbo; pizza $17-32; ☺11:30am-10pm; ⓢA/C to High St) Legendary pizza maestro Patsy Grimaldi has returned to Brooklyn, with delicious thin-crust perfection in both classic and creative combos (like the No 1, with mozzarella, *scamorza affumicata,* pancetta, scallions and Oregon-grown white truffles in olive oil). It's in Dumbo, close to the ever-developing Brooklyn waterfront.

Zenkichi   Japanese $$

(Map p255; ☏718-388-8985; www.zenkichi.com; 77 N 6th St, at Wythe Ave, Williamsburg; small plates $7-18, tasting menu $75; ☺6pm-midnight Mon-Sat, 5:30-11:30pm Sun; ⓢL to Bedford Ave) A temple of refined Japanese cuisine, Zenkichi presents beautifully prepared dishes in an atmospheric setting that has wowed foodies from far and wide. The recommendation here is the *omakase,* a seasonal eight-course tasting menu featuring highlights such as winter fruit with tofu sauce and deep-fried Suzuki striped bass, onion and carrot in a sweet, rich vinaigrette sauce topped with chili pepper.

Roberta's   Pizza $$

(Map p255; ☏718-417-1118; www.robertaspizza. com; 261 Moore St, near Bogart St, Bushwick; pizzas $12-19; ☺11am-midnight Mon-Fri, from 10am Sat & Sun; ☌; ⓢL to Morgan Ave) This hipster-saturated warehouse restaurant in Bushwick consistently produces some of the best pizza in NYC. Service can be lackadaisical and the waits long (lunch is best), but the brick-oven pies are the right combination of chewy and fresh. The

classic margherita is sublimely simple; more adventurous palates can opt for the seasonal hits such as Speckenwolf (mozzarella, *speck,* crimini and onion).

Rabbit Hole   Modern American $$

(Map p255; ☏718-782-0910; www.rabbithole restaurant.com; 352 Bedford Ave, btwn S 3rd & S 4th Sts, Williamsburg; mains breakfast $10-14, dinner $13-22; ☺9am-11pm; ☌; ⓢL to Bedford Ave, J/M/Z to Marcy Ave) A warm and inviting spot in South Williamsburg, the very charming Rabbit Hole is a fine spot to disappear into, particularly if you're craving breakfast (served till 5pm). There's casual cafe-seating up front for good coffee and even better house-made pastries. Head to the back or the relaxing rear garden for creamy eggs Benedict or fresh fruit and granola.

Olmsted   Modern American $$

(Map p254; ☏718-552-2610; www.olmstednyc. com; 659 Vanderbilt Ave, btwn Prospect Pl & Park Pl; small plates $13-19, large plates $20-24; ☺5-10:30pm; ⓢB/Q to 7th Ave) Chef-owner Greg Baxtrom creates seasonally inspired dishes so skillfully done that even Manhattanites will cross the river for dinner at this extremely popular Prospect Heights restaurant. Olmsted's locavore credentials are evident: the menu, a 'living wall' of grass inside and a chicken coop in the backyard garden. When the wait is long, the latter is a great place for drinks.

✪ Queens

Pye Boat Noodle   Thai $

(☏718-685-2329; 35-13 Broadway, Astoria; noodles $10-13; ☺11:30am-10:30pm, to 11pm Fri & Sat; ☌; ⓢN/W to Broadway, M, R to Steinway) Young Thai waitresses in matching fedoras greet you at this cute place decked out like an old-fashioned country house. The specialty is rich, star-anise-scented boat noodles, topped with crispy pork cracklings. There's also delicate seafood *yen ta fo* (mild seafood soup, tinted pink), a rarity in NYC – good with a side of papaya salad (off-menu request: add funky fermented crab).

TREASURE HUNT

Begin your shopping adventure

Treasure Hunt

New Yorkers live in a city of temptation. Candy-colored fashion boutiques, cutting-edge music shops, atmospheric antique stores – no matter what your weakness, you'll come face to face with all the objects your heart desires and plenty of curiosities you never even knew existed.

Shopping here isn't just about collecting pretty, fanciful things. It's also about experiencing the city in all its variety and connecting to New York's many subcultures: from browsing classic soul LPs at an East Village record store to jostling among fashion insiders at a Nolita sample sale, you'll find your tribe here in NYC. There are shops for old-fashioned toys, punk-rock handmade jewelry, antiquarian books, vegan clothing, gently used designer clothing, decoupage home decorations and artist monographs – indeed, if you can think of it, there's most likely a shop for it.

In This Section

Useful Websites

Women's Wear Daily (www.wwd.com) Informative fashion site with its finger on the pulse.

New York Magazine (www.nymag.com) Trustworthy opinions on the Big Apple's best places to swipe your plastic.

The Glamourai (www.theglamourai. com) Glossy downtown fashion blog that's packed with cutting-edge style ideas.

Upper West Side & Central Park
The Upper West Side is chain-store central,
so local flavor can be hard to find, but there
are some good shopping stops (p158)

Upper East Side
Madison Ave (from 60th St
to 72nd St) features one of the
globe's glitziest stretches
of retail (p157)

Midtown
Epic department stores, global chains
and the odd in-the-know treasure (p156)

**West Village, Chelsea &
Meatpacking District**
Boutiques and high-end shopping around Bleecker,
Washington, Hudson and W 14th Streets (p153)

**Union Square, Flatiron
District & Gramercy**
This big block of neighborhoods
harbors its own retail gems (p155)

SoHo & Chinatown
West Broadway is a veritable outdoor
mall of encyclopedic proportions (p147)

East Village & Lower East Side
Treasure trove of vintage wares
and design goods (p150)

Financial District & Lower Manhattan
A trickle of gems, from vintage film posters and
hard-to-find vino to hipster-chic threads (p146)

Brooklyn
A healthy mix of independent
boutiques and thrift stores (p159)

Opening Hours

In general, most businesses are open
from 10am to around 7pm on weekdays
and 11am to around 8pm Saturdays.
Sundays can be variable – some stores
stay closed while others keep weekday
hours. Stores tend to stay open later in
the neighborhoods downtown. Small
boutiques often have variable hours –
many open at noon.

Sales

Clothing sales happen throughout the
year, usually at the end of each season,
when old stock needs to be moved out.
There are also big sales during the holidays, particularly in the weeks leading
up to Christmas.

The Best...

Shop till you drop in New York City's best stores.

For Women

Verameat (p152) Exquisite jewelry that treads between beauty and whimsy.

Beacon's Closet (p159) Valhalla for vintage lovers at multiple locations.

MiN New York (p148) Unique perfumes in an apothecary-like setting.

For Children

Dinosaur Hill (p152) In the East Village, you'll find fun and creative toys, books and music that will inspire young minds.

Books of Wonder (p155) Great gift ideas for kids, plus in-store readings at this shop near Union Square.

Fashion Boutiques

Steven Alan (p146) Stylish, heritage-inspired fashion, with branches around NYC, including downtown.

Marc by Marc Jacobs (p155) A downtown and uptown favorite, particularly the West Village locations.

Rag & Bone (p147) Beautifully tailored clothes for men and women, in SoHo and elsewhere.

John Varvatos (pictured above; p151) Rugged but worldly wearables in a former downtown rock club.

Opening Ceremony (p147) Head-turning, cutting-edge threads and kicks for the fashion avant-garde in SoHo.

Bookshops

Strand Book Store (p153) Hands-down NYC's best used bookstore.

McNally Jackson (pictured above; p148) Great SoHo spot for book browsing and author readings.

Housing Works Book Store (p150) Used books and a cafe in an atmospheric setting in Nolita.

192 Books (p155) The perfect neighborhood book shop in Chelsea.

Homewares & Design Stores

Shinola (pictured above; p146) Unusual accessories from a cutting-edge Detroit design house in Tribeca.

A&G Merch (p159) Clever decorating ideas from this artful Williamsburg shop.

Magpie (p158) Ecofriendly curios to feather your nest, in the Upper West Side.

Unique Souvenirs & Gifts

De Vera (pictured above; p148) Beautiful glasswares and art objects.

Obscura Antiques (p150) A cabinet of curiosities packed with strange and eerie objects.

Top Hat (p151) Lovely collectible objects from around the globe.

Bowne Stationers & Co (p146) Score anything from vintage New York posters to city-themed stationery at this heritage printer.

For Men

By Robert James (p152) Rugged menswear by a celebrated new local designer.

Nepenthes New York (p157) Japanese collective selling covetable, in-the-know labels.

Odin (p147) Tiny downtown men's boutique for one-of-a-kind pieces.

★ Lonely Planet's Top Choices

Barneys (p156) Serious fashionistas shop (or at least browse) at Barneys, well known for its spot-on collections of in-the-know labels.

Brooklyn Flea (p152) Brooklyn's collection of flea markets offers plenty of vintage furnishings, retro clothing and bric-a-brac, plus great food stalls.

ABC Carpet & Home (p155) Spread over six floors like a museum, ABC is packed with treasures large (furniture) and small (designer jewelry, global gifts).

MoMA Design & Book Store (p156) The perfect one-stop shop for coffee-table tomes, art prints, edgy jewelry and 'Where-did-you-get-that?' homewares.

⑥ Financial District & Lower Manhattan

Century 21   Fashion & Accessories
(Map p244; ☎212-227-9092; www.c21stores.
com; 22 Cortlandt St, btwn Church St & Broadway;
☺7:45am-9pm Mon-Fri, 10am-9pm Sat, 11am-
8pm Sun; ⑤A/C, J/Z, 2/3, 4/5 to Fulton St, R to
Cortlandt St) For penny-pinching fashionistas,
this giant cut-price department store is
dangerously addictive. Physically dangerous
as well, considering the elbows you might
have to throw to ward off the competition
bee-lining for the same rack. Not everything
is a knockout or a bargain, but persistence
pays off. You'll also find accessories, shoes,
cosmetics, homewares and toys.

Philip Williams Posters   Vintage
(Map p244; ☎212-513-0313; www.postermuseum.
com; 122 Chambers St, btwn Church St & W
Broadway; ☺10am-7pm Mon-Sat; ⑤A/C, 1/2/3
to Chambers St) You'll find nearly half a million
posters in this cavernous treasure trove,
from oversized French advertisements for
perfume and cognac to Soviet film posters
and retro-fab promos for TWA. Prices
range from $15 for small reproductions to
$500,000 for rare, showpiece originals like
an AM Cassandre Toulouse-Lautrec. There's
a second entrance at 52 Warren St.

Shinola   Fashion & Accessories
(Map p246; ☎917-728-3000; www.shinola.com;
177 Franklin St, btwn Greenwich & Hudson Sts;
☺11am-7pm Mon-Sat, noon-6pm Sun; ⑤1 to
Franklin St) Well known for its coveted wrist-
watches, Detroit-based Shinola branches
out with a super-cool selection of Made-in-
USA life props. Bag anything from leather
iPad cases, journal covers and toiletry bags,
to grooming products, jewelry and limited-
edition bicycles with customized bags.
Added bonuses include complimentary
monogramming of leather goods and stationery, and an in-house espresso bar, **Smile
Newstand** (Map p246; ☎917-728-3023; www.
thesmilenyc.com; ☺7am-7pm Mon-Fri, 8am-7pm
Sat, 8am-6pm Sun; 🛜).

Steven Alan   Fashion & Accessories
(Map p246; ☎212-343-0692; www.stevenalan.
com; 103 Franklin St, btwn Church St & W
Broadway; ☺11am-7pm Mon-Sat, noon-6pm Sun;
⑤A/C/E to Canal St; 1 to Franklin St) New York
designer Steven Alan mixes his hip, heritage-inspired threads for men and women
with a beautiful edit of clothes from in-
die-chic labels like France's Arpenteur and
Scandinavia's Acne and Norse Projects.
Accessories include hard-to-find fragrances, bags, jewelry and a selection of shoes
by cognoscenti brands such as Common
Projects and Isabel Marant Étoile.

**Bowne Stationers
& Co**   Gifts & Souvenirs
(Map p244; ☎646-628-2707; 211 Water St, btwn
Beekman & Fulton Sts; ☺11am-7pm; ⑤2/3, 4/5,
A/C, J/Z to Fulton St) Suitably set in cobbled
South Street Seaport and affiliated with the
attached **South Street Seaport Museum**
(Map p244; www.southstreetseaportmuseum.
org; printing press & shop free), this 18th-
century veteran stocks reproduction
vintage New York posters and NYC-themed
notepads, pencil cases, cards, stamps
and even wrapping paper. At the printing workshop you can order customized
business cards or hone your printing skills
in monthly classes (see the museum website's Events page).

Citystore   Gifts & Souvenirs
(Map p244; ☎212-386-0007; http://a856-
citystore.nyc.gov; Municipal Bldg, North Plaza, 1
Centre St, at Chambers St; ☺10am-5pm Mon-Fri;
⑤J/Z to Chambers St, 4/5/6 to Brooklyn Bridge-
City Hall) Score all manner of New York
memorabilia, from authentic taxi medal-
lions (going the way of the public phone-
booth in the age of Uber?), manhole-cover
coasters and subway-themed socks to
NYPD baseball caps and books about
NYC. Curious, though less relevant for the
average visitor, are the binders of New York
City building codes and other regulations
for sale.

🛍 SoHo & Chinatown

Opening Ceremony Fashion, Shoes
(Map p246; ☎212-219-2688; www.openingceremony.us; 35 Howard St, btwn Broadway & Lafayette St; 🕐11am-8pm Mon-Sat, noon-7pm Sun; [S]N/Q/R/W, J/Z, 6 to Canal St) Unisex Opening Ceremony is famed for its never-boring edit of A-list indie labels. The place showcases a changing roster of names from across the globe, both established and emerging; complementing them is Opening Ceremony's own avant-garde creations. No matter who's hanging on the racks, you can always expect show-stopping, 'where-did-you-get-that?!' threads that are street-smart, bold and refreshingly unexpected.

Rag & Bone Fashion & Accessories
(Map p246; ☎212-219-2204; www.rag-bone.com; 119 Mercer St, btwn Prince & Spring Sts; 🕐11am-8pm Mon-Sat, noon-7pm Sun; [S]N/R to Prince St) Downtown label Rag & Bone is a hit with many of New York's coolest, sharpest dressers – both men and women. Detail-oriented pieces range from clean-cut shirts and blazers and graphic tees to monochromatic sweaters, feather-light strappy dresses, leather goods and Rag & Bone's highly prized jeans. The tailoring is generally impeccable, with accessories including shoes, hats, bags and wallets.

Odin Fashion & Accessories
(Map p246; ☎212-966-0026; www.odinnewyork.com; 161 Grand St, btwn Lafayette & Centre Sts; 🕐11am-8pm Mon-Sat, noon-7pm Sun; [S]6 to Spring St, N/R to Prince St) Odin's flagship men's boutique carries hip downtown labels such as Thom Browne, Rag & Bone and Public School NYC. Rubbing shoulders with them is a select edit of imports, among them Nordic labels Acne and Won Hundred. Other in-store tempters include fragrances, jewelry from Brooklyn creatives such as Naval Yard and Uhuru, and street-smart footwear from cult labels such as Common Projects.

3x1 Fashion & Accessories
(Map p246; ☎212-391-6969; www.3x1.us; 15 Mercer St, btwn Howard & Grand Sts; 🕐11am-7pm Mon-Sat, noon-6pm Sun; [S]N/Q/R/W, J/Z, 6 to

Exterior of Barneys (p156)

Canal St) Design your most flattering pair of jeans at this bespoke denim factory/showroom, with three levels of service. Quick, on-the-spot 'ready-to-wear' lets you choose the hem for ready-to-wear denim (women's from $195, men's from $245); 'custom' has you choose the fabric and detailing for an existing fit ($625 to $850); and 'full bespoke' ($1500) designs your perfect pair from scratch.

McNally Jackson — Books

(Map p246; ☎212-274-1160; www.mcnallyjackson.com; 52 Prince St, btwn Lafayette & Mulberry Sts; ⏱10am-10pm Mon-Sat, to 9pm Sun; Ⓢ N/R to Prince St, 6 to Spring St) Bustling indie MJ stocks an excellent selection of magazines and books, covering contemporary fiction, food writing, architecture and design, art and history. If you can score a seat, the in-store cafe is a fine spot to settle in with some reading material or to catch one of the readings and book signings held here.

MiN New York — Cosmetics

(Map p246; ☎212-206-6366; www.min.com; 117 Crosby St, btwn Jersey & Prince Sts; ⏱11am-7pm Tue-Sat, noon-6pm Mon & Sun; Ⓢ B/D/F/M to Broadway-Lafayette St, N/R to Prince St) This chic, library-like apothecary curates an extraordinary, rotating collection of rare and exclusive perfumes, grooming products and scented candles. Esteemed and historic European lines aside, look out for artisanal American fragrances from the likes of Strangelove NYC and the Vagabond Prince, as well as MiN's own line of coveted hair products.

De Vera — Antiques

(Map p246; ☎212-625-0838; www.devera objects.com; 1 Crosby St, at Howard St; ⏱11am-7pm Tue-Sat; Ⓢ N/Q/R/W, J/Z, 6 to Canal St) Federico de Vera travels the globe in search of rare and exquisite jewelry, carvings, lacquerware and other *objets d'art* for this jewel-box of a store. Illuminated vitrines display works such as 200-year-old Buddhas, Venetian glassware and gilded, inlaid boxes from the Meiji period, while oil paintings and carvings along the walls complete the museum-like experience.

Will Leather Goods Fashion & Accessories

(Map p246; ☎212-925-2824; www.willleathergoods.com; 29 Prince St, at Mott St; 🕐11am-7pm; [S]N/R to Prince St, 6 to Spring St) Beautifully crafted, classically styled leather goods fill this family-owned Oregon import. While you'll find everything from wallets and belts to pet leashes, it's the bags that take the breath away – made using American and Italian leathers, including satchels, briefcases, messenger bags, jet-setter duffles and clutches. The store also sells vintage pieces: 1930s basketball or US Postal Service mail bag, anyone?

MoMA Design Store Gifts & Souvenirs

(Map p246; ☎646-613-1367; www.momastore.org; 81 Spring St, at Crosby St; 🕐10am-8pm Mon-Sat, 11am-7pm Sun; [S]N/R to Prince St, 6 to Spring St) The Museum of Modern Art's downtown retail space carries a huge collection of sleek, smart and clever objects for the home, office and wardrobe. You'll find modernist alarm clocks, sculptural vases and jewelry, surreal lamps and svelte kitchenware, plus brainy games, hand puppets, fanciful scarves, coffee-table books and loads of other unique gift ideas.

Screaming Mimi's Vintage

(Map p246; ☎212-677-6464; www.screamingmimis.com; 240 W 14th St, btwn Seventh & Eighth Aves; 🕐noon-8pm Mon-Sat, 1-7pm Sun; [S]A/C/E/L to 8th Ave-14th St) If you dig vintage threads, you may just scream, too. This funtastic shop carries an excellent selection of yesteryear pieces, organized – ingeniously – by decade, from the '50s to the '90s. (Ask to see the small, stashed-away collection of clothing from the 1920s through '40s.)

Uniqlo Fashion & Accessories

(Map p246; ☎877-486-4756; www.uniqlo.com; 546 Broadway, btwn Prince & Spring Sts; 🕐10am-9pm Mon-Sat, 11am-8pm Sun; [S]N/R to Prince St, 6 to Spring St) This enormous, three-story Japanese emporium, the company's first location in the US, owes its popularity to good-looking, good-quality apparel at discount prices. You'll find Japanese denim, Mongolian cashmere, graphic T-shirts,

★ Top Five Vintage Stops

Screaming Mimi's (p149)

Brooklyn Flea (p152)

No Relation Vintage (p151)

Edith Machinist (p152)

Beacon's Closet (p159)

SORBIS / SHUTTERSTOCK ©

SPENCER PLATT / GETTY IMAGES ©

From left: MoMA Design Store; Uniqlo; Moo Shoes (p152)

Obscura Antiques

This small cabinet of curiosities pleases both lovers of the macabre and inveterate antique hunters

elegant skirts, high-tech thermals and endless racks of colorful ready-to-wear items – with most things falling below the $100 mark.

Housing Works Book Store Books

(Map p246; ☎212-334-3324; www.housingworks.org/bookstore; 126 Crosby St, btwn E Houston & Prince Sts; 🕐9am-9pm Mon-Fri, 10am-5pm Sat & Sun; [S]B/D/F/M to Broadway-Lafayette St, N/R to Prince St) Relaxed, earthy and featuring a great selection of second-hand books, vinyl, CDs and DVDs you can buy for a good cause (proceeds go to the city's HIV-positive and AIDS-infected homeless population), this creaky hide-away is a very local place to while away a few quiet afternoon hours browsing or sitting in the on-site cafe.

🛍 East Village & Lower East Side

Still House Homewares

(Map p246; ☎212-539-0200; www.stillhousenyc.com; 117 E 7th St, btwn First Ave & Ave A; 🕐noon-8pm; [S]6 to Astor Pl) Step into this petite, peaceful boutique to browse sculptural glassware and pottery: handblown vases, geometric tabletop objects, ceramic bowls and cups, and other finery for the home. You'll also find minimalistic jewelry, delicately bound notebooks and small framed artworks for the wall.

Obscura Antiques Antiques

(Map p246; ☎212-505-9251; www.obscuraantiques.com; 207 Ave A, btwn E 12th & 13th Sts; 🕐noon-8pm Mon-Sat, to 7pm Sun; [S]L to 1st Ave) This small cabinet of curiosities pleases both lovers of the macabre and inveterate antique hunters. Here you'll find taxidermied animal heads, tiny rodent skulls and skeletons, butterfly displays in glass boxes, photos of dead people, disturbing little (dental?) instruments, German landmine flags (stackable so tanks could see them), old poison bottles and glass eyes.

John Varvatos Fashion & Accessories

(Map p246; ☎212-358-0315; www.johnvarvatos.com; 315 Bowery, btwn E 1st & 2nd Sts; 🕒noon-8pm Mon-Fri, 11am-8pm Sat, noon-6pm Sun; [S]F to 2nd Ave, 6 to Bleecker St) Set in the hallowed halls of former punk club **CBGB** (Map p246), this John Varvatos store goes to great lengths to tie fashion to rock and roll, with records, '70s audio equipment and even electric guitars for sale alongside JV's denim, leather boots, belts and graphic tees. Sales associates dressed in Varvatos' downtown cool seem far removed from the Bowery's gritty past.

Top Hat Gifts & Souvenirs

(Map p246; ☎212-677-4240; www.tophatnyc.com; 245 Broome St, btwn Ludlow & Orchard Sts; 🕒noon-8pm; [S]B/D to Grand St) Sporting curios from around the globe, this whimsical little shop is packed with intrigue: from vintage Italian pencils and handsomely miniaturized leather journals to beautifully carved wooden bird-whistles. Looking for an endless rain album, a toy clarinet, Japanese fabrics, a crumpled map of the night sky or geometric Spanish cups and saucers? You'll find all these and more here.

No Relation Vintage Vintage

(Map p246; ☎212-228-5201; www.norelationvintage.com; 204 First Ave, btwn E 12th & 13th Sts; 🕒noon-8pm Mon-Thu & Sun, to 9pm Fri & Sat; [S]L to First Ave) Among the many vintage shops of the East Village, No Relation is a winner for its wide-ranging collections that run the gamut from denim and leather jackets to flannels, sneakers, candy-colored T-shirts, varsity jackets, clutches and more. Sharpen your elbows: hipster crowds flock here on weekends.

Tokio 7 Fashion & Accessories

(Map p246; ☎212-353-8443; www.tokio7.net; 83 E 7th St, near First Ave; 🕒noon-8pm; [S]6 to Astor Pl) This revered, hip consignment shop has good-condition designer labels for men and women at some fairly hefty prices. The Japanese-owned store often features lovely pieces by Issey Miyake and Yohji Yamamoto, as well as a well-curated selection of Dolce & Gabbana, Prada, Chanel and other top labels.

NYC Icons

A few stores in this city have cemented their status as NYC legends. This city just wouldn't quite be the same without them. For label hunters, **Century 21** (p146) is a Big Apple institution, with clothing by D&G, Prada, Marc Jacobs and many others at low prices. Book lovers of the world unite at the **Strand** (p153), the city's biggest and best bookseller. Run by Hasidic Jews and employing mechanized whimsy, **B&H Photo Video** (p157) is a mecca for digital and audio geeks. For secondhand clothing, home furnishings and books, good-hearted **Housing Works** (p155), with many locations around town, is a perennial favorite.

Exterior of Century 21
TOOYKRUB / SHUTTERSTOCK ©

Reformation Clothing

(Map p246; ☎646-448-4925; www.thereformation.com; 156 Ludlow St, btwn Rivington & Stanton Sts; 🕒noon-8pm Mon-Sat, to 7pm Sun; [S]F to Delancey St or 2nd Ave, J/M/Z to Essex St) 🌿 This stylish boutique sells beautifully designed garments with minimal environmental impact. Aside from their green credentials, they sell unique tops, blouses, sweaters and dresses, with fair prices in comparison to other Lower East Side boutiques.

Flea Markets & Vintage Adventures

As much as New Yorkers gravitate towards all that's shiny and new, it can be infinitely fun to rifle through closets of unwanted wares and threads. The most popular flea market is the **Brooklyn Flea** (Map p255; www.brooklynflea.com; 90 Kent Ave, btwn N 7th & N 10th Sts, Williamsburg; ⊙10am-5pm Sat Apr-Oct), housed in all sorts of spaces throughout the year. The East Village is the city's de facto neighborhood for secondhand and vintage stores – the uniform of the unwavering legion of hipsters.

Browsing at Brooklyn Flea
JOE TABACCA / SHUTTERSTOCK ©

Verameat   Jewelry
(Map p246; ☎212-388-9045; www.verameat. com; 315 E 9th St, btwn First & Second Aves; ⊙10am-9pm; ⓢ6 to Astor Pl, F to 2nd Ave) Designer Vera Balyura creates exquisite little pieces with a dark sense of humor in this delightful little shop on 9th St. Tiny, artfully wrought pendants, rings, earrings and bracelets appear almost too precious... until a closer inspection reveals zombies, godzilla robots, animal heads, dinosaurs and encircling claws – bringing a whole new level of miniaturized complexity to the realm of jewelry.

Dinosaur Hill   Toys
(Map p246; ☎212-473-5850; www.dinosaurhill. com; 306 E 9th St, btwn First & Second Aves; ⊙11am-7pm; ⓢ6 to Astor Pl) A small, old-fashioned toy store that's inspired more by imagination than Disney movies, this shop has loads of great gift ideas: Czech mari-

onettes, shadow puppets, micro building blocks, calligraphy sets, toy pianos, art and science kits, kids' music CDs from around the globe, and wooden blocks in half-a-dozen different languages, plus natural-fiber clothing for infants.

By Robert James   Fashion & Accessories
(Map p246; ☎212-253-2121; www.byrobert james.com; 74 Orchard St, btwn Broome & Grand Sts; ⊙noon-8pm Mon-Sat, to 6pm Sun; ⓢF to Delancey St, J/M/Z to Essex St) Rugged, beautifully tailored menswear is the mantra of Robert James, who sources and manufactures right here in NYC (the design studio is just upstairs). The racks are lined with slim-fitting denim, handsome button-downs, and classic-looking sports coats. Lola, James' black lab, sometimes roams the store. He also has a store in Williamsburg.

Moo Shoes   Shoes
(Map p246; ☎212-254-6512; www.mooshoes. com; 78 Orchard St, btwn Broome & Grand Sts; ⊙11:30am-7:30pm Mon-Sat, noon-6pm Sun; ⓢF to Delancey St, J/M/Z to Essex St) This earth- and animal-friendly boutique sells surprisingly stylish microfiber (faux leather) shoes, handbags and wallets. Look for elegant ballet flats from Love Is Mighty, rugged men's Oxfords by Novacas, and sleek Matt & Nat wallets.

A-1 Records   Music
(Map p246; ☎212-473-2870; www.a1recordshop. com; 439 E 6th St, btwn First Ave & Ave A; ⊙1-9pm; ⓢF to 2nd Ave) One of the last of the many record stores that once graced the East Village, A-1 has been around for over two decades. The cramped aisles, filled with a large selection of jazz, funk and soul, draw vinyl fans and DJs from far and wide.

Edith Machinist   Vintage
(Map p246; ☎212-979-9992; www.edith machinist.com; 104 Rivington St, btwn Ludlow & Essex Sts; ⊙noon-7pm Tue-Thu, to 6pm Sun, Mon & Fri; ⓢF to Delancey St, J/M/Z to Essex St) To properly strut about the Lower East Side, you've got to dress the part. Edith

Machinist can help you get that rumpled but stylish look in a hurry – a bit of vintage glam via knee-high soft suede boots, 1930s silk dresses and ballet-style flats.

John Derian
Homewares

(Map p246; ☏212-677-3917; www.johnderian. com; 6 E 2nd St, btwn Bowery & Second Ave; ⏱11am-7pm Tue-Sun; ⓢF to 2nd Ave) John Derian is famed for its decoupage: pieces from original botanical and animal prints stamped under glass. The result is a beautiful collection of one-of-a-kind plates, paperweights, coasters, lamps, bowls and vases.

ⓐ West Village, Chelsea & Meatpacking District

Strand Book Store
Books

(Map p246; ☏212-473-1452; www.strandbooks. com; 828 Broadway, at E 12th St; ⏱9:30am-10:30pm Mon-Sat, from 11am Sun; ⓢL, N/Q/R/W, 4/5/6 to 14th St-Union Sq) Beloved and legendary, the iconic Strand embodies downtown NYC's intellectual bona fides –

a bibliophile's Oz, where generations of book lovers carrying the store's trademark tote bags happily lose themselves for hours. In operation since 1927, the Strand sells new, used and rare titles, spreading an incredible 18 miles of books (over 2.5 million of them) among three labyrinthine floors.

Story
Gifts & Souvenirs

(Map p250; www.thisisstory.com; 144 Tenth Ave, btwn W 18th & 19th Sts; ⏱11am-7pm Tue, Wed, Fri-Sun, to 8pm Thu; ⓢC/E to 23rd St; 1 to 18th St) This high-concept shop near the High Line (p52) functions like a gallery, showcasing new themes and products every month or two. The 2000-sq-ft space covers all the bases, from crafty jewelry and eye-catching accessories to lovely stationery, imagination-inspiring toys for kids, thick coffee-table books, environmentally friendly soaps and whimsical souvenirs.

plush BG, at this location since 1928, heads the fashion race...

Streetview of Bergdorf Goodman (p157)

LITTLENY / SHUTTERSTOCK ©

Top Five NYC Souvenirs

Here Personal Globe

Francesco Toselli's geometric globe from the MoMA Design & Book Store (p156) is a great keepsake for those who love to travel.

Local Wears

Add something NYC-made to your wardrobe, like some rugged outer-wear of By Robert James (p152).

Antique Print

Reproductions of NYC at Bowne Stationers & Co (p146) make great art-work when framed – and a fine reminder of the Big Apple experience.

Subway Map Umbrella

Bring a smile to passers-by with an umbrella emblazoned with NY's iconic transport system. Available at Citystore (p146).

NYC in Print

Pick up a beautifully illustrated coffee-table book cov-ering NYC at the Strand Book Store (p153), New York's biggest and best indie bookseller.

Marc by Marc Jacobs Fashion & Accessories

(Map p246; ☎212-924-0026; www.marcjacobs.com; 403 Bleecker St, btwn Bank & W 11th Sts; 🕒11am-7pm Mon-Sat, noon-6pm Sun; [S]A/C/E to 14th St, L to 8th Ave) At home in this well-heeled neighborhood, this Marc Jacob's outpost sells the designer's women's line. The store's large front windows allow easy peeking – assuming there's not a sale, during which you'll only see hordes of fawning shoppers. There's also **BookMarc** (for books, stationary and knickknacks) at No 400.

Personnel of New York Fashion & Accessories

(Map p246; ☎212-924-0604; www.personnelofnewyork.com; 9 Greenwich Ave, btwn Christopher & W 10th St; 🕒noon-7pm Mon-Sat, to 6pm Sun; [S]A/C/E, B/D/F/M to W 4th St-Washington Sq, 1 to Christopher St-Sheridan Sq) This small, delightful indie shop sells women's designer clothing from unique labels from the East and West Coasts and beyond. Look for easy-to-wear Sunja Link dresses, soft pullover sweaters by Ali Golden, statement-making jewelry by Marisa Mason, comfy canvas sneakers by Shoes Like Pottery and couture pieces by Rodebjer.

192 Books Books

(Map p250; ☎212-255-4022; www.192books.com; 192 Tenth Ave, btwn W 21st & 22nd Sts; 🕒11am-7pm; [S]C/E to 23rd St) Located right in the gallery district is this small indie bookstore, with sections on fiction, history, travel, art and criticism. Its rotating art exhibits are a special treat, during which the owners organize special displays of books that relate thematically to the featured show or artist. Weekly book readings feature acclaimed (often NYC-based) authors.

Housing Works Thrift Shop Vintage

(Map p250; ☎718-838-5050; www.housingworks.org; 143 W 17th St, btwn Sixth & Seventh Aves; 🕒10am-7pm Mon-Sat, noon-6pm Sun; [S]1 to 18th St) With its swank window displays, this shop looks more boutique than thrift, but its selections of clothes, accessories, furniture, books and records are great value. All proceeds benefit the charity serving the city's HIV-positive and AIDS-infected homeless communities. There are 13 other branches around town.

McNulty's Tea & Coffee Co, Inc Food & Drinks

(Map p246; ☎212-242-5351; www.mcnultys.com; 109 Christopher St, btwn Bleecker & Hudson Sts; 🕒10am-9pm Mon-Sat, 1-7pm Sun; [S]1 to Christopher St-Sheridan Sq) Just down from a few sex shops, sweet McNulty's, with worn wooden floorboards, fragrant sacks of coffee beans and large glass jars of tea, flaunts a different era of Greenwich Village. It's been selling gourmet teas and coffees here since 1895.

🔒 Union Square, Flatiron District & Gramercy

ABC Carpet & Home Homewares

(Map p250; ☎212-473-3000; www.abchome.com; 888 Broadway, at E 19th St; 🕒10am-7pm Mon-Wed, Fri & Sat, to 8pm Thu, 11am-6:30pm Sun; [S]4/5/6, N/Q/R/W, L to 14th St-Union Sq) A mecca for home designers and decorators brainstorming ideas, this beautifully curated, seven-level temple to good taste heaves with all sorts of furnishings, small and large. Shop for easy-to-pack knickknacks, textiles and jewelry, as well as statement furniture, designer lighting, ceramics and antique carpets.

Books of Wonder Books

(Map p250; ☎212-989-3270; www.booksofwonder.com; 18 W 18th St, btwn Fifth & Sixth Aves; 🕒10am-7pm Mon-Sat, 11am-6pm Sun; 👪; [S]F/M to 14th St, L to 6th Ave) Devoted to children's and young-adult titles, this wonderful bookstore is a great place to take young ones on a rainy day, especially when a kids' author is giving a reading or a storyteller is on hand. There's an impressive range of NYC-themed picture books, plus a section dedicated to rare and vintage children's books and limited-edition children's book artwork.

Sample Sales

While clothing sales happen year-round – usually when seasons change and old stock must be moved out – sample sales are held frequently, mostly in the huge warehouses in the Fashion District of Midtown or in SoHo. While the original sample sale was a way for designers to get rid of one-of-a-kind prototypes that weren't quite up to snuff, most sample sales these days are for high-end labels to get rid of overstock at wonderfully deep discounts. For the latest sample sales, check out **NY Racked** (http://ny.racked.com/sales). Consignment stores are another fine place to look for top (gently used) fashions at reduced prices.

LELAND BOBBE / GETTY IMAGES ©

Bedford Cheese Shop Food

(Map p250; ☎718-599-7588; www.bedfordcheeseshop.com; 67 Irving Pl, btwn E 18th & 19th Sts; ⏰8am-9pm Mon-Sat, to 8pm Sun; [S]4/5/6, N/Q/R/W, L to 14th St-Union Sq) Whether you're after local, raw cow's-milk cheese washed in absinthe or garlic-infused goat's-milk cheese from Australia, chances are you'll find it among the 200-strong selection at this outpost of Brooklyn's most celebrated cheese vendor. Pair the cheesy goodness with artisanal charcuterie, deli treats and ready-to-eat sandwiches ($8 to $11), as well as a proud array of Made-in-Brooklyn edibles.

Idlewild Books Books

(Map p246; ☎212-414-8888; www.idlewildbooks.com; 170 Seventh Ave S, at Perry St; ⏰noon-8pm Mon-Thu, to 6pm Fri-Sun; [S]1 to Christopher St-Sheridan Sq, 2/3 to 14th St-7th Ave) Named after JFK Airport's original moniker, this indie travel bookshop gets feet seriously itchy. Books are divided by region and cover guidebooks as well as fiction, travelogues, history, cookbooks and other stimulating fare for delving into different corners of the world. The store also runs popular language classes in French, Italian, Spanish and German; see the website for details.

DSW Shoes

(Map p246; ☎212-674-2146; www.dsw.com; 40 E 14th St, btwn University Pl & Broadway; ⏰10am-9:30pm Mon-Sat, to 8pm Sun; [S]4/5/6, N/Q/R/W, L to 14th St-Union Sq) If your idea of paradise involves a great selection of cut-price kicks, make a beeline for this sprawling unisex chain. Shoes range from formal to athletic, with no shortage of popular and higher-end labels. Unobstructed views of Union Square Park are a bonus.

Midtown

MoMA Design & Book Store Gifts, Books

(Map p252; ☎212-708-9700; www.momastore.org; 11 W 53rd St, btwn Fifth & Sixth Aves; ⏰9:30am-6:30pm Sat-Thu, to 9pm Fri; [S]E, M to 5th Ave-53rd St) The flagship store at the Museum of Modern Art (p48) is a fab spot for souvenir shopping. Besides gorgeous books (from art and architecture tomes to pop-culture readers and kids' picture books), you'll find art prints and posters and one-of-a-kind knickknacks. For furniture, lighting, homewares, jewelry, bags and MUJI merchandise, head to the MoMA Design Store (p149) across the street.

Barneys Department Store

(Map p252; ☎212-826-8900; www.barneys.com; 660 Madison Ave, at E 61st St; ⏰10am-8pm Mon-Fri, to 7pm Sat, 11am-7pm Sun; [S]N/R/W to

5th Ave-59th St) Serious fashionistas swipe their plastic at Barneys, respected for its collections of top-tier labels like Isabel Marant Étoile, Mr & Mrs Italy, and Lanvin. For (slightly) less expensive deals geared to a younger market, shop street-chic brands on the 8th floor. Other highlights include a basement cosmetics department and Genes, a futuristic cafe with touch-screen communal tables for online shopping.

Bergdorf Goodman
Department Store

(Map p252; 212-753-7300; www.bergdorfgood man.com; 754 Fifth Ave, btwn W 57th & 58th Sts; 10am-8pm Mon-Sat, 11am-7pm Sun; N/R/W to 5th Ave-59th St, F to 57th St) Not merely loved for its Christmas windows (the city's best), plush BG, at this location since 1928, heads the fashion race, led by its industry-leading fashion director Linda Fargo. A mainstay of ladies who lunch, its drawcards include exclusive collections of Tom Ford and Chanel shoes and a coveted women's shoe department. The men's store is across the street.

Bloomingdale's
Department Store

(Map p252; 212-705-2000; www.blooming dales.com; 1000 Third Ave, at E 59th St; 10am-8:30pm Mon-Sat, 11am-7pm Sun; ; 4/5/6 to 59th St, N/R/W to Lexington Ave-59th St) Blockbuster Bloomie's is something like the Metropolitan Museum of Art of the shopping world – historic, sprawling, overwhelming and packed with bodies, but you'd be sorry to miss it. Raid the racks for clothes and shoes from a who's who of US and global designers, including many 'new-blood' collections. Refueling pit stops include a branch of cupcake heaven Magnolia Bakery.

Uniqlo
Fashion & Accessories

(Map p252; 877-486-4756; www.uniqlo.com; 666 Fifth Ave, at E 53rd St; 10am-9pm Mon-Sat, 11am-8pm Sun; E, M to 5th Ave-53rd St) Uniqlo is Japan's answer to H&M and this is its showstopping 89,000-sq-ft flagship mega-store. Grab a mesh bag at the entrance and let the elevators whoosh you up to the

3rd floor to begin your retail odyssey. The forte here is affordable, fashionable, quality basics, from T-shirts and undergarments to Japanese denim, cashmere sweaters and super-light, high-tech parkas.

Nepenthes New York
Fashion & Accessories

(Map p250; 212-643-9540; www.nepenthesny. com; 307 W 38th St, btwn Eighth & Ninth Aves; noon-7pm Mon-Sat, to 5pm Sun; A/C/E to 42nd St-Port Authority Bus Terminal) Occupying an old sewing shop in the Garment District, this cult Japanese collective stocks edgy menswear from the likes of Engineered Garments and Needles, known for their quirky detailing and artisanal production value (think tweed lace-up hem pants). Accessories include bags and satchels, gloves, eyewear and footwear.

B&H Photo Video
Electronics

(Map p250; 212-444-6615; www.bhphoto video.com; 420 Ninth Ave, btwn W 33rd & 34th Sts; 9am-6pm Mon-Thu, to 1pm Fri, 10am-5pm Sun, closed Sat; A/C/E to 34th St-Penn Station) Visiting NYC's most popular camera shop is an experience in itself – it's massive and crowded, and bustling with black-clad (and tech-savvy) Hasidic Jewish salesmen. Your chosen item is dropped into a bucket, which then moves up and across the ceiling to the purchase area (which requires wait-ing in another line).

Upper East Side

Encore
Clothing

(Map p252; 212-879-2850; www.encoreresale. com; 1132 Madison Ave, btwn E 84th & 85th Sts; 10am-6:30pm Mon-Sat, noon-6pm Sun; 4/5/6 to 86th St) This exclusive con-signment store has been emptying out Upper East Side closets since the 1950s. (Jacqueline Kennedy Onassis used to sell her clothes here.) Expect to find a gently worn selection of name brands such as Louboutin, Fendi and Dior. Prices are high, but infinitely better than retail.

Homage to Luxury

One of the world's fashion capitals, NYC is ever setting trends for the rest of the country to follow. For checking out the latest designs hitting the streets, it's worth browsing some of the city's best-loved boutiques around town – regardless of whether you intend to spend. A few favorites include Opening Ceremony, Issey Miyake, Marc Jacobs, Steven Alan, Rag & Bone, John Varvatos, By Robert James and Piperlime.

If time is limited, or you simply want to browse a plethora of labels in one go, then head to those heady conglomerations known worldwide as department stores. New York has a special blend of alluring draws – in particular don't miss **Barneys** (p156), **Bergdorf Goodman** (p157), **Macy's** (Map p250; ☑212-695-4400; www.macys.com; 151 W 34th St, at Broadway; ◷10am-10pm Mon-Sat, 11am-9pm Sun; ⓈB/D/F/M, N/Q/R/W to 34th St-Herald Sq) and **Bloomingdale's** (p157).

Holiday window displays at Macy's
LITTLENY / SHUTTERSTOCK ©

Blue Tree
Fashion, Homewares

(Map p252; ☑212-369-2583; www.bluetreeny. bigcartel.com; 1283 Madison Ave, btwn E 91st & 92nd Sts; ◷10am-6pm Mon-Fri, 11am-6pm Sat; Ⓢ4/5/6 to 86th St) This charming (and expensive) little boutique, owned by actress Phoebe Cates Kline (of *Fast Times at Ridgemont High*), sells a dainty array of women's clothing, cashmere scarves, Lucite objects, whimsical accessories and quirky home design.

ⓐ Upper West Side & Central Park

Flying Tiger Copenhagen
Homewares

(Map p252; ☑646-998-4755; www.flyingtiger. com; 424 Columbus Ave, btwn W 80th & 81st St; ◷9am-8pm Mon-Sat, 10am-6pm Sun; ⚑; ⓈB, C to 81st St-Museum of Natural History) In the market for well-designed, quirky and inexpensive doodads and tchotchkes? This Danish import will scratch that itch. Something of a miniature Ikea, with items grouped thematically (kitchen, kids, arts and crafts, etc) – you could never have imagined the things you didn't know you needed. Remove the price tag and friends will think you've spent too much on a gift.

Magpie
Arts & Crafts

(Map p252; ☑212-579-3003; www.magpienew york.com; 488 Amsterdam Ave, btwn W 83rd & 84th Sts; ◷11am-7pm Mon-Sat, to 6pm Sun; Ⓢ1 to 86th St) ⚑ When you're short of gift ideas stop by this charming little outpost, where you'll find a wide range of ecofriendly objects. Elegant stationery, beeswax candles, hand-painted mugs, organic cotton scarves, recycled resin necklaces, hand-dyed felt journals and wooden earth puzzles are a few things that may catch your eye. Most products are fair-trade, made of sustainable materials or are locally designed and made.

ⓐ Harlem & Upper Manhattan

Flamekeepers Hat Club
Fashion & Accessories

(☑212-531-3542; 273 W 121st St, at St Nicholas Ave; ◷noon-7pm Tue & Wed, to 8pm Thu-Sat, to 6pm Sun; ⓈA/C, B/D to 125th St) Sharpen your kudos at this sassy little hat shop owned by affable Harlem local Marc Williamson. His carefully curated stock is a hat-lover's dream: buttery Barbisio fedoras from Italy, Selentino top hats from the Czech Republic and woolen patchwork caps from Ireland's

Hanna Hats of Donegal. Prices range from $85 to $350, with an optional customization service for true individualists.

Trunk Show Designer Consignment Vintage
(☎212-662-0009; www.trunkshowconsignment.com; 275-277 W 113th St, at Eighth Ave; 🕒by appointment only 1-8:30pm Tue-Fri, to 7:30pm Sat, to 6:30pm Sun; [S]B, C to 110th St-Cathedral Parkway, 2/3 to 110th St-Central Park North) Step into this hot little consignment store in Harlem for a unisex edit of fabulous pre-loved finds. With merchandise delivered every second day, you're pretty much assured of a couture catch, whether it's a John Varvatos leather coat, a Valentino frock or a pair of Lanvin python pumps. Opening times can vary, so consider calling ahead.

Brooklyn

Artists & Fleas Market
(Map p255; www.artistsandfleas.com; 70 N 7th Ave, btwn Wythe & Kent Aves, Williamsburg; 🕒10am-7pm Sat & Sun; [S]L to Bedford Ave) At this popular artists, designers and vintage flea market in Williamsburg, in operation for over a decade, you'll find an excellent selection of crafty goodness. More than 100 vendors sell their wares, which includes vintage clothing, records, paintings, photographs, hats, handmade jewelry, one-of-a-kind T-shirts, canvas bags and more. There's also a smaller location (open daily) inside the Chelsea Market (p130).

Beacon's Closet Vintage
(Map p255; ☎718-486-0816; www.beaconscloset.com; 74 Guernsey St, btwn Nassau & Norman Aves, Greenpoint; 🕒11am-8pm; [S]L to Bedford Ave; G to Nassau Ave) Twenty-something groovers find this massive 5500-sq-ft warehouse of vintage clothing part goldmine, part grit. Lots of coats, polyester tops and '90s-era T-shirts are handily displayed by color, but the sheer mass can take time to conquer. You'll also find shoes of all sorts, flannels, hats, handbags, chunky jewelry and brightly hued sunglasses.

Rough Trade Music
(Map p255; ☎718-388-4111; www.roughtradenyc.com; 64 N 9th St, btwn Kent & Wythe Aves, Williamsburg; 🕒11am-11pm Mon-Sat, to 9pm Sun; [S]L to Bedford Ave) This sprawling, 10,000-sq-ft record store – a London import – stocks thousands of titles on vinyl and CD. It also has in-store DJs, listening stations, art exhibitions, and coffee and doughnuts from Brompton Bike Cafe. A small concert hall onsite hosts live bands throughout the week (admission varies).

A&G Merch Homewares
(Map p255; ☎718-388-1779; www.aandgmerch.com; 111 N 6th St, btwn Berry & Wythe Sts, Williamsburg; 🕒noon-7pm; [S]L to Bedford Ave) A&G Merch is a fun little shop to explore, with its mix of whimsy and elegance. Check out antique plates adorned with animal heads (Uncle Herb the lion), rustic wicker baskets, cast-iron whale bookends, silver tree-branch-like candleholders, brassy industrial table lamps and more goods to give your nest that artfully rustic Brooklyn look.

Buffalo Exchange Clothing
(Map p255; ☎718-384-6901; www.buffaloexchange.com; 504 Driggs Ave, at N 9th St, Williamsburg; 🕒11am-8pm Mon-Sat, noon-7pm Sun; [S]L to Bedford Ave) This new and used clothing shop is a go-to spot for Brooklynites on a budget – featuring clothes (designer and not), shoes, jewelry and accessories. It's a generally well-curated collection, though you'll still want to bank on spending some quality time here. There are four other locations throughout the city.

Spoonbill & Sugartown Books
(Map p255; ☎718-387-7322; www.spoonbillbooks.com; 218 Bedford Ave, btwn N 5th & N 4th Sts, Williamsburg; 🕒10am-10pm; [S]L to Bedford Ave) Williamsburg's favorite bookshop has an intriguing selection of art and coffee-table books, cultural journals, used and rare titles, and locally made works not found elsewhere. Check the website for upcoming readings and book-launch parties.

BAR OPEN

Thirst-quenching venues, craft-beer culture and beyond

Bar Open

Considering that 'Manhattan' is thought to be a derivation of the Munsee word manahactanienk ('place of general inebriation'), it shouldn't be surprising that New York truly lives up to its nickname: 'the city that never sleeps.' You'll find all species of thirst-quenching venues here, from award-winning cocktail lounges and historic dive bars to an ever-growing number of specialty tap rooms and wine bars. Then there's the city's legendary club scene, spanning everything from celebrity staples to gritty, indie hangouts.

In the land where the term 'cocktail' was born, mixed drinks are still stirred with the utmost gravitas. The city's craft beer culture is equally dynamic, with an ever-expanding booty of breweries, bars and shops showcasing local artisanal brews. No matter what your poison, NYC has you covered.

In This Section

Opening Hours

Opening times vary. While some dive bars open as early as 8am, most drinking establishments get rolling around 5pm. Numerous bars stay open until 4am, while others close at around 1am early in the week and at 2am from Thursday to Saturday. Clubs generally operate from 10pm to 4am or 5am.

Harlem & Upper Manhattan 🚇
A burgeoning mix of speakeasy-style bars,
hipster hangouts and old-school dives with
soul-stirring jazz and blues (p176)

Upper West Side & Central Park 🚇
The Upper West Side has its moments, with some
good beer halls, cocktail lounges and wine bars (p176)

Upper East Side
🚇 Times are changing here with
Brooklyn-style cocktail lounges
and gastropubs opening their
doors in recent years (p175)

🚇 **Midtown**
Rooftop bars with skyline views, historic cocktail
salons and rough-n-ready dive bars (p173)

West Village, Chelsea &
Meatpacking District
Jet-setters flock here for wine bars,
backdoor lounges and gay hangouts (p170) 🚇

🚇 **Union Square, Flatiron District & Gramercy**
Vintage drinking dens, swinging cocktail bars
and a string of fun student hangouts (p173)

SoHo & Chinatown
From reformed speakeasies to secretive cocktail
dens, an air of history and mystique surrounds 🚇
many of this neighborhood's drinking holes (p166)

🚇 **East Village & Lower East Side**
Lower East Side is cool and edgy. East Village
is brimming with dive-bar options (p167)

🚇 **Financial District &**
Lower Manhattan
Specialist beer and brandy bars, and
revered cocktail hot spots (p166)

🚇 **Brooklyn**
Brooklyn offers everything on the nightlife
spectrum with Williamsburg as its heart (p176)

Costs/Tipping

If you grab a beer at the bar, bartenders
will expect at least a $1 tip *per drink;* tip
$2 to $3 for fancier cocktails. Sit-down
bars with waitstaff may expect more of
a standard restaurant-style 18% to 20%
tip, particularly if you snacked along
with your boozing.

Useful Blogs & Websites

New York Magazine (www.nymag.
com/nightlife) Myriad nightlife options
by the people who know best.

Thrillist (www.thrillist.com) An on-the-
ball round up of what's hot on the NYC
bar scene.

Urbandaddy (www.urbandaddy.com)
Up-to-the-minute info on bar and restaurant openings.

Time Out (www.timeout.com/newyork/
nightlife) Reviews of where to drink and
dance.

The Best...

Drinking and Nightlife spots to sip the night away

Dance Clubs & House DJs

Cielo (pictured below; p172) A thumping, modern classic in the Meatpacking District.

Le Bain (p172) Well-dressed crowds still pack this favorite near the High Line.

Berlin (p168) Yesteryear's free-spirited dance days live on at this concealed East Village bolthole.

For Spirits

Rum House (p175) Unique, coveted rums and a pianist to boot in Midtown.

Mayahuel (p170) A sophisticated East Village temple to mescal and tequila.

Dead Rabbit (pictured above; p166) NYC's finest collection of rare Irish whiskeys in the Financial District.

For Beer

Spuyten Duyvil (p177) A much-loved Williamsburg spot serving unique, high-quality crafts.

Immigrant (p169) Wonderful beers and service in a skinny East Village setting.

Old Town Bar & Restaurant (p173) Lively old-school drinking den with good drafts on hand.

Wine Selection

Terroir Tribeca (p166) An enlightened, encyclopedic wine list in trendy Tribeca.

La Compagnie des Vins Surnaturels (p167) A love letter to Gallic wines steps away from Little Italy.

Barcibo Enoteca (p176) Go-to spot for vino-philes before or after a show at the nearby Lincoln Center.

Dive Bars

Spring Lounge (p167) Soaks, ties and cool kids unite at this veteran Nolita rebel.

Jimmy's Corner (p175) Boxing legends grace the walls at this lowdown bar off Times Square.

Paris Blues (p176) A welcoming, music-filled watering hole in Harlem.

Classic Date Bars

Pegu Club (p166) Made-from-scratch concoctions in a Burma-inspired SoHo hideaway.

Ten Bells (p168) Candlelit beauty with great drinks and tapas in the Lower East Side.

Buvette (p170) A buzzing, candlelit wine bar on a tree-lined West Village street.

★ Lonely Planet's Top Choices

Little Branch (p172) Speakeasy-chic is all the craze, but no one does it quite like this West Village hideout.

Maison Premiere (p176) Absinthe, juleps and oysters shine bright at this Big Easy tribute in Williamsburg.

Employees Only (p170) Award-winning barkeeps and arresting libations in the timeless West Village.

Financial District & Lower Manhattan

Dead Rabbit Cocktail Bar
(Map p244; ☎646-422-7906; www.deadrabbitnyc.com; 30 Water St, btwn Broad St & Coenties Slip; 🕐taproom 11am-4am, parlor 5pm-2am Mon-Sat, to midnight Sun; [S]R to Whitehall St, 1 to South Ferry) Named in honor of a dreaded Irish-American gang, this most-wanted rabbit is regularly voted one of the world's best bars. Hit the sawdust-sprinkled taproom for specialty beers, historic punches and pop-inns (lightly hopped ale spiked with different flavors). Come evening, scurry upstairs to the cozy parlor for meticulously researched cocktails. The Wall Street crowd packs the place after work.

Pier A Harbor House Bar
(Map p244; ☎212-785-0153; www.piera.com; 22 Battery Pl, Battery Park; 🕐11am-4am; 📶; [S]4/5 to Bowling Green, R to Whitehall St, 1 to South Ferry) Looking dashing after a major renovation, Pier A is a super-spacious, casual eating and drinking house right on New York Harbor. If the weather's fine, try for a seat on the waterside deck – picnic benches, sun umbrellas and an eyeful of New York skyline offer a brilliant spot for sipping craft beers or one of the house cocktails on tap.

The 2nd-floor cocktail bar **BlackTail** opened in 2016 and is curiously themed around American bars in Cuba during Prohibition; it has an intimate feel with polished wood paneling and leather couches.

Keg No 229 Beer Hall
(Map p244; ☎212-566-2337; www.kegno229.com; 229 Front St, btwn Beekman St & Peck Slip; 🕐11am-midnight Sun-Wed, to 1am Thu-Sat; [S]A/C, J/Z, 2/3, 4/5 to Fulton St, R to Cortlandt St) From Butternuts Pork Slap to New Belgium Fat Tire, this bar's battalion of drafts, bottles and cans are a Who's Who of boutique American brews. One fun, potentially costly twist: if you lose count, some drafts are available for 'self-pour'.

Across the street is **Bin No 220**, its wine-loving sibling.

Weather Up Cocktail Bar
(Map p246; ☎212-766-3202; www.weatherupnyc.com; 159 Duane St, btwn Hudson St & W Broadway; 🕐5pm-1am Mon-Wed, to 2am Thu-Sat, to 10pm Sun; [S]1/2/3 to Chambers St) Simultaneously cool and classy: softly lit subway tiles, amiable and attractive barkeeps and seductive cocktails make for a bewitching trio at Weather Up. Sweet-talk the staff over a Tequila Torchlight (tequila, honey, fresh lemon juice and hot sauce). Failing that, comfort yourself with some satisfying bites like oysters and steak tartare.

Terroir Tribeca Wine Bar
(Map p246; ☎212-625-9463; www.wineisterroir.com; 24 Harrison St, at Greenwich St; 🕐4pm-midnight Mon & Tue, to 1am Wed-Sat, to 11pm Sun; [S]1 to Franklin St) Award-winning Terroir keeps oenophiles upbeat with its well-versed, well-priced wine list. Drops span the Old World and New, among them natural wines and inspired offerings from smaller producers. Best of all, there's a generous selection of wines by the glass, making a global wine tour a whole lot easier.

SoHo & Chinatown

Genuine Liquorette Cocktail Bar
(Map p246; ☎212-726-4633; www.genuineliquorette.com; 191 Grand St, at Mulberry St; 🕐6pm-midnight Tue & Wed, to 2am Thu-Sat; [S]J/Z, N/Q/R/W, 6 to Canal St, B/D to Grand St) What's not to love about a jamming basement bar with canned cocktails and a Farah Fawcett–themed restroom? You're even free to grab bottles and mixers and make your own drinks (bottles are weighed before and after you're done). At the helm is prolific mixologist Eben Freeman, who regularly invites New York's finest barkeeps to create cocktails using less-celebrated hooch.

Pegu Club Cocktail Bar
(Map p246; ☎212-473-7348; www.peguclub.com; 77 W Houston St, btwn W Broadway & Wooster St; 🕐5pm-2am Sun-Wed, to 4am Thu-Sat; [S]B/D/F/M to Broadway-Lafayette St, C/E to Spring St) Dark, elegant Pegu Club (named after a legendary gentleman's club in colonial-era

Cocktail Fever

These days, NYC's kicking cocktail scene is big on rediscovered recipes, historical anecdotes and vintage speakeasy style. Once obscure bartenders such as Harry Johnson and Jerry Thomas are now born-again legends, their vintage concoctions revived by a new generation of braces-clad mixologists. Historic ingredients such as Crème de Violette, Old Tom gin and Batavia Arrack are back in vogue. In the Financial District, cocktail bar **Dead Rabbit** (p166) has gone one further, reintroducing the 17th-century practice of pop-inns, drinks that fuse ale, liqueurs, spices and botanicals.

Then there are the city's revered single-spirit establishments, among them tequila- and mescal-focused **Mayahuel** (p170) in the East Village, the gin-centric **Drunken Munkey** (p175) in the Upper East Side, and the self-explanatory **Rum House** (p175) in Midtown.

Appletini cocktails
MICHAEL MARQUAND / GETTY IMAGES ©

Rangoon) is an obligatory stop for cocktail connoisseurs. Sink into a velvet lounge and savor seamless libations such as the silky smooth Earl Grey MarTEAni (tea-infused gin, lemon juice and raw egg white). Grazing options are suitably Asian-esque, among them duck wontons and Mandalay coconut shrimp.

Spring Lounge Bar
(Map p246; ☎212-965-1774; www.thespringlounge.com; 48 Spring St, at Mulberry St; ⏰8am-4am Mon-Sat, from noon Sun; [S]6 to Spring St, R/W to Prince St) This neon-red rebel has never let anything get in the way of a good time. In Prohibition days, it peddled buckets of beer. In the '60s its basement was a gambling den. These days, it's best known for its kooky stuffed sharks, early-start regulars and come-one, come-all late-night revelry. Perfect last stop on a bar-hopping tour of the neighborhood.

Apothéke Cocktail Bar
(Map p246; ☎212-406-0400; www.apothekenyc.com; 9 Doyers St; ⏰6:30pm-2am Mon-Sat, 8pm-2am Sun; [S]J/Z to Chambers St, 4/5/6 to Brooklyn Bridge-City Hall) It takes a little effort to track down this former opium-den-turned-apothecary bar on Doyers St. Inside, skilled barkeeps work like careful chemists, using local, seasonal produce from greenmarkets to produce intense, flavorful 'prescriptions.' Their cocktail ingredient ratio is always on point, such as the pineapple-cilantro blend in the Sitting Buddha, one of the best drinks on the menu.

La Compagnie des Vins Surnaturels Wine Bar
(Map p246; ☎212-343-3660; www.compagnienyc.com; 249 Centre St, btwn Broome & Grand Sts; ⏰5pm-1am Mon-Wed, to 2am Thu & Fri, 3pm-2am Sat, to 1am Sun; [S]6 to Spring St, R/W to Prince St) A snug mélange of Gallic-themed wallpaper, svelte armchairs and tea lights, La Compagnie des Vins Surnaturels is an offshoot of a Paris bar by the same name. Head sommelier Theo Lieberman steers an impressive, French-heavy wine list, with some 600 drops and no shortage of arresting labels by the glass. A short, sophisticated menu includes house-made charcuterie and chicken rillettes.

East Village & Lower East Side

Bar Goto Bar
(Map p246; ☎212-475-4411; www.bargoto.com; 245 Eldridge St, btwn E Houston & Stanton Sts; ⏰5pm-midnight Tue-Thu & Sun, to 2am Fri & Sat; [S]F to 2nd Ave) Maverick mixologist Kenta

Goto has cocktail connoisseurs spellbound at his eponymous hot spot. Expect meticulous, elegant drinks that revel in Goto's Japanese heritage (the sake-spiked Sakura Martini is utterly smashing), paired with authentic, Japanese comfort bites such as *okonomiyaki* (savory pancakes).

Ten Bells   Bar
(Map p246; ☎212-228-4450; www.tenbellsnyc.com; 247 Broome St, btwn Ludlow & Orchard Sts; ⏰5pm-2am Mon-Fri, from 3pm Sat & Sun; ⓢF to Delancey St, J/M/Z to Essex St) This charmingly tucked-away tapas bar has a grotto-like design, with flickering candles, dark tin ceilings, brick walls and a U-shaped bar that's an ideal setting for a conversation with a new friend.

Angel's Share   Bar
(Map p246; ☎212-777-5415; 2nd fl, 8 Stuyvesant St, near Third Ave & E 9th St; ⏰6pm-1:30am Sun-Wed, to 2:30am Thu-Sat; ⓢ6 to Astor Pl) Show up early and snag a seat at this hidden gem, behind a Japanese restaurant on the same floor. It's quiet and elegant, with seriously talented mixologists serving up creative cocktails, plus a top flight collec-

tion of whiskeys. You can't stay if you don't have a table or a seat at the bar, and they tend to go fast.

Berlin   Club
(Map p246; ☎646-827-3689; 25 Ave A, btwn First & Second Aves; ⏰8pm-4am; ⓢF to 2nd Ave) Like a secret bunker hidden beneath the ever-gentrifying streets of the East Village, Berlin is a throwback to the neighborhood's more riotous days of wildness and dancing. Once you find the unmarked entrance, head downstairs to the grotto-like space with vaulted brick ceilings, a long bar and tiny dance floor, with funk and rare grooves spilling all around.

Wayland   Bar
(Map p246; ☎212-777-7022; www.thewayland nyc.com; 700 E 9th St, cnr Ave C; ⏰5pm-4am; ⓢL to 1st Ave) Whitewashed walls, weathered floorboards and salvaged lamps give this urban outpost a Mississippi flair, which goes well with the live music (bluegrass, jazz, folk) featured Monday to Wednesday nights. The drinks, though, are the real draw – try the 'I Hear Banjos', made of apple-pie moonshine, rye whiskey and applewood

From left: Bourbon cocktails; Woman drinking white wine; Making cocktails at Apothéke (p167); Lit-up sign for Rum House (p175)

smoke, which tastes like a campfire (but slightly less burning).

Rue B
Bar

(Map p246; ☎212-358-1700; www.ruebnyc188. com; 188 Ave B, btwn E 11th & 12th Sts; ⊙noon-4am; ⛇L to 1st Ave) There's live jazz (and the odd rockabilly group) every night from about 8:30pm at this tiny, amber-lit drinking den on a bar-dappled stretch of Ave B. A young, celebratory crowd packs the small space – so mind the tight corners, lest the trombonist end up in your lap. B&W photos of jazz greats and other NYC icons enhance the ambience.

Immigrant
Bar

(Map p246; ☎646-308-1724; www.theimmigrant nyc.com; 341 E 9th St, btwn First & Second Aves; ⊙5pm-1am Sun-Wed, to 2am Thu & Fri, to 3am Sat; ⛇L to 1st Ave, 6 to Astor Pl) Wholly unpretentious, these twin boxcar-sized bars could easily become your neighborhood local if you decide to stick around town. The staff are knowledgeable and kind, mingling with faithful regulars while dishing out tangy olives and topping up glasses with imported snifters.

Ten Degrees Bar
Wine Bar

(Map p246; ☎212-358-8600; www.10degrees bar.com; 121 St Marks Pl, btwn First Ave & Ave A; ⊙noon-4am; ⛇F to 2nd Ave, L to 1st Ave or 3rd Ave) This small, candlelit St Marks charmer is a great spot to start out the night. Come from noon to 8pm for two-for-one drink specials (otherwise, it's $11 to $15 for cocktails), or get half-priced bottles of wine on Monday night. Go for the couches up front or grab a tiny table in the back nook.

Pouring Ribbons
Cocktail Bar

(Map p246; ☎917-656-6788; www.pouring ribbons.com; 2nd fl, 225 Avenue B, btwn E 14th & 13th Sts; ⊙6pm-2am; ⛇L to 1st Ave) Finding such a well-groomed and classy spot up a flight of stairs in Alphabet City is as refreshing as their drinks. Gimmicks and pretension are kept low; the flavors are exceptional. The encyclopedic cocktail menu could sate any appetite and includes a handy 'drink decider'. Also, check out what could possibly be the largest collection of Chartreuse in NYC.

Club Life

New Yorkers are always looking for the next big thing, so the city's club scene changes faster than a New York minute. Promoters drag revelers around the city for weekly events held at all of the finest addresses, and when there's nothing on, it's time to hit the dancefloor stalwarts.

When clubbing it never hurts to plan ahead; having your name on a guest list can relieve unnecessary frustration and disappointment. If you're an uninitiated partier, dress like you're not. If you're fed the 'private party' line, try to bluff – chances are high that you've been bounced. Also, don't forget a wad of cash as many nightspots (even the swankiest ones) often refuse credit cards, and in-house ATMs scam a fortune in fees.

NISIAN HUGHES / GETTY IMAGES ©

Death & Co Lounge

(Map p246; ☎212-388-0882; www.deathandcompany.com; 433 E 6th St, btwn First Ave & Ave A; 🕒6pm-2am Sun-Thu, to 3am Fri & Sat; [S]F to 2nd Ave, L to 1st Ave, 6 Astor Pl) Relax amid dim lighting and thick wooden slatting and let the skilled bartenders work their magic as they shake, rattle and roll some of the most perfectly concocted cocktails (from $15) in town. It's always packed – you have to give your phone number and return when they call to let you know a table has opened up.

Mayahuel Cocktail Bar

(Map p246; ☎212-253-5888; www.mayahuelny.com; 304 E 6th St, at Second Ave; 🕒6pm-2am; [S]L to 3rd Ave or 1st Ave, 6 to Astor Pl) About as far from your typical Spring Break tequila (and mezcal) bar as you can get, Mayahuel is more like the cellar of a monastery. Devotees of the fermented agave can seriously indulge themselves by experimenting with dozens of varieties (all cocktails $15). In between drinks, snack on quesadillas and tamales.

Barrio Chino Cocktail Bar

(Map p246; ☎212-228-6710; www.barriochinonyc.com; 253 Broome St, btwn Ludlow & Orchard Sts; 🕒11:30am-4:30pm & 5:30pm-1am; [S]F, J/M/Z to Delancey-Essex Sts) An eatery that spills easily into a party scene, with an airy Havana-meets-Beijing vibe and a focus on fine sipping tequilas. Or stick with fresh blood-orange or black-plum margaritas, guacamole and chicken tacos.

West Village, Chelsea & Meatpacking District

Employees Only Bar

(Map p246; ☎212-242-3021; www.employeesonlynyc.com; 510 Hudson St, btwn W 10th & Christopher Sts; 🕒6pm-4am; [S]1 to Christopher St-Sheridan Sq) Duck behind the neon 'Psychic' sign to find this hidden hangout. Bartenders are ace mixologists, fizzing up crazy, addictive libations like the Ginger Smash and the Mata Hari. Great for late-night drinking and eating, courtesy of the on-site restaurant that serves till 3:30am – house-made chicken soup is ladled out to stragglers. The bar gets busier as the night wears on.

Buvette Wine Bar

(Map p246; ☎212-255-3590; www.ilovebuvette.com; 42 Grove St, btwn Bedford & Bleecker Sts; 🕒7am-2am Mon-Fri, from 8am Sat & Sun; [S]1 to Christopher St-Sheridan Sq, A/C/E, B/D/F/M to W 4th St-Washington Sq) The rustic-chic decor here (think delicate tin tiles and a swooshing marble counter) makes it the perfect place for a glass of wine – no matter the time of day. For the full experience at this self-proclaimed *gastrotèque*, grab a seat at one of the surrounding tables and nibble on small plates while enjoying old-world wines (mostly from France and Italy).

Happiest Hour Cocktail Bar

(Map p246; ☎212-243-2827; www.happiesthournyc.com; 121 W 10th St, btwn Greenwich St & Sixth Ave; 🕑5pm-late Mon-Fri, from 2pm Sat & Sun; [S]A/C/E, B/D/F/M to W 4th St-Washington Sq, 1 to Christopher St-Sheridan Sq) A super-cool, tiki-licious cocktail bar splashed with palm prints, '60s pop and playful mixed drinks. The crowd tends to be button-down after-work types and online daters. Beneath sits its serious sibling, **Slowly Shirley**, an art deco–style subterranean temple to beautifully crafted, thoroughly researched libations.

Pier 66 Maritime Bar

(Map p250; ☎212-989-6363; www.pier66maritime.com; Pier 66, at W 26th St; 🕑noon-midnight May-Oct; [S]C/E to 23rd St) Salvaged from the bottom of the sea (or at least the Chesapeake Bay), the Lightship *Frying Pan* and the two-tiered dockside bar where it's moored are fine go-to spots for a sundowner. On warm days, the rustic open-air space brings in the crowds, who laze on deck chairs and drink ice-cold beers ($7 for a microbrew; $25 for a pitcher).

Bell Book & Candle Bar

(Map p246; ☎212-414-2355; www.bbandcnyc.com; 141 W 10th St, btwn Waverley Pl & Greenwich Ave; 🕑5:30pm-2am Sun-Wed, to 4am Thu-Sat; [S]A/C/E, B/D/F/M to W 4th St-Washington Sq, 1 to Christopher St-Sheridan Sq) Step down into this candlelit gastropub for strong, inventive drinks (try the *canela* margarita, with cinnamon-infused tequila) and hearty late-night pub grub. A 20-something crowd gathers around the small, packed bar (for $1 oysters and happy-hour drink specials early in the night), though there's a lot more seating in the back, with big booths ideal for larger groups.

Not well known is a hidden table behind the bar, where the wallpaper is plastered with figures of women showing off full-frontal nudity. The bartender passes drinks

What's not to love about a jamming basement bar with canned cocktails...?

Genuine Liquorette (p166)

CABECA DE MARMORE / SHUTTERSTOCK ©

through a little hole in the wall as if you're hosting your own top-secret party.

Bathtub Gin Cocktail Bar

(Map p250; ☎646-559-1671; www.bathtubginnyc.com; 132 Ninth Ave, btwn W 18th & 19th Sts; 🕐5pm-2am Sun-Wed, to 4am Thu-Sat; [S]A/C/E, L to 14th St-8th Ave, C/E to 23rd St) Amid New York City's obsession with speakeasy-styled hangouts, Bathtub Gin manages to poke its head above the crowd with its super-secret front door hidden on the wall of an unassuming cafe (the Stone Street Coffee Company). Once inside, chill seating, soft background beats and kindly staff make it a great place to sling back bespoke cocktails with friends.

Little Branch Cocktail Bar

(Map p246; ☎212-929-4360; 20 Seventh Ave S, at Leroy St; 🕐7pm-3am; [S]1 to Houston St) If it weren't for lines later in the evening, you'd never guess that a charming drinking den lurked beyond the plain metal door positioned at this triangular intersection – walk downstairs to find a basement bar that feels like a kickback to Prohibition times. Locals clink glasses and sip inventive, artfully prepared cocktails, with live jazz performances Sunday through Thursday nights.

Marie's Crisis Bar

(Map p246; ☎212-243-9323; 59 Grove St, btwn Seventh Ave & Bleecker St; 🕐4pm-3am Mon-Thu, to 4am Fri & Sat, to midnight Sun; [S]1 to Christopher St-Sheridan Sq) Aging Broadway queens, wide-eyed out-of-town gay boys, giggly tourists and various other fans of musical theater assemble around the piano here and take turns belting out campy show tunes, often joined by the entire crowd – and the occasional celebrity. It's old-school fun, no matter how jaded you might be when you go in.

Cielo Club

(Map p246; ☎212-645-5700; www.cieloclub.com; 18 Little W 12th St, btwn Ninth Ave & Washington St; cover charge $15-25; 🕐11am-7pm & 10pm-4am Mon-Sat; [S]A/C/E, L to 14th St-8th Ave) This long-running club boasts a largely attitude-free crowd and an excellent sound system. Join dance lovers on TOCA Tuesdays, when DJ Tony Touch spins classic hip hop, soul and funk. Other nights feature various DJs from Europe, who mix entrancing, seductive sounds that pull everyone to their feet.

The Manhattan

Legend has it that the city's namesake drink, Manhattan – a blend of whiskey, sweet vermouth and bitters – began life on the southeastern corner of 26th St and Madison Ave, at the long-gone Manhattan Club. The occasion was a party in 1874, allegedly thrown by Jennie Churchill (mother of British Prime Minister Winston) to celebrate Samuel J Tilden's victory in the New York gubernatorial election. One of the barmen decided to create a drink to mark the occasion, naming it in honor of the bar.

A Manhattan cocktail
WESLEY HITT / GETTY IMAGES ©

Le Bain Club

(Map p246; ☎212-645-7600; www.standardhotels.com; 444 W 13th St, btwn Washington St & Tenth Ave; 🕐10pm-4am Wed-Fri, from 2pm Sat, 2pm-midnight Sun; [S]A/C/E, L to 14th St-8th Ave) The sweeping rooftop venue at the tragically hip Standard Hotel, Le Bain sees a garish parade of party promoters who do their thang on any day of the week. Brace yourself for skyline views, a dance floor with a giant Jacuzzi built right into it and an eclectic crowd getting wasted on pricey snifters.

⊖ Union Square, Flatiron District & Gramercy

Flatiron Lounge   Cocktail Bar

(Map p250; ☑212-727-7741; www.flatironlounge.
com; 37 W 19th St, btwn Fifth & Sixth Aves;
⊘4pm-2am Mon-Wed, to 3am Thu, to 4am Fri,
5pm-4am Sat; 🛜; S F/M, R/W, 6 to 23rd St)
Head through a dramatic archway and into
a dark, swinging, deco-inspired fantasy of
lipstick-red booths, racy jazz tunes and
sassy grown-ups downing seasonal drinks.
The Lincoln Tunnel (dark rum, applejack,
maple syrup and bitters) is scrumptious.
Happy-hour cocktails go for $10 a pop
(4pm to 6pm weekdays).

Old Town Bar & Restaurant   Bar

(Map p250; ☑212-529-6732; www.oldtownbar.
com; 45 E 18th St, btwn Broadway & Park Ave S;
⊘11:30am-1am Mon-Fri, noon-2am Sat, 1pm-
midnight Sun; S 4/5/6, N/Q/R/W, L to 14th St-
Union Sq) It still looks like 1892 in here, with
the mahogany bar, original tile floors and
tin ceilings – the Old Town is an old-world
drinking-man's classic (and -woman's: Madonna lit up at the bar here – when lighting
up in bars was still legal – in her 'Bad Girl'
video). There are cocktails around, but most
come for beers and a burger.

Pete's Tavern   Bar

(Map p250; ☑212-473-7676; www.petestavern.
com; 129 E 18th St, at Irving Pl; ⊘11am-2:30am;
S 4/5/6, N/Q/R/W, L to 14th St-Union Sq) With
its original 19th-century mirrors, pressed-
tin ceiling and rosewood bar, this dark,
atmospheric watering hole has all the
earmarks of a New York classic. You can
get a respectable prime-rib burger here
and choose from 17 draft beers, joined by
everyone from post-theater couples and
Irish expats to no-nonsense NYU students
and the odd celebrity (see photos by the
restrooms).

Raines Law Room   Cocktail Bar

(Map p250; www.raineslawroom.com; 48 W 17th
St, btwn Fifth & Sixth Aves; ⊘5pm-2am Mon-Wed,
to 3am Thu-Sat, 7pm-1am Sun; S F/M to 14th St, L

to 6th Ave, 1 to 18th St) A sea of velvet drapes
and overstuffed leather lounge chairs, the
perfect amount of exposed brick, expertly
crafted cocktails using meticulously
aged spirits – these folks are as serious
as a mortgage payment when it comes
to amplified atmosphere. Reservations
(recommended) are only accepted Sunday
to Tuesday. Whatever the night, style up for
a taste of a far more sumptuous era.

⊖ Midtown

Bar SixtyFive   Cocktail Bar

(Map p252; ☑212-632-5000; www.rainbow
room.com; 30 Rockefeller Plaza, entrance on
W 49th St; ⊘5pm-midnight Mon-Fri, 4-9pm
Sun; S B/D/F/M to 47th-50th Sts-Rockefeller
Center) Not to be missed, sophisticated
SixtyFive sits on level 65 of the GE Building
at Rockefeller Center (p84). Dress well (no
sportswear or guests under 21) and arrive
by 5pm for a seat with a multi-million-dollar
view. Even if you don't score a table on the
balcony or by the window, head outside to
soak up that sweeping New York panorama.

Waylon   Bar

(Map p252; ☑212-265-0010; www.thewaylon.
com; 736 Tenth Ave, at W 50th St; ⊘noon-4am;
S C/E to 50th St) Slip on your spurs, partner,
there's a honky-tonk in Hell's! Celebrate
Dixie at this saloon-style watering hole,
where the jukebox keeps good folks dancing to Tim McGraw's broken heart, where
the barkeeps pour American whiskeys and
tequila, and where the grub includes Texan-
style Frito pie and country-fried steak
sandwiches.

Lantern's Keep   Cocktail Bar

(Map p252; ☑212-453-4287; www.thelanterns
keep.com; Iroquois Hotel, 49 W 44th St, btwn Fifth
& Sixth Aves; ⊘5-11pm Mon, to midnight Tue-Fri,
7pm-1am Sat; S B/D/F/M to 42nd St-Bryant
Park) Can you keep a secret? If so, cross
the lobby of the **Iroquois Hotel** (Map p252;
☑212-840-3080; www.iroquoisny.com) and
slip into this dark, intimate cocktail salon.
Its specialty is classic drinks, shaken and

New York City in a Glass

Fresh ginger

Ice cubes

3/4 oz fresh lemon juice

1.5 fl oz Scotch whisky
(such as Chivas Regal)

1.5 fl oz malt whisky
(such as Laphroaig)

Two spoonfuls of
Blossom honey

A New York Penicillin

MARK SHALNY / SHUTTERSTOCK ©

How to Make a Penicillin

Mash the ginger at the bottom of a mixer. Stir honey and whisky together in the mixer until the honey is dissolved. Add the lemon juice. Shake with ice and strain into an ice-filled glass. Garnish with a ginger wedge.

History of a Bespoke Cocktail

Invented in 2005 at **Milk & Honey** (www.mlkhny.com/newyork) in the Lower East Side, the Penicillin quickly became one of the top new drinks of NYC. At its essence, this complex libation, with elements of smoke, sweetness and tanginess embodies the city's thirst for bespoke cocktails. Whimsically named (creator Sam Ross jokingly referenced its curative powers), the cocktail is found all across the city. **Brooklyn Brewery** (p177) even made a limited-edition beer in honor of the scotch-based drink.

Right: Patrons at Attaboy
AURORA PHOTOS / ALAMY ©

★ NYC's Top Places for a Penicillin

Attaboy (Map p246; 134 Eldridge St, btwn Delancy & Broome Sts; ⊗6:45pm-4am; Ⓢ B/D to Grand St)
Little Branch (p172)
Death & Co (p170)
North End Grill (Map p244; ☏646-747-1600; www.northendgrillnyc.com; 104 North End Ave, at Murray St; mains lunch $19-37, dinner $27-44; ⊗11:30am-10pm Mon-Thu, to 10:30pm Fri, 11am-10:30pm Sat, 11am-9pm Sun; ☏; Ⓢ1/2/3, A/C to Chambers St, E to World Trade Center)
Employees Only (p170)

stirred by passionate, personable mixologists. If you're feeling spicy, request a Gordon's Breakfast, a fiery mélange of gin, Worcestershire sauce, hot sauce, muddled lime and cucumber, salt and pepper. Reservations are recommended.

Industry   Gay

(Map p252; ☑646-476-2747; www.industry-bar. com; 355 W 52nd St, btwn Eighth & Ninth Aves; ◎4pm-4am; ⑤C/E, 1 to 50th St) What was once a parking garage is now one of the hottest gay bars in Hell's Kitchen – a slick, 4000-sq-ft watering hole with handsome lounge areas, a pool table and a stage for top-notch drag divas. Head in between 4pm and 9pm for the two-for-one drinks special or squeeze in later to party with the eye-candy party hordes. Cash only.

Rum House   Cocktail Bar

(Map p252; ☑646-490-6924; www.therumhouse nyc.com; 228 W 47th St, btwn Broadway & Eighth Ave; ◎noon-4am; ⑤N/R/W to 49th St) This sultry, revamped slice of old New York is revered for its cognoscenti rums and whiskeys. Savor them straight up or mixed in impeccable cocktails like a classic Dark & Stormy (rum, ginger beer and lime). Adding to the magic is nightly live music, spanning solo piano tunes to jaunty jazz trios and sentimental torch divas.

Jimmy's Corner   Bar

(Map p252; ☑212-221-9510; 140 W 44th St, btwn Sixth & Seventh Aves; ◎11:30am-4am Mon-Fri, from 12:30pm Sat, from 3pm Sun; ⑤N/Q/R/W, 1/2/3, 7 to 42nd St-Times Sq, B/D/F/M to 42nd St-Bryant Park) This welcoming, completely unpretentious dive off Times Square is run by an old boxing trainer – as if you wouldn't guess by all the framed photos of boxing greats (and lesser-known fighters, too). The jukebox, which covers Stax to Miles Davis (plus Lionel Ritchie's most regretful moments), is kept low enough for post-work gangs to chat away.

❷ Upper East Side

Penrose   Bar

(Map p252; ☑212-203-2751; www.penrosebar. com; 1590 Second Ave, btwn E 82nd & 83rd Sts; ◎noon-4am Mon-Fri, 10am-4am Sat & Sun; ⑤4/5/6, Q to 86th St) The Penrose, famous for their pickle martinis and fried pickles, brings a dose of style to the Upper East Side, with craft beers, exposed brick walls, vintage mirrors, reclaimed wood details and friendly bartenders. It's packed with a young neighborhood crowd on weekends, but you can usually get a seat along the wall or in the back.

Daisy   Bar

(Map p252; ☑646-964-5756; www.thedaisynyc. com; 1641 Second Ave, at E 85th St; ◎4pm-2am Mon & Tue, 11:30am-4am Wed-Sun; ⑤4/5/6, Q to 86th St) Billing itself as an 'agave gastropub,' the Daisy serves up mescal cocktails and creative, Latin-inspired drinks (Michelada) and dishes (rice with duck) alongside bistro fare like duck-fat fries and grilled octopus. Unlike most other UES bars, there are no TVs or bros here – it's a laid-back, low-lit spot, with good grooves, skilled bartenders and a friendly crowd.

Drunken Munkey   Lounge

(Map p252; ☑646-998-4600; www.drunken munkeynyc.com; 338 E 92nd St, btwn First & Second Aves; ◎11am-2am Mon-Thu & Sun, to 3am Fri & Sat; ⑤6, Q to 96th St) This playful lounge channels colonial-era Bombay with vintage wallpaper, cricket-ball door handles and jauntily attired waitstaff. The monkey chandeliers may be pure whimsy, but the craft cocktails and tasty curries (small, meant for sharing) are serious business. Gin, not surprisingly, is the drink of choice. Try the Bramble: Bombay gin, blackberry liqueur and fresh lemon juice and blackberries.

❷ Upper West Side & Central Park

Manhattan Cricket Club Lounge

(Map p252; ☎646-823-9252; www.mccnewyork. com; 226 W 79th St, btwn Amsterdam Ave & Broadway; ☺6pm-late; ⑤1 to 79th St) Above an Australian bistro (p138), this elegant drinking lounge is modeled on the classy Anglo-Aussie cricket clubs of the early 1900s. Sepia-toned photos of batsmen adorn the gold brocaded walls, while mahogany bookshelves and Chesterfield sofas create a fine setting for quaffing well-made (but pricey) cocktails. It's a guaranteed date-pleaser.

West End Hall Beer Garden

(☎212-662-7200; www.westendhall.com; 2756 Broadway, btwn W 105th & 106th Sts; ☺3pm-midnight Mon-Wed, to 2am Thu & Fri, 11am-4am Sat, to midnight Sun; ⑤1 to 103rd St) Beer drinkers of the Upper West Side have much to celebrate at this grand beer hall that showcases craft brews from around Belgium, Germany, the US and beyond. There are around 20 drafts on rotation along with another 30 bottle choices, most of which go nicely with the meaty menu of sausages, schnitzel, pork sliders and an excellent truffle burger.

Dead Poet Bar

(Map p252; ☎212-595-5670; www.thedeadpoet. com; 450 Amsterdam Ave, btwn W 81st & 82nd Sts; ☺noon-4am; ⑤1 to 79th St) This skinny, mahogany-paneled pub has been a neighborhood favorite since the turn of the millennium, with a mix of locals and students nursing pints of Guinness. Cocktails named after dead poets, including a Walt Whitman Long Island Iced Tea ($12) and a Pablo Neruda spiced-rum sangria ($11). Funny – we always pegged Neruda as a pisco sour kind of guy.

Barcibo Enoteca Wine Bar

(Map p252; ☎212-595-2805; www.barcibo enoteca.com; 2020 Broadway, at W 69th St; ☺4:30pm-12:30am Tue-Fri, from 3:30pm Sat-Mon; ⑤1/2/3 to 72nd St) Just north of Lincoln Center, this casual-chic marble-table spot is ideal for sipping, with a long list of vintages from all over Italy, including 40 different varieties sold by the glass. There is a short menu of small plates and light meals. The staff is knowledgeable; ask for recommendations.

❷ Harlem & Upper Manhattan

Ginny's Supper Club Cocktail Bar

(☎212-421-3821, brunch reservations 212-792-9001; www.ginnyssupperclub.com; 310 Malcolm X Blvd, btwn W 125th & 126th Sts, Harlem; ☺6pm-11pm Thu, to 3am Fri & Sat, brunch 10:30am-2pm Sun; ⑤2/3 to 125th St) Looking straight out of *Boardwalk Empire,* this roaring basement supper club is rarely short of styled-up regulars sipping cocktails, nibbling on soul and global bites – from the Red Rooster (p138) kitchen upstairs – and grooving to live jazz from 7:30pm Thursday to Saturday and DJ-spun beats from 11pm Friday and Saturday. Don't miss the weekly Sunday gospel brunch (reservations recommended).

Paris Blues Bar

(☎917-257-7831; 2021 Adam Clayton Powell Jr Blvd, at W 121st St, Harlem; ☺noon-3am; ⑤A/C, B to 116th St, 2/3 to 125th St) This down-home dive is named after the 1961 Sidney Poitier and Paul Newman flick about two expats living and loving in Paris. It's worn in places and the booze selection is limited, but it makes up for it with buckets of charm, generous pours and nightly jazz gigs from around 9pm. A free buffet of comfort-food standards is sometimes available.

❷ Brooklyn

Maison Premiere Cocktail Bar

(Map p255; ☎347-335-0446; www.maison premiere.com; 298 Bedford Ave, btwn S 1st & Grand Sts, Williamsburg; ☺4pm-2am Mon-Thu, to 4am Fri, 11am-4am Sat, to 4pm Sun; ⑤L to Bedford Ave) We kept expecting to see Dorothy Parker stagger into this old-timey place, which features an elegant bar full of syrups and essences, suspended bartenders and a jazzy soundtrack to further channel the French Quarter New Orleans vibe. The cocktails are serious business: the epic list includes more than a dozen absinthe drinks, various juleps and an array of specialty cocktails.

Hotel Delmano   Cocktail Bar
(Map p255; ☑718-387-1945; www.hoteldelmano. com; 82 Berry St, at N 9th St, Williamsburg; ⊗5pm-2am Mon-Fri, 2pm-2am Sat & Sun; ⓢL to Bedford Ave) This low-lit cocktail bar aims for a speakeasy vibe, with old, smoky mirrors, unpolished floorboards and vintage chandeliers. Nestle into one of the nooks in the back or have a seat at the curving, marble-topped bar and watch mustachioed barkeeps whip up a changing array of inventive cocktails (rye, gin and mescal are favored spirits).

Spuyten Duyvil   Bar
(Map p255; ☑718-963-4140; www.spuytenduy vilnyc.com; 359 Metropolitan Ave, btwn Havemayer & Roebling Sts, Williamsburg; ⊗5pm-late Mon-Fri, from noon Sat & Sun; ⓢL to Lorimer St, G to Metropolitan Ave) This low-key Williamsburg bar looks like it was pieced together from a rummage sale. The ceilings are painted red, there are vintage maps on the walls and the furniture consists of tattered armchairs. But the beer selection is staggering, the locals from various eras are chatty and there's a decent-sized patio with leafy trees that's open in good weather.

Rocka Rolla   Bar
(Map p255; 486 Metropolitan Ave, btwn Union Ave & Rodney St; ⊗noon-4am; ⓢG to Metropolitan Ave) This Midwestern-throwback rock 'n' roll bar with cheap drinks and a hard-partying late-night crowd is located appropriately enough on a gritty stretch beneath the Brooklyn-Queens Expwy overpass. The owners, who also run Skinny Dennis (p178), look to the late '70s and early '80s for inspiration: think AC/DC on the jukebox, a Farrah Fawcett poster for decor and $3 goblets of Budweiser.

 Borough Brews

Beer brewing was once a thriving industry in the city – by the 1870s, Brooklyn boasted a belly-swelling 48 breweries. By the eve of Prohibition in 1919, the borough was one of the country's leading beer peddlers. However, by the end of Prohibition in 1933, most breweries had shut shop. And while the industry rose from the ashes in WWII, local flavor gave in to big-gun Midwestern brands.

Today, Brooklyn is once more a catchword for a decent brewski as a handful of craft breweries put integrity back on tap. Head of the pack is **Brooklyn Brewery** (Map p255; ☑718-486-7422; www. brooklynbrewery.com; 79 N 11th St, btwn Berry St & Wythe Ave, Williamsburg). The brewery's comrades-in-craft include **SixPoint Craft Ales** (www.sixpoint.com), **Threes Brewing** (www.threesbrewing. com) and **Other Half Brewing Co** (www. otherhalfbrewing.com). Justifiably famed for its piney, hoppy Imperial IPA Green Diamonds, Other Half Brewing Co gets its hops and malts from local farms.

Up-and-coming Queens is home to nanobrewery **Transmitter Brewing** (www.transmitterbrewing.com) and beachborn **Rockaway Brewing Company** (www.rockawaybrewco.com). The borough's dominant player remains **SingleCut Beersmiths** (www.singlecutbeer.com), whose launch in 2012 saw Queens welcome its first brewery since Prohibition. Its offerings include unusual takes on lager, among them the Jan White Lagrrr, brewed with coriander, chamomile flowers, oranges, matzo and Sichuan peppercorns. Further north, the Bronx lays claim to **Bronx Brewery** (☑718-402-1000; www.thebronxbrewery.com; 856 E 136th St, btwn Willow & Walnut Aves) and **Gun Hill Brewing Co** (www.gunhillbrewing.com), the latter making waves with its Void of Light, a jet-black, roastalicious stout.

★ **Top Five Cocktail Bars**

Dead Rabbit (p166)

Pegu Club (p166)

Flatiron Lounge (p173)

Bar Sixtyfive (p173)

Lantern's Keep (p173)

From left: Pete's Tavern (p173); Cosmopolitan cocktail; Jimmy's Corner (p175)

Skinny Dennis   Bar

(Map p255; www.skinnydennisbar.com; 152 Metropolitan Ave, btwn Wythe Ave & Berry St, Williamsburg; ☺noon-4am; ⓈL to Bedford Ave) No need to fly to Austin – you can get your honky-tonk right here in Billyburg at this roadhouse saloon on bustling Metropolitan Ave. Aside from Kinky Friedman posters, a reverential painting of Willie Nelson, peanut shells on the floor and a Patsy Cline–heavy jukebox in the corner, you'll find country crooners playing nightly to a garrulous, beer-swilling crowd.

Der Schwarze Köelner   Pub

(Map p254; ☏347-841-4495; www.dsk-brooklyn. com; 710 Fulton St, cnr Hanson Pl, Fort Greene; ☺5pm-1am Mon, noon-1am Tue, Wed & Sun, to 2am Thu & Sun, to 4am Fri & Sat; ⓈC to Lafayette Ave, G to Fulton St) This casual beer garden with checkered floors, lots of windows and a lively, mixed crowd is located just a few blocks away from the Brooklyn Academy of Music (p190). There are 18 beers on tap, all of which go swimmingly with a hot *brezel* (soft German pretzel). A variety of other snacks are served all night.

Royal Palms   Bar

(Map p254; ☏347-223-4410; www.royalpalms shuffle.com; 514 Union St, btwn Third Ave & Nevins St, Gowanus; ☺6pm-midnight Mon-Thu, to 2am Fri, noon-2am Sat, noon-10pm Sun; ⓈR to Union St) If you're hankering for some sport but don't want to sweat or drift too far from the bar stool, Royal Palms is for you. Inside this 17,000-sq-ft space, you'll find 10 full shuffleboard courts ($40 per hour), plus board games (massive Jenga, oversize Connect Four), draft brews, cocktails and snacks provided by a food truck (a different rotation each week).

Dardy Bar   Bar

(Map p255; ☏718-599-2455; www.dardybar. com; 245 S 1st St, btwn Roebling & Havemeyer Sts; ☺5pm-2am; ⓈG to Metropolitan Ave) Two musicians from a band called the Dardys created this friendly, divey hangout slightly off the beaten path in South Williamsburg. Cheap beer (two-for-one drafts from 5pm to 8pm), simple bar food like hot dogs and nachos and kitschy games like shuffleboard and Connect Four draw a mostly young neighborhood crowd. If it's cramped inside, try the narrow back patio.

SERGI REBOREDO / ALAMY ©

Radegast Hall & Biergarten Beer Hall

(Map p255; ☎718-963-3973; www.radegasthall.com; 113 N 3rd St, at Berry St, Williamsburg; 🕒noon-2am Mon-Fri, from 11am Sat & Sun; [S]L to Bedford Ave) An Austro-Hungarian beer hall in Williamsburg offers up a huge selection of Bavarian brews as well as a kitchen full of munchable meats. You can hover in the dark, woody bar area or sit in the adjacent hall, which has a retractable roof and communal tables to feast at – perfect for pretzels, sausages and burgers. Live music every night.

Rookery Bar

(www.therookerybar.com; 425 Troutman St, btwn St Nicholas & Wyckoff Aves, Bushwick; 🕒noon-4am; [S]L to Jefferson St) A mainstay of the burgeoning Bushwick scene is the industrial-esque Rookery on mural-lined Troutman Ave. Come for cocktails, craft brews, reconfigured pub fare (curried-goat shepherds pie, oxtail sloppy joe), obscure electro-pop and a relaxed vibe. High ceilings give the space an airy feel and the back patio is a great spot, afternoon or evening, in warm weather.

Pine Box Rock Shop Bar

(Map p255; ☎718-366-6311; www.pineboxrockshop.com; 12 Grattan St, btwn Morgan Ave & Bogart St, Bushwick; 🕒4pm-4am Mon-Fri, 2pm-4am Sat & Sun; [S]L to Morgan Ave) The cavernous Pine Box is a former Bushwick casket factory that has 17 drafts to choose from (all vegan), as well as spicy, pint-sized Bloody Marys. Run by a friendly musician couple, the walls are filled with local artwork, and a performance space in the back hosts regular gigs.

🍷 Queens

Dutch Kills Bar

(☎718-383-2724; www.dutchkillsbar.com; 27-24 Jackson Ave., Long Island City; specialty cocktails from $13, beer and wine from $6; 🕒5pm-2am; [S]E, M, or R train to Queens Plaza, G train to Court Square) When you step into Dutch Kills you are stepping back in time. This speakeasy style bar is all about atmosphere and amazing craft cocktails. Their menu of specialty drinks is extensive, but if you're looking for an old standard, you can trust the expert bartenders to deliver.

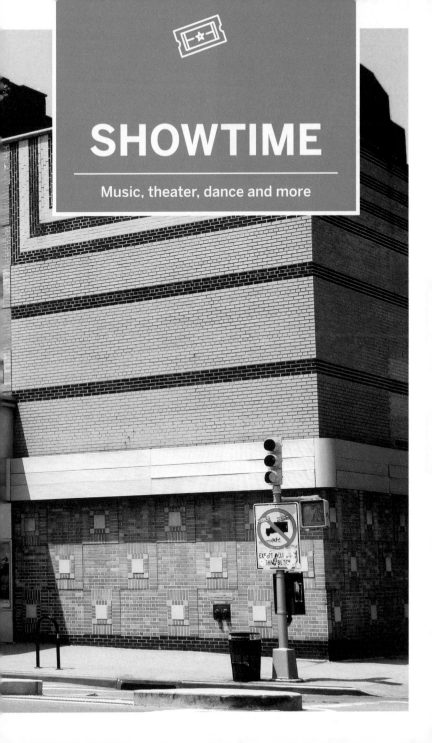

SHOWTIME

Music, theater, dance and more

Showtime

Dramatically lit stages, basement jazz joints, high-ceilinged dance halls, and opera houses set for melodramatic tales – for more than a century, New York City has been America's capital of cultural production. And while gentrification has pushed many artists out to the city's fringes and beyond, New York nonetheless remains a nerve center for music, theater and dance.

When it comes to entertainment, the city is perhaps best known for its Broadway musicals. These are presented in any one of 40 official Broadway theaters – lavish early 20th-century jewels that surround Times Square – and are a major component of cultural life in New York. Beyond Broadway, you'll find experimental downtown playhouses, the hallowed concert halls of the Met, and live music joints scattered in all corners of the city. The biggest challenge is deciding where to begin.

In This Section

Showtime Tickets

To purchase tickets for shows, you can either head directly to the venue's box office, or use one of several ticket agencies such as **Telecharge** (www.telecharge.com) or **Ticketmaster** (www.ticketmaster.com).

For cut-price same-day Broadway tickets, visit a **TKTS Booth** (www.tdf.org). And for non-Broadway entertainment (comedy, cabaret, performance art, music, dance and downtown theater), check out **SmartTix** (www.smarttix.com).

Billboards in Times Square (p62)

The Best...

Live Music

Brooklyn Bowl (p192) Great line-up of funk, indie rock and global beats, plus beer and bowling!

Jazz at Lincoln Center (p188) Glittering evening views of Central Park and world-class musical acts.

Carnegie Hall (p188) Legendary concert hall, blessed with perfect acoustics.

Brooklyn Academy of Music (p190) This hallowed theater hosts cutting-edge works.

Village Vanguard (p185) Legendary West Village jazz club.

Smalls (p186) Tiny West Village basement joint that evokes the feel of decades past.

Barbès (p192) Obscure but celebratory rhythms from around the globe in Park Slope.

Birdland (p188) Sleek Midtown space that hosts big-band sounds, Afro-Cuban jazz and more.

Minton's (p190) Swanky crowds, bewitching brass and a Sunday jazz brunch in Harlem.

✪ Financial District & Lower Manhattan

Flea Theater   Theater
(Map p246; ☑tickets 212-352-3101; www.theflea.
org; 20 Thomas St, btwn Church St & Broadway;
ⓢA/C/E, 1/2/3, J/M/Z to Chambers St, 4/5/6 to
City Hall) One of NYC's top off-off-Broadway
companies, Flea is famous for performing
innovative and timely new works. Spring
2017 is the inaugural season in its new
space (four blocks south of the old one).
Luminaries including Sigourney Weaver and
John Lithgow have trod the boards here, and
the year-round program also includes music
and dance performances.

✪ SoHo & Chinatown

Film Forum   Cinema
(Map p246; ☑212-727-8110; www.filmforum.com;
209 W Houston St, btwn Varick St & Sixth Ave; ⓢ1
to Houston St) This three-screen nonprofit
cinema screens an astounding array of
independent films, revivals and career
retrospectives from greats such as Orson

Welles. Theaters are small (as are the
screens), so get there early for a good viewing spot. Showings are often combined with
director talks or other film-themed discussions attended by hardcore cinephiles.

Joe's Pub   Live Music
(Map p246; ☑212-539-8778, tickets 212-967-
7555; www.joespub.com; Public Theater, 425
Lafayette St, btwn Astor Pl & 4th St; ⓢ6 to Astor
Pl, R/W to 8th St-NYU) Part bar, part cabaret
and performance venue, intimate Joe's
serves up both emerging acts and top-shelf
performers. Past entertainers have included
Patti LuPone, Amy Schumer, Leonard Co-
hen and British songstress Adele (in fact, it
was right here that Adele gave her very first
American performance, back in 2008).

✪ East Village & Lower East Side

Metrograph   Cinema
(Map p246; ☑212-660-0312; www.metrograph.
com; 7 Ludlow St, btwn Canal & Hester Sts; tickets
$15; ⓢF to East Broadway, B/D to Grand St)

Jazz club Village Vanguard

The newest movie mecca for downtown cinephiles, this two-screen theater with red velvet seats shows curated art-house flicks. Most you'll never find at any multiplex, though the odd mainstream pic is occasionally screened. In addition to movie geeks browsing the bookstore, you'll find a stylish and glamorous set at the bar or in the upstairs restaurant.

La MaMa ETC
Theater

(Map p246; ☑212-352-3101; www.lamama.org; 74a E 4th St, btwn Bowery & Second Ave; tickets from $20; ⓢF to Second Ave) A long-standing home for onstage experimentation (the ETC stands for Experimental Theater Club), La MaMa is now a three-theater complex with a cafe, an art gallery and a separate studio building that features cutting-edge dramas, sketch comedy and readings of all kinds. Ten $10 tickets are available for each show. Book early to score a deal!

New York Theatre Workshop
Theater

(Map p246; ☑212-460-5475; www.nytw.org; 79 E 4th St, btwn Second & Third Aves; ⓢF to 2nd Ave) For more than thirty years this innovative production house has been a treasure trove for those seeking cutting-edge, contemporary plays with purpose. It was the originator of two big Broadway hits, *Rent* and *Urinetown* – plus it's where the musical *Once* had its off-Broadway premiere – and offers a constant supply of high-quality drama.

✪ West Village, Chelsea & Meatpacking District

Sleep No More
Theater

(Map p250; ☑866-811-4111; www.sleepnomore nyc.com; 530 W 27th St, btwn Tenth & Eleventh Aves; tickets from $105; ⓒ7pm-midnight Mon-Sat; ⓢC/E to 23rd St) One of the most immersive theater experiences ever conceived, *Sleep No More* is a loosely based retelling of *Macbeth* set inside a series of Chelsea warehouses that have been redesigned to look like the 1930s-era McKittrick Hotel and its hopping jazz bar.

 Comedy

A good laugh is easy to find in the Big Apple, where comedians sharpen their stand-up, practice new material and hope to get scouted by a producer or agent. The best spots for some chuckles are downtown, particularly around Chelsea and Greenwich Village. Several festivals, including **Comic Con** (www. newyorkcomiccon.com), draw big names throughout the year. You can also snag seats to tapings of America's popular late-night variety shows.

Comic Con attendee dressed as the Joker
SAM ARONOV / SHUTTERSTOCK ©

Village Vanguard
Jazz

(Map p246; ☑212-255-4037; www.village vanguard.com; 178 Seventh Ave, at W 11th St; cover around $33; ⓒ7:30pm-12:30am; ⓢ1/2/3 to 14th St) Possibly the city's most prestigious jazz club, the Vanguard has hosted literally every major star of the past 50 years. It started as a home to spoken-word performances and occasionally returns to its roots, but most of the time it's just big, bold jazz all night long.

Blue Note
Jazz

(Map p246; ☑212-475-8592; www.bluenote. net; 131 W 3rd St, btwn Sixth Ave & MacDougal St; ⓢA/C/E, B/D/F/M to W 4th St-Washington Sq) This is by far the most famous (and expensive) of the city's jazz clubs. Most shows are $15 to $30 at the bar or $25 to $45 at a table, but can rise for the biggest stars. There's also jazz brunch on Sundays at 11:30am. Go on an off night, and don't talk – all attention is on the stage!

Smalls Jazz

(Map p246; ☎646-476-4346; www.smallslive.com; 183 W 10th St, btwn W 4th St & Seventh Ave S; cover $10-20; 🕐7:30pm-4am Mon-Thu, from 4:30pm Fri-Sun; [S]1 to Christopher St-Sheridan Sq) Living up to its name, this cramped but appealing basement jazz den offers a grab-bag collection of jazz acts who take the stage nightly. Cover for the evening is $20 (or $10 if you arrive after 12:30am), with a come-and-go policy if you need to duck out for a bite.

Duplex Cabaret

(Map p246; ☎212-255-5438; www.theduplex.com; 61 Christopher St, at Seventh Ave S; cover $10-25; 🕐4pm-4am; [S]1 to Christopher St-Sheridan Sq) Cabaret, karaoke and campy dance moves are par for the course at the legendary Duplex. Pictures of Joan Rivers line the walls, and the performers like to mimic her sassy form of self-deprecation while getting in a few jokes about audience members as well. It's a fun and unpretentious place, and certainly not for the bashful.

Upright Citizens Brigade Theatre Comedy

(UCB; Map p250; ☎212-366-9176; www.ucbtheatre.com; 307 W 26th St, btwn Eighth & Ninth Aves; free-$10; 🕐7pm-midnight; [S]C/E to 23rd St) Comedy sketch shows and improv reign at this below-ground 74-seat venue, which gets drop-ins from casting directors and often features well-known figures from TV. Getting in is cheap, and so is the beer and wine. You'll find quality shows happening nightly, from about 7:30pm, though the Sunday night Asssscat Improv session is always a riot.

IFC Center Cinema

(Map p246; ☎212-924-7771; www.ifccenter.com; 323 Sixth Ave, at W 3rd St; tickets $15; [S]A/C/E, B/D/F/M to W 4th St-Washington Sq) This art-house cinema in NYU-land has a solidly curated lineup of new indies, cult classics and foreign films. Catch shorts, documentaries, '80s revivals, director-focused series, weekend classics and frequent special series, such as cult favorites (*The Shining*, *Taxi Driver*, *Aliens*) at midnight.

Cherry Lane Theater   Theater

(Map p246; ☎212-989-2020; www.cherrylane theater.org; 38 Commerce St, off Bedford St; Ⓢ1 to Christopher St-Sheridan Sq) A theater with a distinctive charm hidden in the West Village, Cherry Lane has a long and distinguished history. Started by poet Edna St Vincent Millay, it has given a voice to numerous playwrights and actors over the years, remaining true to its mission of creating 'live' theater that's accessible to the public. Readings, plays and spoken-word performances rotate frequently.

Comedy Cellar   Comedy

(Map p246; ☎212-254-3480; www.comedycellar. com; 117 MacDougal St, btwn W 3rd St & Minetta Lane; cover $12-24; Ⓢ A/C/E, B/D/F/M to W 4th St-Washington Sq) This long-established basement comedy club in Greenwich Village features mainstream material and a good list of regulars (Colin Quinn, Judah Friedlander, Wanda Sykes), plus occasional high-profile drop-ins like Dave Chappelle, Jerry Seinfeld and Amy Schumer. Its success continues: Comedy Cellar now boasts

another location at the Village Underground around the corner on W 3rd St.

Joyce Theater   Dance

(Map p250; ☎212-691-9740; www.joyce.org; 175 Eighth Ave, at W 19th St; Ⓢ C/E to 23rd St; A, L to 14th St-8th Ave; 1 to 18th St) A favorite among dance junkies thanks to its excellent sight lines and offbeat offerings, this is an intimate venue, seating 472 in a renovated cinema. Its focus is on traditional modern companies such as Martha Graham, Stephen Petronio Company and Parsons Dance, as well as global stars such as Dance Brazil, Ballet Hispanico and MalPaso Dance Company.

Le Poisson Rouge   Live Music

(Map p246; ☎212-505-3474; www.lepoisson rouge.com; 158 Bleecker St, btwn Sullivan & Thompson Sts; Ⓢ A/C/E, B/D/F/M to W 4th St-Washington Sq) This high-concept art space hosts a highly eclectic lineup of live music, with the likes of Deerhunter, Marc Ribot and Yo La Tengo performing in past years. There's a lot of experimentation and cross-genre pollination between classical, folk music, opera and more.

★ **Top Five Broadway Shows**

Book of Mormon (p59)

Hamilton (p59)

Kinky Boots (p60)

An American in Paris (p60)

Matilda (p60)

From left: Blue Note (p185); Signs for *Hamilton* at Richard Rodgers Theatre; Keren Ann performs at Le Poisson Rouge

New York City Ballet performers

HIROYUKI ITO / GETTY IMAGES ©

Today, the company has 90 dancers and is the largest ballet organization in the US...

Midtown

Jazz at Lincoln Center Jazz

(Map p252; ☎tickets to Dizzy's Club Coca-Cola 212-258-9595, tickets to Rose Theater & Appel Room 212-721-6500; www.jazz.org; Time Warner Center, Columbus Circle, Broadway at W 59th St; [S]A/C, B/D, 1 to 59th St-Columbus Circle) Perched atop the Time Warner Center, Jazz at Lincoln Center consists of three state-of-the-art venues: the mid-sized **Rose Theater**; the panoramic, glass-backed **Appel Room**; and the intimate, atmospheric **Dizzy's Club Coca-Cola**. It's the last of these that you're most likely to visit, given its nightly shows. The talent is often exceptional, as are the dazzling Central Park views.

Jazz Standard Jazz

(Map p250; ☎212-576-2232; www.jazzstandard.com; 116 E 27th St, btwn Lexington & Park Aves; [S]6 to 28th St) Jazz luminaries like Ravi Coltrane, Roy Haynes and Ron Carter have played at this sophisticated club. The service is impeccable, and the food is great. There's no minimum and it's programmed by Seth Abramson, a guy who really knows his jazz.

Carnegie Hall Live Music

(Map p252; ☎212-247-7800; www.carnegiehall.org; 881 Seventh Ave, at W 57th St; 🕐tours 11:30am, 12:30pm, 2pm & 3pm Mon-Fri, 11:30am & 12:30pm Sat Oct-Jun; [S]N/R/W to 57th St-7th Ave) This legendary music hall may not be the world's biggest, nor grandest, but it's definitely one of the most acoustically blessed venues around. Opera, jazz and folk greats feature in the Isaac Stern Auditorium, with edgier jazz, pop, classical and world music in the popular Zankel Hall. The intimate Weill Recital Hall hosts chamber-music concerts, debut performances and panel discussions.

Birdland Jazz, Cabaret

(Map p252; ☎212-581-3080; www.birdlandjazz.com; 315 W 44th St, btwn Eighth & Ninth Aves; cover $25-50; 🕐5pm-1am; 📶; [S]A/C/E to 42nd St-Port Authority Bus Terminal) This bird's got a slick look, not to mention the legend – its name dates from bebop legend Charlie Parker (aka 'Bird'), who headlined at the previous location on 52nd St, along with Miles, Monk and just about everyone else (you can see their photos on the walls). Covers run from $25 to $50 and the lineup is always stellar.

New Victory Theater Theater

(Map p252; ☎646-223-3010; www.newvictory.org; 209 W 42nd St, btwn Seventh & Eighth Aves; 👪; [S]N/Q/R/W, S, 1/2/3, 7 to Times Sq-42nd St, A/C/E to 42nd St-Port Authority Bus Terminal) Budding thespians and dancers flock to the upbeat energy of this kid-focused theater. New Victory puts on comedy, dance, music, puppetry and drama shows for the 12-and-under set, and hosts an array of offerings for teenagers. Events also include theater workshops, ranging from acting classes to clowning and hip hop lessons.

✪ Upper West Side & Central Park

Metropolitan Opera House Opera

(Map p252; ☎tickets 212-362-6000, tours 212-769-7028; www.metopera.org; Lincoln Center, Columbus Ave at W 64th St; [S]1 to 66th St-Lincoln Center) New York's premier opera company is the place to see classics such as *Carmen*, *Madame Butterfly* and *Macbeth*, not to mention Wagner's *Ring Cycle*. It also hosts premieres and revivals of more contemporary works, such as John Adams' *The Death of Klinghoffer*. The season runs from September to April.

New York City Ballet Dance

(Map p252; ☎212-496-0600; www.nycballet.com; Lincoln Center, Columbus Ave at W 63rd St; 👪; [S]1 to 66th St-Lincoln Center) This prestigious ballet company was first directed by renowned Russian-born choreographer George Balanchine back in the 1940s. Today, the company has 90 dancers and is the largest ballet organization in the US, performing 23 weeks a year at Lincoln Center's **David H Koch Theater**. During the holidays the troop is best known for its annual production of *The Nutcracker*.

Musical Metropolis

This is the city where jazz players such as Ornette Coleman, Miles Davis and John Coltrane pushed the limits of improvisation in the '50s. It's where various Latin sounds – from cha-cha-cha to rumba to mambo – came together to form the hybrid we now call salsa, where folk singers such as Bob Dylan and Joan Baez crooned protest songs in coffeehouses, and where bands such as the New York Dolls and the Ramones tore up the stage in Manhattan's gritty downtown. It was the ground zero of disco. And it was the cultural crucible where hip-hop was nurtured and grew – then exploded.

The city remains a magnet for musicians to this day. The local indie rock scene is especially vibrant: groups including the Yeah Yeah Yeahs, LCD Soundsystem and Animal Collective all emerged out of NYC. Williamsburg is at the heart of the action, packed with clubs and bars, as well as indie record labels and internet radio stations. The best venues for rock include the **Music Hall of Williamsburg** (p193) and the **Brooklyn Bowl** (p192), as well as Manhattan's **Bowery Ballroom** (Map p246; ☎212-533-2111; www.boweryballroom.com; 6 Delancey St, at Bowery St; [S]J/Z to Bowery, B/D to Grand St).

VNV Nation performs at Music Hall of Williamsburg

KATHYHYDE / SHUTTERSTOCK ©

New York
Philharmonic   Classical Music
(Map p252; ☑212-875-5656; www.nyphil.org;
Lincoln Center, Columbus Ave at W 65th St; ♿;
Ⓢ1 to 66 St-Lincoln Center) The oldest professional orchestra in the US (dating back to
1842) holds its season every year at **David
Geffen Hall** (known as Avery Fisher until
2015); newly installed music director Jaap
van Zweden took over from Alan Gilbert in
2017. The orchestra plays a mix of classics
(Tchaikovsky, Mahler, Haydn) and contemporary works, as well as concerts geared
towards children.

Symphony Space   Live Music
(Map p252; ☑212-864-5400; www.symphony
space.org; 2537 Broadway, btwn W 94th & 95th
Sts; Ⓢ1/2/3 to 96th St) Symphony Space is
a multidisciplinary gem supported by the
local community. It often hosts three-day
series that are dedicated to one musician,
and also has an affinity for world music,
theater, film, dance and literature (with
appearances by acclaimed writers).

Film Society of
Lincoln Center   Cinema
(Map p252; ☑212-875-5367; www.filmlinc.com;
Ⓢ1 to 66th St-Lincoln Center) The Film Society
is one of New York's cinematic gems, provid-
ing an invaluable platform for a wide gamut
of documentary, feature, independent,
foreign and avant-garde art pictures. Films
screen in one of two facilities at Lincoln
Center: the **Elinor Bunin Munroe Film
Center** (Map p252; ☑212-875-5232), a more
intimate, experimental venue, or the **Walter
Reade Theater** (Map p252; ☑212-875-5601),
with wonderfully wide, screening room–
style seats.

Beacon Theatre   Live Music
(Map p252; ☑212-465-6500; www.beacon
theatre.com; 2124 Broadway, btwn W 74th & 75th
Sts; Ⓢ1/2/3 to 72nd St) This historic 1929
theater is a perfect medium-size venue
with 2829 seats (not a terrible one in the
house) and a constant flow of popular acts
from ZZ Top to Wilco (plus comedians like
Jerry Seinfeld and Patton Oswalt). A 2009

restoration left the gilded interiors – a mix
of Greek, Roman, Renaissance and rococo
design elements – totally sparkling.

✪ Harlem & Upper
Manhattan

Minton's   Jazz
(☑212-243-2222; www.mintonsharlem.com; 206
W 118th St, btwn St Nicholas Ave & Adam Clayton
Powell Jr Blvd; ⊗6-11pm Wed-Sat, noon-3pm &
6-10pm Sun; ⒮B/C, 2/3 to 116th St) Birthplace
of bebop, this Harlem jazz-and-dinner club
is a musical holy grail. Everyone from Dizzy
Gillespie to Louis Armstrong have jammed
here, and dinner (mains $18 to $34) or
Sunday brunch ($12 to $18) in its tinted-
mirror dining room is an experience to
behold. Book ahead, dress to impress and
savor Southern flavors while toe-tapping to
live, honey-sweet jazz.

✪ Brooklyn

Brooklyn Academy
of Music   Performing Arts
(BAM; Map p254; ☑718-636-4100; www.bam.org;
30 Lafayette Ave, at Ashland Pl, Fort Greene; 🎧;
ⓈB/D, N/Q/R, 2/3, 4/5 to Atlantic Ave-Barclays
Center) Several venues make up this vibrant
performing-arts complex, a major driver of
the cultural revitalization of the neighborhood and Brooklyn as a whole. The Italian
Renaissance-style **Peter J Sharp Building**
houses the **Howard Gilman Opera House**
(opera, dance, music and more) and the
Rose Cinemas, which screen first-run,
indie and foreign films.

St Ann's Warehouse   Theater
(Map p254; ☑718-254-8779; www.stanns
warehouse.org; 45 Water St, Brooklyn Bridge Park,
Dumbo; ⒮A/C to High St) This avant-garde
performance company hosts innovative
theater and dance happenings that attract
the Brooklyn literati. The calendar has featured rock opera, genre-defying music by
new composers, and strange and wondrous
puppet theater. In 2015, St Ann's moved
from its old home several blocks away to

★ Performing Arts

The classics are alive and well at **Lincoln Center** (p76). Here, the **Metropolitan Opera** (p189) delivers a wide array of celebrated operas. The **New York Philharmonic** (p190) is also based here. **Carnegie Hall** (p188) also offers wonderful – and more intimate – spaces to enjoy great classical music.

Clockwise from top: A New York Philharmonic performance; The cast of Broadway's *Chicago* performs; Restaurant at the Metropolitan Opera House

On Broadway & Beyond

In the early 20th century, clusters of theaters settled into the area around Times Square and began producing popular plays and suggestive comedies. By the 1920s, these messy works had evolved into on-stage spectacles like *Show Boat*, an all-out Oscar Hammerstein production about the lives of performers on a Mississippi steamboat. In 1943, Broadway had its first runaway hit – *Oklahoma!* – that remained on stage for a record 2212 performances.

Today, Broadway musicals are shown in one of 40 official Broadway theaters. If you're on a budget, look for off-Broadway productions. These tend to be more intimate, inexpensive, and often just as good.

NYC bursts with theatrical offerings beyond Broadway, from Shakespeare to David Mamet to rising experimental playwrights including Young Jean Lee. In addition to Midtown staples such as **Playwrights Horizons** (Map p250; ☎212-279-4200; www.playwrightshorizons.org; 416 W 42nd St, btwn Ninth & Tenth Aves, Midtown West) and **Second Stage Theatre** (Tony Kiser Theatre; Map p252; ☎tickets 212-246-4422; www.2st.com; 305 W 43rd St, at Eighth Ave, Midtown West), the **Lincoln Center** (p76) theaters and smaller companies such as **Soho Rep** (Soho Repertory Theatre; Map p246; ☎212-941-8632; sohorep.org; 46 Walker St, btwn Church St & Broadway) are important hubs for works by modern and contemporary playwrights.

Across the East River, **Brooklyn Academy of Music** (BAM; p190), **PS 122** (Map p246; ☎212-477-5829; www.ps122.org; 150 First Ave, at E 9th St; L to 1st Ave) and **St Ann's Warehouse** (p190) all offer edgy programming. Numerous festivals, such as **FringeNYC** (p13), **Next Wave Festival** (p14) and the biennial **Performa** (www.performa-arts.org; 🕒Nov) offer brilliant opportunities to catch new work.

this location in the historic Tobacco Warehouse (p108) in Brooklyn Bridge Park.

Nitehawk Cinema Cinema

(Map p255; www.nitehawkcinema.com; 136 Metropolitan Ave, btwn Berry & Wythe Sts, Williamsburg; [S]L to Bedford Ave) This triplex has a fine lineup of first-run and indie films, a good sound system and comfy seats, but Nitehawk's big draw is that you can dine and drink while watching a movie. Munch on hummus plates, sweet-potato risotto balls or short-rib empanadas, matched by a Blue Point toasted lager, a Negroni or a movie-themed cocktail invention.

Barbès Live Music

(Map p254; ☎718-965-9177; www.barbesbrooklyn.com; 376 9th St, at Sixth Ave, Park Slope; suggested donation for live music $10; 🕒5pm-2am Sun-Thu, to 4am Fri & Sat; [S]F to 7th Ave) This compact and festive bar and performance space, named after a North African neighborhood in Paris, is owned by a French musician and longtime Brooklyn resident, Olivier Conan, who sometimes takes the stage with his Latin-themed band Las Rubias del Norte. The lineup here is impressive and eclectic, with Afro-Peruvian grooves, West African funk and French *chanson*, among other sounds.

Bell House Live Music

(Map p254; ☎718-643-6510; www.thebellhouseny.com; 149 7th St, btwn Second & Third Aves, Gowanus; 🕒5pm-4am; 📶; [S]F, G, R to 4th Ave-9th St) A big, old venue in the mostly barren neighborhood of Gowanus, the Bell House features high-profile live performances, indie rockers, DJ nights, comedy shows and burlesque parties. The handsomely converted warehouse has a spacious concert area, plus a friendly little bar in the front room with flickering candles, leather armchairs and 10 or so beers on tap.

Brooklyn Bowl Live Music

(Map p255; ☎718-963-3369; www.brooklynbowl.com; 61 Wythe Ave, btwn N 11th & N 12th Sts, Williamsburg; 🕒6pm-2am Mon-Fri, from 11am Sat & Sun; [S]L to Bedford Ave, G to Nassau Ave) This

Carnegie Hall (p188)

23,000-sq-ft venue inside the former Hecla Iron Works Company combines bowling (p202), microbrews, food and groovy live music. In addition to the live bands that regularly tear up the stage, there are NFL game days, karaoke and DJ nights. Aside from weekends (11am to 6pm), it's age 21 and up.

Jalopy Live Music

(Map p254; ☎718-395-3214; www.jalopy.biz; 315 Columbia St, at Woodhull St, Red Hook; 🕒4pm-9pm Mon, noon-midnight Tue-Sun; [S]F, G to Carroll St) This fringe Carroll Gardens/Red Hook banjo shop has a fun DIY space with cold beer for its bluegrass, country and ukulele shows, including a no-cover feel-good Roots 'n' Ruckus show on Wednesday nights.

Music Hall of Williamsburg Live Music

(Map p255; www.musichallofwilliamsburg.com; 66 N 6th St, btwn Wythe & Kent Aves, Williamsburg; tickets $15-40; [S]L to Bedford Ave) This popular Williamsburg music venue is *the* place to see indie bands in Brooklyn. (For many groups traveling through New York, this is their one and only spot.) It's intimate and the programming is solid. Artists who have played here include rapper Kendrick Lamar and indie folk band Bon Iver.

This legendary music hall may not be the world's biggest, but it's definitely one of the most acoustically blessed...

LoftOpera Opera

(☎347-915-5638; www.loftopera.com; tickets from $30) True to its name, this iconoclastic Brooklyn-based outfit performs condensed operas at lofts in Gowanus and unconventional spaces elsewhere in Brooklyn. Even if you're not an opera fan, it's an extraordinary experience witnessing a first-rate performance in a disused garage with graffiti while sipping a $5 beer. Visit the website for tickets and venues.

ACTIVE NEW YORK

Sports, biking, tours and more

Active New York

Although hailing cabs in New York City can feel like a blood sport, and waiting on subway platforms in summer heat is steamier than a sauna, New Yorkers still love to stay active in their spare time. And considering how limited the green spaces are in the city, it's surprising for some visitors just how active the locals can be. Non-rainy days see New Yorkers taking to the paths of Central Park, cycling along Hudson River Park and joining in pick-up basketball games on outdoor courts across town.

For those who prefer their sport sitting down, there's a packed calendar of athletic artistry, with over half a dozen pro teams playing within the metropolitan area. Football, basketball, baseball, hockey, tennis – there's lots of excitement right on your doorstep.

In This Section

What to Watch & When

Baseball season runs from April to October. Basketball follows on its heels, running from October to May or June. It overlaps a bit with football season (August to January) and pro hockey (September to April). Meanwhile, the US Open is America's biggest tennis event, happening in late August and September.

Rock climbing at Brooklyn Boulders (p199)

The Best...

NYC Activities Spots

Central Park (p36) The city's wondrous playground has rolling hills, forested paths, an open meadow and a beautiful lake.

Chelsea Piers Complex (p199) Every activity imaginable – from kickboxing to ice hockey – under one gigantic roof.

Brooklyn Bridge Park (p106) This brand new green space is Brooklyn's pride and joy.

Prospect Park (p102) Escape the crowds at Brooklyn's gorgeous park, with trails, hills, a canal, lake and meadows.

NYC Sports Teams

New York Yankees One of the country's most successful baseball teams.

New York Giants Football powerhouse that, despite the name, plays their home games in New Jersey.

New York Knicks See the Knicks sink a few three-pointers at Madison Square Garden.

Brooklyn Nets The hot new NBA team in town and symbol of Brooklyn's resurgence.

New York Mets NYC's other baseball team play their games at Citi Field in Queens.

Sporting Arenas

Yankee Stadium Stadium

(☎718-293-4300, tours 646-977-8687; www.newyork.yankees.mlb.com; E 161st St, at River Ave; tours $20; [S]B/D, 4 to 161st St-Yankee Stadium) The Boston Red Sox like to talk about their record of eight World Series championships in the last 90 years...well, the Yankees have won a mere 27 in that period. The team's magic appeared to have moved with them across 161st St to the new Yankee Stadium, where they played their first season in 2009 – winning the World Series there in a six-game slugfest against the Phillies. The Yankees play from April to October.

Madison Square Garden Spectator Sport

(Map p250; www.thegarden.com; 4 Pennsylvania Plaza, Seventh Ave btwn 31st & 33rd Sts; [S]A/C/E, 1/2/3 to 34th St-Penn Station) NYC's major performance venue – part of the massive complex housing Penn Station (p235) – hosts big-arena performers, from Kanye West to Madonna. It's also a sports arena, with **New York Knicks** (www.nba.com/knicks.com) and **New York Liberty** (www.liberty.wnba.com) basketball games and **New York Rangers** (www.nhl.com/rangers) hockey games, as well as boxing and events like the Annual Westminster Kennel Club Dog Show.

Barclays Center Spectator Sport

(Map p254; ☎917-618-6100; www.barclayscenter.com; cnr Flatbush & Atlantic Aves, Prospect Heights; [S]B/D, N/Q/R, 2/3, 4/5 to Atlantic Ave-Barclays Center) The (currently woeful) Brooklyn Nets in the NBA (formerly the New Jersey Nets) now hold court at this high-tech stadium that opened in 2012. Basketball aside, Barclays also stages major concerts and big shows – Bruce Springsteen, Justin Bieber, Barbara Streisand, Cirque de Soleil, Disney on Ice...

NYC's major performance venue hosts big-arena performers and sporting events...

Washington Capitals vs New York Rangers at Madison Square Garden

PAUL BERESWILL / STRINGER / GETTY IMAGES ©

Speaking of ice, Brooklyn hockey fans now have a home team: the **New York Islanders** (www.nhl.com/islanders) began playing their home games here in 2015. Poor sight lines and fan-base dissatisfaction mean the Islanders aren't likely to be at Barclays for long, however.

Health & Fitness

Chelsea Piers Complex Health & Fitness

(Map p250; ☎212-336-6666; www.chelseapiers.com; Pier 62, at W 23rd St; 👪; 🚌M23 to Chelsea Piers, [S]C/E to 23rd St) This massive waterfront sports center caters to the athlete in everyone. You can set out to hit a bucket of golf balls at the four-level driving range, skate on the complex's indoor ice rinks or rack up a few strikes in a jazzy bowling alley. There's Hoop City for basketball, a sailing school for kids, batting cages, a huge gym facility with an indoor swimming pool (day passes for nonmembers are $60), indoor **rock-climbing** walls – the works.

Brooklyn Boulders Climbing

(Map p254; ☎347-834-9066; www.brooklynboulders.com; 575 Degraw St, at Third Ave, Boerum Hill; day pass $32, shoe rental $7; 🕓7am-midnight Mon-Fri, 8am-10pm Sat & Sun; [S]R to Union St) Brooklyn's biggest indoor climbing arena is housed in an airy and vibrant space on an industrial block in the Gowanus neighborhood. Ceilings top out at 30ft inside this 18,000-sq-ft facility, and its caves and freestanding 17ft boulder and climbing walls offer numerous routes for beginners and experts. There are overhangs of 15°, 30° and 45°. Climbing classes are available.

Central Park Tennis Center Tennis

(Map p252; ☎212-316-0800; www.centralparktenniscenter.com; Central Park, btwn W 94th & 96th Sts; 🕓6:30am-dusk Apr-Nov; [S]B, C to 96th St) This daylight-hours-only facility has 26 clay courts for public use and four hard courts for lessons. You can buy single-play tickets ($15) here, and can reserve a court if you pick up a $15 permit at the **Arsenal** (Map p252; ☎212-360-8163; www.nycgovparks.org; Central Park, at Fifth Ave & E 64th St; 🕓9am-5pm Mon-Fri; [S]N/R/W to 5th Ave-59th St) [FREE]. The least busy times are roughly from noon to 4pm on weekdays. Closest park entrance is Central Park West and 96th St.

Jivamukti Yoga

(Map p246; ☎212-353-0214; www.jivamuktiyoga.com; 841 Broadway, 2nd fl, btwn E 13th & 14th Sts; classes $15-22; 🕓classes 7am-8:30pm Mon-Fri, 7:45am-8pm Sat & Sun; [S]4/5/6, N/Q/R/W, L to 14th St-Union Sq) Considered *the* yoga spot in Manhattan, Jivamukti – in a 12,000-sq-ft locale on Union Sq – is a posh place for Vinyasa, Hatha and Ashtanga

Baseball

New York is one of the last remaining corners of the USA where baseball reigns supreme over football and basketball. Tickets start at around $20 – a great deal for seeing the home teams playing in their recently opened stadiums. The two Major League Baseball teams play 162 games during the regular season from April to October, when the playoffs begin.

New York Yankees (p198) The Bronx Bombers are the USA's greatest dynasty, with over two dozen World Series championship titles since 1900.

New York Mets (www.mlb.com/mets) In the National League since 1962, the Mets remain New York's 'new' baseball team, and won the pennant in 2015.

New York Yankees baseball game

EXAMEDIA PHOTOGRAPHY / SHUTTERSTOCK ©

Biking the Big Apple

NYC has taken enormous strides in making the city more bike friendly, adding hundreds of miles of bike lanes in recent years. That said, we recommend that the uninitiated stick to the less hectic trails in the parks and along the waterways, such as Central Park, Prospect Park, the Manhattan Waterfront Greenway and the Brooklyn Waterfront Greenway.

The new **Citi Bike** (www.citibikenyc.com) is handy for quick jaunts, but for longer rides, you'll want a proper rental. **Bike & Roll** (www.bikenewyorkcity.com) has loads of outdoor hire spots, including at **Central Park** (p36) by Columbus Circle.

Cycling through Central Park
JAVEN / SHUTTERSTOCK ©

classes. The center's 'open' classes are suitable for both rookies and experienced practitioners, and there's an organic **vegan cafe** on site, too. Gratuitous celebrity tidbit: Uma's little bro Dechen Thurman teaches classes here.

New York Trapeze School
Adventure Sports

(Map p246; ☎212-242-8769; www.newyork. trapezeschool.com; Pier 40, at West Side Hwy; per class $50-70; ⊙Apr-Oct; ⓢ1 to Houston St) Fulfill your circus dreams flying from trapeze to trapeze in this open-air tent by the river. It's open from April to October and located on top of Pier 40. The school also has an indoor facility in South Williamsburg, Brooklyn, that's open year-round. Call or check the website for daily class times. There's a one-time $22 registration fee.

🌀 Spas & Steam Rooms

Great Jones Spa
Spa

(Map p246; ☎212-505-3185; www.greatjones spa.com; 29 Great Jones St, btwn Lafayette St & Bowery; ⊙9am-10pm; ⓢ6 to Bleecker St, B/D/F/M to Broadway-Lafayette St) Don't skimp on the services at this downtown feng shui–designed place, whose offerings include Moroccan rose sea-salt scrubs and stem-cell facials. If you spend over $100 per person (not difficult: hour-long massages start at $145, hour-long facials start at $135), you get access to the water lounge with thermal hot tub, sauna, steam room and cold plunge pool (swimwear required).

Russian & Turkish Baths
Bathhouse

(Map p246; ☎212-674-9250; www.russian turkishbaths.com; 268 E 10th St, btwn First Ave & Ave A; per visit $45; ⊙noon-10pm Mon-Tue & Thu-Fri, from 10am Wed, from 9am Sat, from 8am Sun; ⓢL to 1st Ave, 6 to Astor Pl) Since 1892, this cramped and grungy downtown spa has been drawing a polyglot and eclectic mix: actors, students, frisky couples, singles-on-the-make, Russian regulars and old-school locals, who all strip down to their skivvies (or the roomy cotton shorts provided) and rotate between steam baths, an ice-cold plunge pool, a sauna and the sundeck. Open to both men and women most hours (wearing shorts is required at these times), though at some times it's men or women only.

🌀 Ice Skating

Lakeside
Ice Skating, Boating

(Map p254; ☎718-462-0010; www.lakeside prospectpark.com; East Dr, Prospect Park, near Ocean & Parkside Aves; ice skating $6-9, skate rental $6; ⊙9am-5:15pm Mon-Thu, to 9pm Fri, 11:30am-9pm Sat, to 5:15pm Sun; 🚻; ⓢB, Q to Prospect Park) Two ice-skating rinks (one open and one covered) in Prospect Park opened in late 2013 as part of Lakeside Center, a $74 million project that reconfigured 26 acres of parkland in a beautiful, ecofriendly showcase. In the summer, kids splash about in wading pools and sprinklers; the other rink features old-school roller skating.

Wollman Skating Rink   Ice Skating

(Map p252; ☎212-439-6900; www.wollman skatingrink.com; Central Park, btwn E 62nd & 63rd Sts; adult Mon-Thu/Fri-Sun $12/19, child $6, skate rentals $9; ☺10am-2:30pm Mon & Tue, to 10pm Wed-Sat, to 9pm Sun Nov-Mar; ⓘ; Ⓢ F to 57 St; N/Q/R/W to 5th Ave-59th St) Larger than the Rockefeller Center skating rink – and allowing all-day skating – this rink at the southeastern edge of Central Park offers magical views. There's locker rental for $5 and a spectator fee of $5. Cash only.

Rink at Rockefeller Center   Ice Skating

(Map p252; ☎212-332-7654; www.therinkatrock center.com; Rockefeller Center, Fifth Ave btwn W 49th & 50th Sts; adult $25-32, child $15, skate rental $12; ☺8:30am-midnight mid-Oct–Apr; ⓘ; Ⓢ B/D/F/M to 47th-50th Sts-Rockefeller Center) From mid-October to April, Rockefeller Plaza is home to New York's most famous ice-skating rink. Carved out of a recessed oval with the 70-story art deco Rockefeller Center (p84) towering above, plus a massive **Christmas tree** (www.rockefellercenter. com; ☺Dec) during the holiday season, it's incomparably magical. It's also undeniably small and crowded. Opt for the first skating period of the day (8:30am) to avoid a long wait. Come summer, the rink becomes a cafe.

⊛ Family Activities

Belvedere Castle   Birdwatching

(Map p252; ☎212-772-0288; Central Park, at W 79th St; ☺10am-4pm; ⓘ; Ⓢ1/2/3, B, C to 72nd St) **FREE** For a DIY birding expedition with kids, borrow a 'Discovery Kit' at Belvedere Castle in Central Park, which comes with binoculars, a bird book, colored pencils and paper – a perfect way to get the kids excited about birds. Picture ID required.

Rockefeller Plaza is home to New York's most famous ice-skating rink

Ice skating at Rockefeller Center

Boaters on Turtle Pond, Central Park (p36)

Brooklyn Bowl   Bowling

(Map p255; ☎718-963-3369; www.brooklyn bowl.com; 61 Wythe Ave, btwn N 11th & N 12th Sts, Williamsburg; lane rental per 30min $25, shoe rental $5; ⏰6pm-2am Mon-Fri, from 11am Sat & Sun; 🚇L to Bedford, G to Nassau Ave) This incredible alley is housed in the 23,000-sq-ft former Hecla Iron Works Company, which provided ornamentation for several NYC landmarks at the turn of the 20th century. There are 16 lanes surrounded by cushy sofas and exposed brick walls. In addition to bowling, Brooklyn Bowl hosts concerts throughout the week, and there's always good food on hand.

🌊 Water Sports

Loeb Boathouse   Boating, Cycling

(Map p252; ☎212-517-2233; www.thecentral parkboathouse.com; Central Park, btwn E 74th & 75th Sts; boating per hr $15, bike rental per hr $9-15; ⏰10am-6pm Apr-Nov; 🚻; 🚇B, C to 72nd St, 6 to 77th St) Central Park's boathouse has a fleet of 100 rowboats, as well as a Venetian-style gondola that seats up to six if you'd

rather someone else do the paddling. Bicycles are also available (helmets included), weather permitting. Rentals require ID and a credit card.

Downtown Boathouse   Kayaking

(Map p246; www.downtownboathouse.org; Pier 26, near N Moore St; ⏰9am-5pm Sat & Sun mid-May–mid-Oct, plus 5-7:30pm Tue-Thu mid-Jun–mid-Sep; 🚇1 to Houston St) FREE New York's most active public boathouse offers free, walk-up 20-minute kayaking sessions (including equipment) in a protected embayment in the Hudson River on weekends and some weekday evenings. For more activities – kayaking trips, stand-up paddle boarding and classes – check out www.hudsonriverpark.org for the four other kayaking locations on the Hudson River. There's also a summer-only kayaking location on Governors Island (p109).

Red Hook Boaters   Kayaking

(www.redhookboaters.org; Louis Valentino Jr Pier Park, Coffey St, Red Hook; ⏰1-5pm Sun Jun-Sep & 6-8pm Thu mid-Jun–mid-Aug; 🚌B61 to Van Dyke St, 🚇F, G to Smith-9th Sts) FREE This boathouse, located in Red Hook, offers free kayaking in the small embayment off Louis Valentino Jr Pier Park. Once in the water, there are beautiful views of lower Manhattan and the Statue of Liberty. Check the website for the latest times before making the trip out.

Schooner Adirondack Cruise

(Map p250; ☎212-627-1825; www.sail-nyc.com; Chelsea Piers Complex, Pier 62 at W 22nd St; tours $52-86; [S]C, E to 23rd St) The two-masted *'Dack* hits the New York Harbor with four two-hour sails daily from May to October. The 1920s-style, 80ft *Manhattan* and 100ft *Manhattan II* yachts offer tours throughout the week. Call or check the website for the latest times.

Tours

Central Park Bike Tours Cycling

(Map p252; ☎212-541-8759; www.centralparkbiketours.com; 203 W 58th St, at Seventh Ave; rentals per 2hr/day $14/28, 2hr tours $49; ⌚9am-8pm; [S]A/C, B/D, 1 to 59th St-Columbus Circle) This place rents out good bikes (helmets, locks and bike map included) and leads two-hour guided tours of Central Park and the Brooklyn Bridge area. See the website for tour times.

Municipal Art Society Walking

(☎212-935-3960; www.mas.org; tours from $25) The Municipal Art Society offers various scheduled tours focusing on architecture and history. Among them is a 75-minute tour of Grand Central Terminal (p236), departing daily at 12:30pm from the station's Main Concourse.

New York City Audubon Walking

(Map p250; ☎212-691-7483; www.nycaudubon.org; 71 W 23rd St, Suite 1523, at Sixth Ave; tours & classes free-$170; [S]F/M to 23rd St) Throughout the year, the New York City Audubon Society runs bird-watching field trips (including seal- and waterbird-spotting on New York Harbor and eagle-watching in the Hudson Valley), lectures and beginners' birding classes.

NYC Running

Central Park's loop roads are best during traffic-free hours, though you'll be in the company of many cyclists and in-line skaters. The 1.6-mile path surrounding the Jacqueline Kennedy Onassis Reservoir (where Jackie O used to run) is for runners and walkers only; access it between 86th and 96th Sts. Running along the Hudson River is a popular path, best from about 30th St to Battery Park in Lower Manhattan. The Upper East Side has a path that runs along FDR Dr and the East River (from 63rd St to 115th St). Brooklyn's Prospect Park has plenty of paths (and a 3-mile loop), while 1.3-mile-long Brooklyn Bridge Park has incredible views of Manhattan (reach it via Brooklyn Bridge to up the mileage). The **New York Road Runners Club** (www.nyrr.org) organizes weekend runs citywide, including the New York City Marathon.

MATT DUTILE / GETTY IMAGES ©

Big Apple Greeter (Accessible) Tours

(☎212-669-8198; www.bigapplegreeter.org) [FREE] The Big Apple Greeter program has more than 50 volunteers with disabilities (visible or invisible) on staff, who are happy to show off their favorite corners of the city. The tours are free and the company has a no-tipping policy. It's best to contact them three to four weeks before your arrival.

REST YOUR HEAD

Top tips for the best accommodations

Rest Your Head

Like the student with the hand up at the front of class, NYC just seems to know how to do everything well, and its lodging scene is no exception. Creative minds have descended upon the 'city that never sleeps' to create memorable spaces for those who might just want to grab a bit of shut-eye during their stay.

In This Section

Prices/Tipping

A 'budget hotel' in NYC generally costs up to $150 for a standard double room including breakfast. For a modest mid-range option, plan on spending $150 to $350. Luxury options run $350 and higher.

Tip the hotel housekeeper $3 to $5 per night, tip porters around $2 per bag. Staff providing service (hailing cabs, room service, concierge help) should be tipped accordingly.

Reservations

Reservations are essential – walk-ins are practically impossible and rack rates are almost always unfavorable relative to online deals. Reserve your room as early as possible and make sure you understand your hotel's cancellation policy. Expect check-in to always be in the middle of the afternoon and check-out in the late morning. Early check-ins are rare, though high-end establishments can often accommodate with advance notice.

Useful Websites

Lonely Planet (lonelyplanet.com/usa/new-york-city/hotels) Accommodation reviews and online booking service.

newyorkhotels.com (www.newyorkhotels.com) The self-proclaimed official website for hotels in NYC.

NYC (www.nycgo.com/hotels) Loads of listings from the NYC Official Guide.

Renting Rooms and Apartments Online

More and more travelers are bypassing hotels and staying in private apartments listed online through companies such as Airbnb. The wealth of options is staggering, with more than 25,000 listings per night scattered in every corner of New York City. If you want a more local, neighborhood-oriented experience, then this can be a great way to go.

There are a few things, however, to keep in mind. First off: many listings are actually illegal. Laws in NYC dictate that apartments can be rented out for less than 30 days only if the occupants are present. Effects on the immediate community are another issue, with some neighbors complaining about noise, security risks and the unexpected transformation of their residence into a hotel of sorts. There are also the larger impacts on the housing market: some landlords are cashing in, knowing they can earn more from holiday rentals than with long-term tenants. Taking thousands of possible rentals off the market is only driving rental prices for NYC residents ever higher.

🛏 Booking Accommodations

In New York City, the average room rate is well over $300. But don't let that scare you, as there are great deals to be had – almost all of which can be found through savvy online snooping. To get the best deals, launch a two-pronged approach: if you don't have your heart set on a particular property, then check out the generic booking websites. If you do know where you want to stay – it might sound simple – but it's best to start at your desired hotel's website. These days it's not uncommon to find deals and package rates directly on the site of your accommodation of choice.

🛏 Room Rates

New York City doesn't have a 'high season' in the common way that beach destinations do. Sure, there are busier times of the year when it comes to tourist traffic, but, with more than 50 million visitors per annum, the Big Apple never needs to worry when it comes to filling up beds. As such, room rates fluctuate based on availability; in fact, most hotels have a booking algorithm in place that spits out a price quote relative to the number of rooms already booked on the same night, so the busier the evening the higher the price goes.

If you're looking to find the best room rates, then flexibility is key – weekdays are often cheaper, and you'll generally find that accommodations in winter months have smaller price tags. If you are visiting over a weekend, try for a business hotel in the Financial District, which tends to empty out when the workweek ends.

🛏 Types of Accommodations

B&Bs & Family-Style Guesthouses

Offer mix-and-match furnishings and some serious savings (if you don't mind eating breakfast with strangers).

Boutique Hotels

Usually have tiny rooms decked out with fantastic amenities and at least one celebrity-filled basement bar, rooftop bar or hip, flashy eatery on-site.

Classic Hotels

Typified by old-fashioned, small-scale European grandeur; these usually cost the same as boutiques and aren't always any larger.

European-Style Travelers' Hotels

Have creaky floors and small, but cheap and clean (if chintzily decorated) rooms, often with a shared bathroom.

Hostels

Functional dorms (bunk beds and bare walls) that are nonetheless communal and friendly. Many have a backyard garden, kitchen and a pretty lounge that make up for the soulless rooms.

Where to Stay

Upper West Side & Central Park

Upper East Side

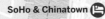

Midtown

Greenwich Village, Chelsea & Meatpacking District

Union Square, Flatiron District & Gramercy

SoHo & Chinatown

East Village & Lower East Side

Financial District & Lower Manhattan

Brooklyn

Neighborhood	For	Against
Financial District & Lower Manhattan	Convenient to Tribeca's nightlife and ferries. Cheap weekend rates at business hotels.	The area can feel impersonal, corporate and even a bit desolate after business hours.
SoHo & Chinatown	Shop to your heart's content right on your doorstep.	Crowds swarm the commercial streets of SoHo almost any time of day.
East Village & Lower East Side	Funky and fun, the area feels the most 'New York' to visitors and Manhattanites alike.	Not a great deal to choose from when it comes to hotels.
Greenwich Village, Chelsea & Meatpacking District	Brilliantly close-to-everything feel in a thriving part of town that has an almost European feel.	Prices soar for traditional hotels, but remain reasonable for B&Bs. Rooms can sometimes be on the small side, even for NYC.
Union Square, Flatiron District & Gramercy	Convenient subway access to anywhere in the city. You're also steps away from the Village and Midtown in either direction.	Prices are high and there's not much in the way of neighborhood flavor.
Midtown	In the heart of the postcard's version of NYC: skyscrapers, museums, shopping and shows.	One of the most expensive areas in the city; expect small rooms. Midtown can often feel touristy and impersonal.
Upper East Side	You're a stone's throw from top-notch museums and the rolling hills of Central Park.	Options are scarce and wallet-busting prices are not uncommon; also not particularly central.
Upper West Side & Central Park	Convenient access to Central Park and the Museum of Natural History.	Tends to swing in the familial direction if you're looking for a livelier scene.
Brooklyn	Better prices; great for exploring some of NYC's most creative neighborhoods.	It can be a long commute to Midtown Manhattan and points north.

Aerial view of Manhattan at sunset

In Focus

Grand Street, Little Italy

New York City Today

With more than 60 million smitten people visiting each year, New York remains a mighty force to be reckoned with. Bold new projects are reshaping the metropolis, while ambitious greenhouse targets attest to a city determined to build a cleaner, greener future. Yet, like any urban destination, the world's 'can-do' capital is not without its challenges, from rising crime rates to social harmony in the Age of Terror.

City of Immigrants

Just hours after Donald Trump was elected president in 2016, Mayor Bill de Blasio took to the podium in City Hall and promised that New York would continue to be a tolerant place, welcoming to immigrants and people of diverse religions, beliefs and sexual orientations. Like other places in America, NYC has had to grapple with big changes in society – stagnant wages, higher healthcare costs and loss of manufacturing jobs. But rather than blame immigrants for their problems, New Yorkers have invested in sectors with promising job growth instead – creating affordable industrial parks (such as the Brooklyn Navy Yard) where small-scale manufacturers can develop new products, and new educational hubs (including Roosevelt Island, which recently opened a $500 million applied sciences campus).

housing
(% of population)

67.5 — Renters

32 — Homeowners

0.05 — Homeless (documented)

if New York City were 100 people

34 would be Caucasian

28 would be Hispanic/Latino

23 would be African American

13 would be Asian

2 would be Other

population per sq mile

= 5000 people

Manhattan

New York State

Anyone with simple math skills can see: immigrants are good for the economy. In NYC, immigrant-founded small businesses produce more than $800 billion in sales and pay over $130 billion in payroll taxes each year. Nearly 40% of New Yorkers are foreign born, which is but one reason why the anti-civil rights rhetoric espoused by Trump and others will never be tolerated here.

Clean & Green

Never one to take things lying down, NYC is fighting climate change with impressive fervor. The city's current goal is to slash citywide greenhouse gas emissions 80% below 2005 levels by the year 2050. The goal complements de Blasio's 'One City, Built to Last,' scheme in which 3000 city-owned buildings will be upgraded with more efficient power, cooling and heating systems by 2025. Private buildings will be given ambitious target reductions, which, if not met voluntarily, will be followed by mandated reductions. Given around three-quarters of NYC's total greenhouse gases are produced by buildings, the program will go a long way to meeting the 2050 targets. De Blasio's recent commitments build on the original New York City Carbon Challenge launched by his predecessor, Michael Bloomberg.

Transforming the Metropolis

Big projects continue to change the New York landscape, in both subtle and grand ways. In early 2017, the new Second Avenue Subway line opened to much fanfare. Although it was first proposed back in the 1920s, it took nearly 100 years before the Second Avenue Subway line became a reality. Or at least a partial reality. The new line runs between 96th and 63rd Sts, only the first phase of a project intended to stretch more than 8 miles. It took nine years and some $4.5 billion to build it. Meanwhile, on the west side of Manhattan, work continues on the mega-project known as the Hudson Yards. This 28-acre development will bring new residential towers, shopping complexes, restaurants and outdoor spaces. At its center will be a new public square, with a 150ft-high honeycomb-like sculpture (opening in late 2018) made of hundreds of interconnected, climbable staircases designed by artist Thomas Heatherwick. The whole Hudson Yards project won't be finished until 2024 and will cost upwards of $20 billion.

Manhattan Bridge

History

This is the tale of a city that never sleeps, of a kingdom where tycoons and world leaders converge, of a place that's seen the highest highs and the most devastating lows. Yet through it all, it continues to reach for the sky (both figuratively and literally). And to think it all started with $24 and a pile of beads...

c AD 1500

About 15,000 Native Americans live in 80 sites around the island. The groups include the feuding Iroquois and Algonquins.

1625–26

The Dutch West India Company imports slaves from Africa to work in the fur trade and construction.

1646

The Dutch found the village of Breuckelen (Brooklyn) on the eastern shore of Long Island, naming it after Breukelen in the Netherlands.

Statue of Liberty (p40)

PETER UNGER / GETTY IMAGES ©

Buying Manhattan

The Dutch West India Company sent 110 settlers to begin a trading post here in 1624. They settled in Lower Manhattan and called their colony New Amsterdam, touching off bloody battles with the unshakable Lenape, a people who had roots on the island dating back 11,000 years. It all came to a head in 1626, when the colony's first governor, Peter Minuit, became the city's first – but certainly not the last – unscrupulous real estate agent by purchasing Manhattan's 14,000 acres from the Lenape for 60 guilders ($24) and some glass beads.

By the time peg-legged Peter Stuyvesant arrived to govern the colony in 1647, the Lenape population had dwindled to about 700. In 1664 the English arrived in battleships. Stuyvesant avoided bloodshed by surrendering without a shot. King Charles II renamed the colony after his brother the Duke of York. New York became a prosperous British port and the population rose to 11,000 by the mid-1700s; however, colonists started to become resentful of British taxation.

1784	**1811**	**1853**
Alexander Hamilton founds America's first bank, the Bank of New York, with holdings of $500,000.	Manhattan's grid plan is developed by Mayor DeWitt Clinton, reshaping the city and laying plans for the future.	The State Legislature authorizes the allotment of public lands for what will later become Central Park.

Tomb sculpture inside Trinity Church

Revolution & War

By the 18th century the economy was so robust that the locals were improvising ways to avoid sharing the wealth with London, and New York became the stage for the fatal confrontation with King George III. Revolutionary battles began in August of 1776, when General George Washington's army lost about a quarter of its men in just a few days. The general retreated, and fire engulfed much of the colony. But soon the British left and Washington's army reclaimed their city. In 1789 the retired general found himself addressing crowds at Federal Hall, gathered to witness his presidential inauguration. Alexander Hamilton, as Washington's secretary of the treasury, began rebuilding New York and working to establish the New York Stock Exchange.

Population Bust, Infrastructure Boom

There were setbacks at the start of the 19th century: the bloody Draft Riots of 1863, cholera epidemics, tensions among 'old' and 'new' immigrants, and poverty and crime in Five Points, the city's first slum. But the city prospered and found resources for mighty public works. Begun in 1855, Central Park was a vision of green reform and a boon to real-estate speculation. It also offered work relief when the Panic of 1857 shattered the nation's finance system. Another vision was realized by German-born engineer John Roebling who designed the Brooklyn Bridge, spanning the East River and connecting lower Manhattan and Brooklyn.

The Burgeoning Metropolis

By the start of the 20th century, elevated trains carried a million people a day in and out of the city. Rapid transit opened up areas of the Bronx and Upper Manhattan. Tenements were overflowing with immigrants arriving from southern Italy and Eastern Europe, who increased the metropolis to about three million. Newly wealthy folks – boosted by an economy jump-started by financier JP Morgan – built splendid mansions on Fifth Ave. Reporter and photographer Jacob Riis illuminated the widening gap between the classes, leading the city to pass much-needed housing reforms.

1863	1882	1883
Civil War draft riots erupt, lasting for three days; order is restored by the Federal Army.	Thomas Edison switches on the city's first electric lights at the JP Morgan bank at 23 Wall St.	The Brooklyn Bridge, built at a cost of $15.5 million (and 27 lives), opens on 24 May.

Factory Tragedy, Women's Rights

Wretched factory conditions – low pay, long hours, abusive employers – in the early 20th century were highlighted by a tragic event in 1911. The infamous Triangle Shirtwaist Company fire saw rapidly spreading flames catch onto the factory's piles of fabrics, killing 146 of the 500 female workers who were trapped behind locked doors. The event led to sweeping labor reforms after 20,000 female garment workers marched to City Hall. Nurse and midwife Margaret Sanger opened the first birth-control clinic in Brooklyn and suffragists held rallies to obtain the vote for women.

The Jazz Age

The 1920s saw the dawning of the Jazz Age, when Prohibition outlawed the sale of alcohol, encouraging bootlegging and speakeasies, as well as organized crime. Congenial mayor James Walker was elected in 1925, Babe Ruth reigned at Yankee Stadium and the Great Migration from the South led to the Harlem Renaissance, when the neighborhood became a center of African American culture and society. Harlem's nightlife attracted the flappers and gin-soaked revelers that marked the complete failure of Prohibition.

Hard Times

The stock market crashed in 1929 and the city dealt with the Great Depression through grit, endurance, rent parties, militancy and public works projects. Texas-born, Yiddish-speaking Mayor Fiorello LaGuardia worked to bring relief in the form of New Deal–funded projects. WWII brought troops to the city, ready to party in Times Square before shipping off to Europe. Converted to war industries, factories hummed, staffed by women and African Americans who had rarely before had access to good, unionized jobs. With few evident controls on business, Midtown bulked up with skyscrapers after the war.

Enter Robert Moses

Working with Mayor La Guardia to usher the city into the modern age was Robert Moses, an urban planner who would influence the physical shape of the city more than anyone else in

Move to the Beats

The 1960s ushered in an era of legendary creativity and anti-establishment expression, with many of its creators centered right downtown in Greenwich Village. One movement was Abstract Expressionism, a large-scale outbreak of American painters – Mark Rothko, Jackson Pollock, Lee Krasner, Helen Frankenthaler and Willem de Kooning among them – who offended and intrigued with incomprehensible squiggles and blotches and exuberant energy. Then there were the writers, such as Beat poets Allen Ginsberg and Jack Kerouac and novelist/playwright Jane Bowles. They gathered in Village coffeehouses to exchange ideas and find inspiration, which was often discovered in the form of folk music from burgeoning big names, such as Bob Dylan.

1913
Though not yet complete, Grand Central Terminal opens for business on 2 February.

1939
The World's Fair opens in Queens. With the future as its theme, the exposition invites visitors to take a look at 'the world of tomorrow.'

1969
Police officers raid the gay-friendly Stonewall Inn, sparking days of rioting and the birth of the modern gay-rights movement.

Interior of the National Museum of the American Indian

SEAN PAVONE / SHUTTERSTOCK ©

★ **Best Sites for Learning About the Past**

Lower East Side Tenement Museum (p98)

National Museum of the American Indian (p44)

Museum of Jewish Heritage (p44)

the 20th century. He was the mastermind behind the Triborough Bridge (now the Robert F Kennedy Bridge), Jones Beach State Park, the Verrazano–Narrows Bridge, the West Side Hwy and the Long Island parkway system – not to mention endless highways, tunnels and bridges, which shifted this mass-transit area into one largely dependent on the automobile.

'Drop Dead'

By the early 1970s deficits had created a fiscal crisis. President Ford refused to lend federal aid – summed up by the *Daily News* headline 'Ford to City, Drop Dead!' Massive layoffs decimated the working class; untended bridges, roads and parks reeked of hard times. The traumatic '70s – which reached a low point in 1977 with a citywide blackout and the existence of serial killer Son of Sam – drove down rents, helping to nourish an alternative culture that transformed the former industrial precincts of SoHo and Tribeca into nightlife districts.

Out of the Ashes

While the stock market boomed for much of the 1980s, neighborhoods struggled with the spread of crack cocaine; the city reeled from the impact of addiction, crime and AIDS. Squatters in the East Village fought back when police tried to clear a big homeless encampment, leading to the Tompkins Square Park riots of 1988. In South Bronx, a wave of arson reduced blocks of apartments to cinders. But amid the smoke, an influential hip-hop culture was born there and in Brooklyn.

Still convalescing from the real-estate crash of the late 1980s, the city faced crumbling infrastructure, jobs leaking south and Fortune 500 companies leaving for suburbia. Then the dot-com market roared in, turning the New York Stock Exchange into a speculator's fun park and the city launched a frenzy of building and partying unparalleled since the 1920s.

With pro-business, law-and-order Rudy Giuliani as mayor, the dingy and destitute were swept from Manhattan's yuppified streets to the outer boroughs, leaving room for Generation X to live the high life. Giuliani grabbed headlines with his campaign to stamp out crime, even kicking the sex shops off notoriously seedy 42nd St.

1977	1988	2001
A summer blackout leaves New Yorkers in the dark for 24 sweltering hours, which leads to rioting around the city.	Squatters riot when cops attempt to remove them from their de facto home in the East Village's Tompkins Square Park.	On September 11, terrorist hijackers fly two planes into the Twin Towers, destroying the World Trade Center and killing nearly 3000 people.

The Naughts in New York

The 10 years after 9/11 were a period of rebuilding – both physically and emotionally. In 2002 Mayor Michael Bloomberg began the unenviable task of picking up the pieces of a shattered city. Much to Bloomberg's pleasure, New York did see a great deal of renovation and reconstruction, especially after the city hit its stride with spiking tourist numbers in 2005. By the latter part of Bloomberg's second term as mayor, the entire city seemed to be under construction, with luxury high-rise condos sprouting up in every neighborhood.

Soon the economy buckled under its own weight in what has largely become known as the Global Financial Crisis (GFC). The city was paralyzed as the cornerstones of the business world were forced to close shop. Although hit less badly than many pockets of the country, NYC still saw a significant dip in real-estate prices and many cranes turned to frozen monuments of a broken economy.

In 2011 the city commemorated the 10th anniversary of the 9/11 attacks with the opening of a remembrance center and a half-built Freedom Tower – a new corporate behemoth – that loomed overhead.

September 11

On September 11, 2001, terrorists flew two hijacked planes into the World Trade Center's Twin Towers, turning the whole complex to dust and rubble and killing nearly 3000 people. Downtown Manhattan took months to recover from the ghastly fumes wafting from the ruins as forlorn missing-person posters grew ragged on brick walls. While the city mourned its dead and recovery crews coughed their way through the debris, residents braved constant terrorist alerts and an anthrax scare. Shock and grief drew people together, uniting the oft-fractious citizenry in a determined effort not to succumb to despair.

Storms & Political Change

New York's resilience would be tested again in 2012 by superstorm Hurricane Sandy. On October 29, cyclonic winds and drenching rain pounded the city, causing severe flooding and property damage in all five boroughs, including to the NYC subway system, Hugh L Carey Tunnel and World Trade Center site. A major power blackout plunged much of Lower Manhattan into surreal darkness, while trading at the New York Stock Exchange was suspended for two days in its first weather-related closure since 1888. In the neighborhood of Breezy Point, Queens, a devastating storm surge hindered the efforts of firefighters confronted with a blaze that reduced over 125 homes to ashes. The fire went down as one of the worst in NYC's history, while the storm itself claimed 44 lives in the city alone.

The winds of political change swept through the city in November 2013, when Bill de Blasio became the city's first Democrat mayor since 1989. The 52-year-old self-proclaimed 'progressive' also became the first white mayor of NYC with an African American spouse.

2008–9	2012	2017
The stock market crashes due to mismanagement by major American financial institutions.	Superstorm Sandy hits NYC in October, cutting power and causing major flooding and property damage.	Massive projects continue, with ongoing work on the 28-acre Hudson Yards, and the opening of the Second Ave Subway line.

Detail of One World Trade Center's (p94) facade

KEV LLEWELLYN / SHUTTERSTOCK ©

Art & Architecture

Peel back the concrete urban landscape, and you discover one of the world's great artistic centers. The city has been a showcase for talents great and small, who've added their mark to the city's canvas – both on its gallery walls and onto its gritty streets in the form of architectural icons that soar above the crowded sidewalks.

An Artistic Heavyweight

That New York claims some of the world's mightiest art museums attests to its enviable artistic pedigree. From Pollock and Rothko, to Warhol and Rauschenberg, the city has nourished many of America's greatest artists and artistic movements.

The Birth of an Arts Hub

In almost all facets of the arts, New York really got its sea legs in the early 20th century, when the city attracted and retained a critical mass of thinkers, artists, writers and poets. It was at this time that the homegrown art scene began to take shape. In 1905 photographer (and husband of artist Georgia O'Keeffe) Alfred Stieglitz opened 'Gallery 291,' a Fifth

Ave space that provided a vital platform for American artists and helped establish photography as a credible art form.

In the 1940s, an influx of cultural figures fleeing the carnage of WWII saturated the city with fresh ideas – and New York became an important cultural hub. Peggy Guggenheim established the Art of this Century gallery on 57th St, a space that helped launch the careers of painters such as Jackson Pollock, Willem de Kooning and Robert Motherwell. These Manhattan-based artists came to form the core of the Abstract Expressionist movement – also known as the New York School – creating an explosive and rugged form of painting that changed the course of modern art as we know it.

An American Avant-Garde

The Abstract Expressionists helped establish New York as a global arts center. Another generation of artists then carried the ball. In the 1950s and '60s, Robert Raus-chenberg, Jasper Johns and Lee Bontecou turned paintings into off-the-wall sculptural constructions that included everything from welded steel to taxidermy goats. By the mid-1960s, pop art – a movement that utilized the imagery and production techniques of popular culture – had taken hold, with Andy Warhol at the helm.

Graffiti & Street Art

Contemporary graffiti as we know it was cultivated in NYC. In the 1970s the graffiti-covered subway train became a potent symbol of the city and work by figures such as Dondi, Blade, and Lady Pink became known around the world. In addition, fine artists such as Jean-Michel Basquiat, Kenny Scharf and Keith Haring began incorporating elements of graffiti into their work.

The movement received new life in the late 1990s when a new genera-tion of artists – many with art-school pedigrees – began using materials such as cut paper and sculptural elements (all illicitly). Well-known New York City artists working in this vein include John Fekner, Stephen 'Espo' Powers, Swoon and the twin-brother duo Skewville.

These days, spray-can and stencil hot spots include the Brooklyn side of the Williamsburg Bridge and the corner of Troutman St and St Nicholas Ave in Bushwick, also in Brooklyn. In Astoria, Queens, explore the Technicolor art-works around Welling Ct and 30th Ave.

By the '60s and '70s, when New York's economy was in the dumps and much of SoHo lay in a state of decay, the city became a hotbed of conceptual and performance art. Gor-don Matta-Clark sliced up abandoned buildings with chainsaws and the artists of Fluxus staged happenings on downtown streets. Carolee Schneemann organized performances that utilized the human body; at one famous 1964 event, she had a crew of nude dancers roll around in an unappetizing mix of paint, sausages and dead fish in the theater of a Greenwich Village church.

Art Today

New York remains the world's gallery capital, with more than 800 spaces showcasing all kinds of art all over the city. The blue-chip dealers can be found clustered in Chelsea and the Upper East Side. Galleries that showcase emerging and mid-career artists dot the Lower East Side, while prohibitive rents have pushed the city's more emerging and experimental scenes further out, with current hot spots including Harlem and the Brooklyn neighborhoods of Bushwick, Greenpoint, Clinton Hill and Bedford-Stuyvesant (Bed-Stuy).

Guggenheim Museum (p80)

★ **Best Architectural Icons**

Brooklyn Bridge (p46)

Chrysler Building (p75)

Grand Central Terminal (p236)

Empire State Building (p66)

Guggenheim Museum (p80)

Architecture

New York's architectural history is a layer cake of ideas and styles – one that is literally written on the city's streets. Humble colonial farmhouses and graceful Federal-style buildings can be found alongside ornate beaux-arts palaces from the early 20th century. There are the unadorned forms of the International Style, and, in recent years, there has been the addition of the torqued forms of deconstructivist architects. For the architecture buff, it's a bricks-and-mortar bonanza.

Beaux-Arts Blockbusters

At the start of the 20th century, New York entered a gilded age. Architects, many of whom trained in France, came back with European design ideas. Gleaming white limestone began to replace all the brownstone, first stories were elevated to allow for dramatic staircase entrances, and buildings were adorned with sculptured keystones and Corinthian columns.

McKim Mead & White's Villard Houses, from 1884 (now the Palace Hotel), show the movement's early roots. Loosely based on Rome's Palazzo della Cancelleria, they channeled the symmetry and elegance of the Italian Renaissance. Other classics include the central branch of the New York Public Library (1911) designed by Carrère and Hastings, the 1902 extension of the Metropolitan Museum of Art by Richard Morris Hunt, and Warren and Wetmore's stunning Grand Central Terminal (1913), which is capped by a statue of Mercury, the god of commerce.

Reaching Skyward

By the time New York settled into the 20th century, elevators and steel-frame engineering had allowed the city to grow up – literally. This period saw a building boom of skyscrapers, starting with Cass Gilbert's neo-Gothic 57-story Woolworth Building (1913). To this day it remains one of the 50 tallest buildings in the United States.

Others soon followed. In 1930, the Chrysler Building, the 77-story art-deco masterpiece designed by William Van Alen, became the world's tallest structure. The following year, the record was broken by the Empire State Building, a clean-lined moderne monolith crafted from Indiana limestone. Its spire was meant to be used as a mooring mast for dirigibles (airships) – an idea that made for good publicity, but which proved to be impractical and unfeasible.

The influx of displaced European architects and other thinkers who had resettled in New York by the end of WWII fostered a lively dialogue between American and European architects. This was a period when urban planner Robert Moses furiously rebuilt vast swaths of New York – to the detriment of many neighborhoods – and designers and artists became obsessed with the clean, unadorned lines of the International Style.

One of the earliest projects in this vein were the UN buildings (1948–52), the combined effort of a committee of architects, including the Swiss-born Le Corbusier, Brazil's Oscar Niemeyer and America's Wallace K Harrison. The Secretariat employed New York's first glass curtain wall – which looms over the ski-slope curve of the General Assembly. Other significant modernist structures from this period include Gordon Bunshaft's Lever House (1950–52), a floating, glassy structure on Park Ave and 54th St, and Ludwig Mies van der Rohe's austere, 38-story Seagram Building (1956–58), located just two blocks to the south.

The New Guard

By the late 20th century, numerous architects began to rebel against the hard-edged, unornamented nature of modernist design. Among them was Philip Johnson. His pink granite AT&T Building (now Sony Tower; 1984) – topped by a scrolled, neo-Georgian pediment – has become a postmodern icon of the Midtown skyline.

What never became an icon was Daniel Libeskind's twisting, angular design for the One World Trade Center (2013) tower, replaced by a boxier architecture-by-committee glass obelisk. On the same site, budget blowouts led to tweaks of Santiago Calatrava's luminous design for the World Trade Center Transportation Hub (2016). According to critics, what should have looked like a dove in flight now resembles a winged dinosaur.

Starchitects on the Line

Frank Gehry's IAC Building (2007) – a billowing, white-glass structure often compared to a wedding cake – is one of a growing number of 'starchitect' creations appearing around railway-turned-urban-park, the High Line. The most prominent of these is Renzo Piano's new Whitney Museum of American Art (2015). Dramatically asymmetrical and clad in blue-gray steel, the building has received significant praise for melding seamlessly with the elevated park. Turning heads eight blocks to the north is 100 Eleventh Ave (2010), a 23-story luxury condominium by French architect Jean Nouvel. Its exuberant arrangement of angled windows is nothing short of mesmerizing, both cutting-edge in its construction and sensitive to the area's heritage. That the facade's patterning evokes West Chelsea's industrial masonry is not coincidental.

The area's next darling is set to be Zaha Hadid's apartment complex at 520 W 28th St. Rising 11 stories, the luxury structure will be the Iraqi-British architect's first residential project in the city, its voluptuous, sci-fi curves to be complemented by a 2500-sq-ft sculpture deck showcasing art presented by Friends of the High Line.

Sir Norman Foster has also bequeathed his cutting-edge style upon the city. The British architect's Hearst Tower (2006) – a glass skyscraper zigzagging its way out of a 1920s sandstone structure – remains a Midtown trailblazer. The building is one of numerous daring 21st-century additions to the city's architectural portfolio, among them Brooklyn's sci-fi arena Barclays Center (2012), Thom Mayne's folded-and-slashed 41 Cooper Square (2009) in the East Village, and Frank Gehry's rippling, 76-story apartment tower New York by Gehry (2011) in the Financial District.

LAZYLLAMA / SHUTTERSTOCK ©

LGBTIQ New York City

New York City is out and damn proud. It was here that the Stonewall Riots took place, that the modern gay rights movement bloomed and that America's first Pride march hit the streets. Yet even before the days of 'Gay Lib,' the city had a knack for all things queer and fabulous, from Bowery sex saloons and Village Sapphic poetry to drag balls in Harlem.

Divas, Drag & Harlem

While Times Square had developed a reputation for attracting gay men – many of them working in the district's theaters, restaurants and speakeasy bars – the hottest gay scene in the 1920s was found further north, in Harlem.

Harlem's drag balls were a hit with both gay and straight New Yorkers in the Roaring Twenties. The biggest of the lot was the Hamilton Lodge Ball, held annually at the swank Rockland Palace on 155th St. Commonly dubbed the Faggot's Ball, it was a chance for both gay men and women to (legally) cross-dress and steal a same-sex dance, and for fashionable 'normals' to indulge in a little voyeuristic titillation. The evening's star attraction was the beauty pageant, which saw the drag-clad competitors compete for the title of 'Queen of the Ball.' Langston Hughes proclaimed it the 'spectacles of color' and the gay writer was one of many members of New York's literati to attend the ball. It was also attended by everyone from prostitutes to high-society families, including the Astors and the Vanderbilts. Even the papers covered the extravaganza with its outrageous frocks the talk of the town.

The Stonewall Revolution

The relative transgression of the early 20th century was replaced with a new conservatism in the following decades, as the Great Depression, WWII and the Cold War took their toll. Conservatism was helped along by Senator Joseph 'Joe' McCarthy, who declared that homosexuals in the State Department threatened America's security and children. Tougher policing aimed to eradicate queer visibility in the public sphere, forcing the scene further underground in the 1940s and '50s. Although crackdowns on gay venues had always occurred, they became increasingly common.

Yet on June 28, 1969, when eight police officers raided the Stonewall Inn – a gay-friendly watering hole in Greenwich Village – patrons did the unthinkable: they revolted. Fed up with both the harassment and corrupt officers receiving payoffs from the bars' owners (who were mostly organized crime figures), they began bombarding the officers with coins, bottles, bricks and chants of 'gay power' and 'we shall overcome.' The cops were also met by a line of high-kicking drag queens and their now legendary chant, 'We are the Stonewall girls, we wear our hair in curls, we wear no underwear, we show our pubic hair, we wear our dungarees, above our nelly knees...'

Their collective anger and solidarity was a turning point, igniting intense and passionate debate about discrimination and forming the catalyst for the modern gay rights movement, not just in New York, but across the US and in countries from the Netherlands to Australia.

In the Shadow of AIDS

LGBT activism intensified as HIV and AIDS hit world headlines in the early 1980s. Faced with ignorance, fear and the moral indignation of those who saw AIDS as a 'gay cancer,' activists such as writer Larry Kramer set about tackling what was quickly becoming an epidemic. Out of his efforts was born ACT UP (AIDS Coalition to Unleash Power) in 1987, an advocacy group set up to fight the perceived homophobia and indifference of then President Ronald Reagan, as well as to end the price gouging of AIDS drugs by pharmaceutical companies.

The epidemic itself had a significant impact on New York's artistic community. Among its most high-profile victims were artist Keith Haring, photographer Robert Mapplethorpe and fashion designer Halston. Yet out of this loss grew a tide of powerful AIDS-related plays and musicals that would not only win broad international acclaim, but would become part of America's mainstream cultural canon. Among these are Tony Kushner's political epic *Angels in America* and Jonathan Larson's rock musical *Rent*. Both works would win Tony Awards and the Pulitzer Prize.

Marriage & the New Millennium

The LGBT fight for complete equality took two massive steps forward in recent years. In 2011, a federal law banning LGBT military personnel from serving openly – the so-called 'Don't Ask, Don't Tell' policy – was repealed after years of intense lobbying. An even bigger victory arrived when in 2015 the US Supreme Court ruled that same-sex marriage is a legal right across the country, striking down the remaining marriage bans in 13 US states.

The Brooklyn Bridge and Manhattan skyline

RUDY SULGAN / GETTY IMAGES ©

NYC on Screen

New York City has a long and storied life on screen. It was on these streets that a bumbling Woody Allen fell for Diane Keaton in Annie Hall, *that Meg Ryan faked her orgasm in* When Harry Met Sally, *and that Sarah Jessica Parker philosophized about the finer points of dating and Jimmy Choos in* Sex & the City. *To fans of American film and television, traversing the city can feel like one big déjà vu of memorable scenes, characters and one-liners.*

Landmarks on Screen

It's not surprising that NYC feels strangely familiar to many first-time visitors – the city itself has racked up more screen time than most Hollywood divas put together and many of its landmarks are as much a part of American screen culture as its red-carpet celebrities. Take the Staten Island Ferry (p236), which takes bullied secretary Melanie Griffith from suburbia to Wall St in *Working Girl* (1988); Battery Park (p41), where Madonna bewitches Aidan Quinn and Rosanna Arquette in *Desperately Seeking Susan* (1985); or the New York County Courthouse, where villains get what they deserve in *Wall Street* (1987) and *Goodfellas* (1990), as well as in small-screen classics such as *Cagney & Lacey*, *NYPD Blue* and *Law & Order*. The latter show, famous for showcasing New York and its characters, is honored with its own road – Law & Order Way – that leads to Pier 62 at Chelsea Piers.

Few landmarks can claim as much screen time as the Empire State Building (p66), famed for its spire-clinging ape in *King Kong* (1933, 2005), as well as for the countless romantic encounters on its observation decks. One of its most famous scenes is Meg Ryan and Tom Hanks' after-hours encounter in *Sleepless in Seattle* (1993). The sequence – which uses the real lobby but a studio-replica deck – is a tribute of sorts to *An Affair to Remember* (1957), which sees Cary Grant and Deborah Kerr make a pact to meet and (hopefully) seal their love atop the skyscraper.

Sarah Jessica Parker is less lucky in *Sex & the City* (2008), when a nervous Chris Noth jilts her and her Vivienne Westwood wedding dress at the New York Public Library (p74). Perhaps he'd seen *Ghost-busters* (1984) a few too many times, its opening scenes featuring the haunted library's iconic marble lions and Rose Main Reading Room. The library's foyer sneakily stands in for the Metropolitan Museum of Art in *The Thomas Crown Affair* (1999), in which thieving playboy Pierce Brosnan meets his match in sultry detective Rene Russo. It's at the fountain in adjacent Bryant Park that DIY sleuth Diane Keaton debriefs husband Woody Allen about their supposedly bloodthirsty elderly neighbor in *Manhattan Murder Mystery* (1993).

Across Central Park (p36) – whose own countless scenes include Barbra Streisand and Robert Redford rowing on its lake in clutch-a-tissue *The Way We Were* (1973) – stands the Dakota Building, used in the classic thriller *Rosemary's Baby* (1968). The Upper West Side is also home to Tom's Restaurant, whose facade was used regularly in *Seinfeld*. Another neighborhood star is the elegant Lincoln Center (p76), where Natalie Portman slowly loses her mind in the psychological thriller *Black Swan* (2010), and where love-struck Brooklynites Cher and Nicolas Cage meet for a date in *Moonstruck* (1987).

The more recent Oscar-winner *Birdman* (2014) shines the spotlight on Midtown's glittering Theater District, in which a long-suffering Michael Keaton tries to stage a Broadway adaptation at the St James Theatre on W44th St.

Hollywood Roots & Rivals

Believe it or not, America's film industry is an East Coast native. Fox, Universal, Metro, Selznick and Goldwyn all originated here in the early 20th century, and long before Westerns were shot in California and Colorado, they were filmed in the (now former) wilds of New Jersey. Even after Hollywood's year-round sunshine lured the bulk of the business west by the 1920s, 'Lights, Camera, Action' remained a common call in Gotham. The heart of the local scene was Queens' still-kicking Kaufman Astoria Studios.

Dancing in the Street

Knives make way for leotards in the cult musical *Fame* (1980), in which New York High School of Performing Arts students do little for the city's traffic woes by dancing on Midtown's streets. The film's graphic content was too much for the city's Board of Education, who banned shooting at the real High School of Performing Arts, then located at 120 W 46th St. Consequently, filmmakers used the doorway of a disused church on the opposite side of the street for the school's entrance, and Haaren Hall (Tenth Ave and 59th St) for interior scenes.

Fame is not alone in turning Gotham into a pop-up dance floor. In *On the Town* (1949), starstruck sailors Frank Sinatra, Gene Kelly and Jules Munshin look straight off a Pride float as they skip, hop and sing their way across this 'wonderful town,' from the base of Lady Liberty (p40) to Rockefeller Plaza (p85) and the Brooklyn Bridge (p46). Another wave of campness hits the bridge when Diana Ross and Michael Jackson cross it in *The Wiz* (1978), a bizarre take on *The Wizard of Oz*, complete with munchkins in Flushing Meadows Corona

Park and an Emerald City at the base of the WTC Twin Towers. The previous year, the bridge provided a rite of passage for a bell-bottomed John Travolta in *Saturday Night Fever* (1977), who leaves the comforts of his adolescent Brooklyn for the bigger, brighter mirror balls of Manhattan. Topping them all, however, is the closing scene in Terry Gilliam's *The Fisher King* (1991), which sees Grand Central Terminal's Main Concourse (p236) turned into a ballroom of waltzing commuters.

NYC on Film

It would take volumes to cover all the films tied to Gotham, so fire up your imagination with the following celluloid hits:

Taxi Driver (Martin Scorsese, 1976) De Niro plays a mentally unstable Vietnam War vet whose violent urges are heightened by the city's tensions.

Manhattan (Woody Allen, 1979) A divorced New Yorker dating a high-school student falls for his best friend's mistress in what is essentially a love letter to NYC. Catch romantic views of the Queensboro Bridge and the Upper East Side.

Desperately Seeking Susan (Susan Seidelman, 1985) A case of mistaken identity leads a bored New Jersey housewife on a wild adventure through Manhattan's subcultural wonderland. Relive mid-80s East Village and long-gone nightclub Danceteria.

Summer of Sam (Spike Lee, 1999) Spike Lee puts NYC's summer of 1977 in historical context by weaving together the Son of Sam murders, the blackout, racial tensions and the misadventures of one disco-dancing Brooklyn couple, including scenes at CBGB (p151) and Studio 54.

Angels in America (Mike Nichols, 2003) This movie version of Tony Kushner's Broadway play recalls 1985 Manhattan: crumbling relationships, AIDS out of control and a closeted Roy Cohn – advisor to President Ronald Reagan – doing nothing about it except falling ill himself. Follow characters from Brooklyn to Lower Manhattan to Central Park.

Party Monster (Fenton Bailey, 2003) Starring Macaulay Culkin, who plays the famed, murderous club kid Michael Alig, this is a disturbing look into the drug-fueled downtown clubbing culture of the late '80s. The former Limelight club is featured prominently.

Precious (Lee Daniels, 2009) This unflinching tale of an obese, illiterate teenager who is abused by her parents takes place in Harlem, offering plenty of streetscapes and New York–ghetto 'tude.

Birdman (Alejandro G Iñárritu, 2014) Oscar-winning black-comedy/drama *Birdman* documents the struggles of a has-been Hollywood actor trying to mount a Broadway show.

NYC's iconic yellow cabs

Survival Guide

Directory A–Z

Customs Regulations

US Customs allows each person over the age of 21 to bring 1L of liquor and 200 cigarettes into the US duty free. Agricultural items including meat, fruits, vegetables, plants and soil are prohibited. US citizens are allowed to import, duty free, up to $800 worth of gifts from abroad, while non-US citizens are allowed to import $100 worth. For updates, check www.cbp.gov.

Discount Cards

The following discount cards offer a variety of passes and perks to some of the city's must sees.Check the websites for more details.

Downtown CulturePass (www.downtownculturepass.org)
Explorer Pass (www.smart destinations.com)
New York CityPASS (www.citypass.com/new-york)
The New York Pass (www.newyorkpass.com)

Electricity

The US electric current is 110V to 115V, 60Hz AC. Outlets are made for flat two-prong plugs (which often have a third, rounded prong for grounding). If your appliance is made for another electrical system (eg 220V), you'll need a step-down converter, which can be bought at hardware stores and drugstores. Most electronic devices (laptops, camera-battery chargers etc) are built for dual-voltage use, however, and will only need a plug adapter.

Insurance

Before traveling, contact your health-insurance provider to find out what types of medical care it will cover outside your hometown (or home country). Overseas visitors should acquire travel insurance that covers medical situations in the US, as non-emergency care for uninsured patients can be very expensive. For non-emergency appointments at hospitals, you'll need proof of insurance or cash. Even with insurance, you'll most likely have to pay up front for non-emergency care and then consult with your insurance company afterwards to get your money reimbursed.

Internet Access

It's rare to find accommodations in New York City that don't offer wi-fi, though it isn't always free. Public parks with free wi-fi include the High Line, Bryant Park, Battery Park, Tompkins Square Park and Union Square Park. Other public areas with free wi-fi include **Columbia University** (www.columbia.edu; Broadway, at W 116th St, Morningside Heights; Ⓢ 1 to 116th St-Columbia University) and **South Street Seaport** (www.southstreet seaport.com). Internet kiosks can be found at the scattering of Staples and FedEx Office locations around the city, and you can also try Apple stores.

LGBTIQ Travelers

From hand-locked married couples on the streets of Hell's Kitchen to a rainbow-hued Empire State Building at Pride, there's no doubt that New York City is one of the world's great gay cities. Indeed, few places come close to matching the breadth and depth of queer offerings here, from cabarets and clubs to festivals and readings.

Money

ATMs are widely available and credit cards are widely accepted. Farmers markets, food trucks and some restaurants and bars are cash-only.

ATMs

ATMs are on practically every corner. You can either use your card at banks – usually in a 24-hour-access lobby, filled with up to a dozen monitors at major branches – or you can opt for the lone wolves, which sit in delis, restaurants, bars and grocery stores, charging fierce service fees that average $3 but can go as high as $5.

Changing Money

Banks and moneychangers, found all over New York City (including at the three major airports), will give you US currency based on the current exchange rate.

Credit Cards

Major credit cards are accepted at most hotels, restaurants and shops throughout New York City.

Opening Hours

Standard business hours are as follows:

Banks 9am to 6pm Monday to Friday, some also 9am to noon Saturday.

Bars 5pm to 4am.

Businesses 9am to 5pm Monday to Friday.

Clubs 10pm to 4am.

Restaurants Breakfast 6am to 11am, lunch 11am to around 3pm, and dinner 5pm to 11pm. Weekend brunch 11am to 4pm.

Shops 10am to 7pm weekdays, 11am to 8pm Saturday, and Sunday can be variable – some stores stay closed while others keep weekday hours. Stores tend to stay open later in the neighborhoods downtown.

Public Holidays

Major NYC holidays and special events may force the closure of many businesses or attract crowds, making dining and accommodations reservations difficult.

New Year's Day January 1

Martin Luther King Day Third Monday in January

Presidents' Day Third Monday in February

Easter March/April

Memorial Day Late May

Gay Pride Last Sunday in June

Independence Day July 4

Labor Day Early September

Rosh Hashanah and Yom Kippur Mid-September to mid-October

Halloween October 31

Thanksgiving Fourth Thursday in November

Christmas Day December 25

New Year's Eve December 31

Safe Travel

Crime rates in NYC are still at their lowest in years. There are few neighborhoods where you might feel apprehensive no matter what time of night it is (they're mainly in the outer boroughs). Subway stations are generally safe, too, though again, especially in the outer boroughs, some can be dicey. There's no reason to be paranoid, but it's better to be safe than sorry, so use common sense: don't walk around alone at night in unfamiliar, sparsely populated areas, especially if you're a woman. Carry your daily walking-around money somewhere inside your clothing or in a front pocket rather than in a handbag or a back pocket, and be aware of pickpockets, particularly in mobbed areas, such as Times Square or Penn Station at rush hour.

Taxes & Refunds

Restaurants and retailers never include the sales tax – 8.875% – in their prices, so beware of ordering the $4.99 lunch special when you only have $5 to your name. Several categories of so-called 'luxury items,' including rental cars and dry-cleaning, carry an additional city surcharge of 5%, so you wind up paying

Practicalities

Newspapers

New York Post (www.nypost.com) The *Post* is known for screaming headlines, conservative political views and its popular Page Six gossip column.

New York Times (www.nytimes.com) 'The gray lady' has become hip in recent years, adding sections on technology, arts and dining out.

Magazines

New York Magazine (www.nymag.com) A biweekly magazine with feature stories and great listings about anything and everything in NYC, plus an indispensable website.

New Yorker (www.newyorker.com) This highbrow weekly covers politics and culture through its famously lengthy works of reportage; it also publishes fiction and poetry.

Time Out New York (www.timeout.com/newyork) A free weekly magazine, with listings on restaurants, arts and entertainment.

Radio

WNYC (820AM & 93.9FM; www.wnyc.org) NYC's public radio station is the local NPR affiliate and offers a blend of national and local talk and interview shows, with a switch to classical music in the day on the FM station.

Smoking

Smoking is strictly forbidden in any location that's considered a public place; this includes subway stations, restaurants, bars, taxis and parks.

an extra 13.875% in total for these services. Clothing and footwear purchases under $110 are tax free; anything over that amount has a state sales tax of 4.5%. Hotel rooms in New York City are subject to a 14.75% tax, plus a flat $3.50 occupancy tax per night. Since the US has no nationwide value-added tax (VAT), there is no opportunity for foreign visitors to make 'tax-free' purchases.

Telephone

Phone numbers within the US consist of a three-digit area code followed by a seven-digit local number. If you're calling long distance, dial 1 + the three-digit area code + the seven-digit number. To make an international call from NYC, call 011 + country code + area code + number. When calling Canada, there is no need to use the 011.

Area Codes

No matter where you're calling within New York City, even if it's just across the street in the same area code, you must always dial 1 + the area code first.

Cell Phones

Most US cell (mobile) phones, besides the iPhone, operate on CDMA, not the European standard GSM – make sure you check compatibility with your phone service provider. North Americans should have no problem, though it's best to check with your service provider about roaming charges.

If you require a cell phone, you'll find many store fronts – most run by Verizon, T-Mobile or AT&T – where you can buy a cheap phone and load it up with prepaid minutes, thus avoiding a long-term contract.

Time

New York City is in the Eastern Standard Time (EST) zone – five hours behind Greenwich Mean Time (London). Almost all of the USA observes daylight-saving time: clocks go forward one hour from the second Sunday in March to the first Sunday in November, when the clocks are turned back one hour (it's easy to remember by the phrase 'spring ahead, fall back').

Toilets

Considering the number of pedestrians, there's a noticeable lack of public restrooms around the city. You'll find spots to relieve yourself in Grand Central Terminal, Penn Station and Port Authority Bus Terminal, and in parks, including Madison Square Park, Battery Park, Tompkins Square Park, Washington Square Park and Columbus Park in Chinatown, plus several places scattered around Central Park. The good bet, though, is to pop into a Starbucks (there's one about every three blocks) or a department store (Macy's, Century 21, Bloomingdale's).

Tourist Information

In this web-based world you'll find infinite online resources to get up-to-the-minute information about New York. In person, try one of the official bureaux of **NYC & Company** (www.nycgo.com):

City Hall (☏212-484-1222; www.nycgo.com; City Hall Park, at Broadway; ☺9am-6pm Mon-Fri, 10am-5pm Sat & Sun; ⎯S⎯4/5/6 to Brooklyn Bridge-

City Hall; R to City Hall; J/Z to Chambers St)

Macy's Herald Square
(☏212-484-1222; www.nycgo.com; Macy's, 151 W 34th St, at Broadway; ☺9am-7pm Mon-Fri, from 10am Sat, from 11am Sun; ⎯S⎯B/D/F/M, N/Q/R/W to 34th St-Herald Sq)

Times Square (☏212-484-1222; www.nycgo.com; Broadway Plaza, btwn W 43rd & 44th Sts; ☺9am-6pm; ⎯S⎯N/Q/R/W, S, 1/2/3, 7 to Times Sq-42nd St)

Neighborhood Tourism Portals

Some of the city's most popular neighborhoods and boroughs have their own websites (either official or 'unofficial') dedicated to exploring the area.

Brooklyn (www.explorebk.com)
Chinatown (www.explorechinatown.com)
Soho (www.sohonyc.com)
Williamsburg (www.freewilliamsburg.com)

Travelers with Disabilities

Federal laws guarantee that all government offices and facilities are accessible to people with disabilities. For information on specific places, you can contact the mayor's **Office for People with Disabilities** (☏212-639-9665, in NYC 311; www.nyc.gov/html/mopd; ☺9am-5pm Mon-Fri), which will send you a free copy of its *Access*

New York guide. Also check out www.nycgo.com/accessibility for a good list of planning tools.

Big Apple Greeter (☏212-669-8198; www.bigapplegreeter.org) ⟨FREE⟩ This excellent program has over 50 volunteers with physical disabilities on staff who are happy to show off their corner of the city.

Accessibility Line (☏511; http://web.mta.info/accessibility/) Call or visit the website for detailed information on subway and bus wheelchair accessibility.

Visas

The US Visa Waiver Program (VWP) allows nationals from 38 countries to enter the US without a visa, provided they are carrying a machine-readable passport. For the up-to-date list of countries included in the program and current requirements, see the **US Department of State website** (http://travel.state.gov/visa).

Citizens of VWP countries need to register with the US Department of Homeland Security three days before their visit. There is a $14 fee for registration application; when approved, the registration is valid for two years or until your passport expires, whichever comes first. Apply online at www.esta.cbp.dhs.gov/esta.

Transportation

Arriving in New York City

With its three bustling airports, two main train stations and a monolithic bus terminal, New York City rolls out the welcome mat for millions of visitors who come to take a bite out of the Big Apple each year.

Direct flights are possible from most major American and international cities. Figure six hours from Los Angeles, seven hours from London and Amsterdam, and 14 hours from Tokyo. Consider getting here by train instead of car or plane to enjoy a mix of bucolic and urban scenery en route, without unnecessary traffic hassles, security checks and excess carbon emissions.

Flights, tours and rail tickets can be booked online at lonelyplanet.com/bookings.

John F Kennedy International Airport

John F Kennedy International Airport (JFK; ☎718-244-4444; www.kennedyairport.com; [S]A to Howard Beach or E, J/Z to Sutphin Blvd-Archer Ave then, JFK Airtrain), 15 miles from Midtown in southeastern Queens, has eight terminals, serves nearly 50 million passengers annually and hosts flights coming and going from all corners of the globe.

Taxi A yellow taxi has a flat rate of around $53 (plus a $4.50 surcharge from 4pm to 8pm weekdays) between JFK and any destination in Manhattan. This fee does not include tolls or tip. Going to/from a destination in Brooklyn, the metered fare should be about $45 (Coney Island) to $65 (downtown Brooklyn). Note that the Williamsburg, Manhattan, Brooklyn and Queensboro–59th St Bridges have no toll either way, while the Queens–Midtown Tunnel and the Hugh L Carey Tunnel (aka the Brooklyn–Battery Tunnel) cost $8.50 going into Manhattan.

Vans & Car Service Shared vans, like those offered by Super Shuttle Manhattan (www.supershuttle.com), cost around $20 to $28 per person, depending on the destination. If traveling to the airport from NYC, car services have set fares from $45.

Express Bus The NYC Airporter (www.nycairporter.com) runs to Grand Central Station, Penn Station or the Port Authority Bus Terminal from JFK. The one-way fare is $18.

Subway The subway is the cheapest but slowest way of reaching Manhattan. From the airport, hop on the AirTrain ($5, payable as you exit) to Sutphin Blvd-Archer Ave (Jamaica Station) to reach the E, J or Z line (or the Long Island Rail Road). To take the A line instead, ride the AirTrain to Howard Beach station. The E train to Midtown has the fewest stops. Expect the journey to take at least 1½ hours to Midtown.

Long Island Rail Road (LIRR) This is by far the most relaxing way to arrive in the city. From the airport, take the AirTrain ($5, as you exit) to Jamaica Station. From there, LIRR trains go frequently to Penn Station in Manhattan or to Atlantic Terminal in Brooklyn (near Fort Greene, Boerum Hill and the Barclay Center). It's about a 20-minute journey from station to station. One-way fares to either Penn Station or Atlantic Terminal cost $7.50 ($10.25 at peak times).

LaGuardia Airport

Used mainly for domestic flights, **LaGuardia** (LGA; ☎718-533-3400; www.panynj.gov; 🚌M60, Q70) is smaller than JFK but only 8 miles from midtown Manhattan; it sees about 26 million passengers per year.

Taxi A taxi to/from Manhattan costs about $40 to $50 for the approximately half-hour ride.

Car Service A car service to LaGuardia costs around $35.

Express Bus The NYC Airporter (www.nycairporter.com) costs $15 and goes to/from Grand Central, Penn Station and the Port Authority Bus Terminal.

Subway & Bus It's less convenient to get to LaGuardia by public transportation than the other airports. The best subway link is the 74 St–Broadway station (7 line, or the E, F, M and R lines at the connecting Jackson Heights-Roosevelt Ave station) in Queens, where you can pick up the Q70 Express Bus (about 10 minutes to the airport).

Climate Change & Travel

Every form of transport that relies on carbon-based fuel generates CO_2, the main cause of human-induced climate change. Modern travel is dependent on planes, which might use less fuel per kilometre per person than most cars but travel much greater distances. The altitude at which aircraft emit gases (including CO_2) and particles also contributes to their climate change impact. Many websites offer 'carbon calculators' that allow people to estimate the carbon emissions generated by their journey and, for those who wish to do so, to offset the impact of the greenhouse gases emitted with contributions to portfolios of climate-friendly initiatives throughout the world. Lonely Planet offsets the carbon footprint of all staff and author travel.

Newark Liberty International Airport

Don't write off New Jersey when looking for airfares to New York. About the same distance from Midtown as JFK (16 miles), **Newark** (EWR; ☎973-961-6000; www.panynj.gov) brings many New Yorkers out for flights (there's some 36 million passengers annually).

Car Service & Taxi A car service runs about $45 to $60 for the 45-minute ride from Midtown – a taxi is roughly the same. You'll have to pay a whopping $15 to get into NYC through the Lincoln (at 42nd St) and Holland (at Canal St) Tunnels and, further north, the George Washington Bridge, though there's no charge going back through to NJ. There are a couple of cheap tolls on New Jersey highways, too, unless you ask your driver to take Hwy 1 or 9.

Subway/Train NJ Transit (www.njtransit.com) runs a rail service (with an AirTrain connection) between Newark airport (EWR) and New York's Penn Station for $13 each way. The trip takes 25 minutes and runs every 20 or 30 minutes from 4:20am to about 1:40am. Hold onto your ticket, which you must show upon exiting at the airport.

Express Bus The Newark Liberty Airport Express (www.newarkairportexpress.com) has a bus service between the airport and Port Authority Bus Terminal, Bryant Park and Grand Central Terminal in Midtown ($16 one-way). The 45-minute ride goes every 15 minutes from 6:45am to 11:15pm and every half hour from 4:45am to 6:45am and 11:15pm to 1:15am.

Port Authority Bus Terminal

For long-distance bus trips, you'll leave and depart from the world's busiest bus station, the **Port Authority Bus Terminal** (☎212-502-2200; www.panynj.gov; 625 Eighth Ave, at W 42nd St; [S]A/C/E to 42nd St-Port Authority Bus Terminal), which sees nearly 70 million passengers each year. Bus companies leaving from here include the following:

Greyhound (www.greyhound.com) Connects New York with major cities across the country.

Peter Pan Trailways (www.peterpanbus.com) Daily express services to Boston, Washington, DC, and Philadelphia.

Short Line Bus (www.shortlinebus.com) Serves northern New Jersey and upstate New York, focusing on college towns such as Ithaca and New Paltz; part of Coach USA.

Penn Station

Train

Penn Station (W 33rd St, btwn Seventh & Eighth Aves; [S]1/2/3, A/C/E to 34th St-Penn Station) is the departure point for all **Amtrak** (www.amtrak.com) trains, including the Acela Express services to Princeton, NJ, and Washington, DC (note that this express service will cost twice as much as a normal fare). All fares vary, based on the day of the week and the time you want to travel. There's no baggage-storage facility at Penn Station.

Long Island Rail Road (http://www.mta.info/lirr) The Long Island Rail Road serves over 300,000 commuters each day, with services from Penn Station to points in Brooklyn and Queens, and on Long Island. Prices are broken down by zones. A peak-hour ride from Penn Station to Jamaica Station (en route to JFK via AirTrain) costs $10.25 if you buy it at the station (or a whopping $16 onboard).

NJ Transit (www.njtransit.com) Also operates trains from Penn Station, with services to the suburbs and the Jersey Shore.

New Jersey PATH (www.panynj. gov/path) An option for getting into NJ's northern points, such as Hoboken and Newark. Trains ($2.75) run from Penn Station along the length of Sixth Ave, with stops at 33rd, 23rd, 14th, 9th and Christopher Sts, as well as at the reopened World Trade Center site.

Budget Buses

A growing number of budget bus lines operate from locations just outside Penn Station:

BoltBus (📞877-265-8287; www.boltbus.com; W 33rd St, between Eleventh & Twelfth Aves; 🛜) Services from New York to Philadelphia, Boston, Baltimore and Washington, DC. The earlier you purchase tickets, the better the deal. Notable for its free wi-fi, which occasionally actually works.

Megabus (http://us.megabus. com; 🛜; ⓢ7 to 34th St-Hudson Yards) Travels from New York to Boston, Washington, DC, and Toronto, among other destinations. Free (sometimes functioning) wi-fi.

Vamoose (📞212-695-6766; www.vamoosebus.com; ⓢ1 to 28th St; A/C/E, 1/2/3 to 34th St-Penn Station) Buses head to Arlington, Virginia, near Washington, DC.

Grand Central Terminal

The last line departing from Grand Central Terminal, the **Metro-North Railroad**

(www.mta.info/mnr) serves Connecticut, Westchester County and the Hudson Valley.

Getting Around

Check the **Metropolitan Transportation Authority** (www.mta.info) website for public transportation information (buses and subway), including a handy travel planner and regular notifications of delays and alternate travel routes during frequent maintenance.

Subway

The New York subway system, run by the Metropolitan Transportation Authority, is iconic, cheap, round-the-clock and often the fastest and most reliable way to get around the city. It's also safer and (a bit) cleaner than it used to be. A single ride, regardless of the distance, is $2.75 with a MetroCard (though if you buy just a one-ride ticket, rather than two or more rides, it's $3). A 7-Day Unlimited Pass costs $32.

It's a good idea to grab a free map from a station attendant. If you have a smartphone, download a useful app (such as the free Citymapper), with subway map and alerts of service outages.

Bicycle

Hundreds of miles of designated bike lanes have been added over the past decade. Add to this

the excellent bike-sharing network **Citi Bike** (www. citibikenyc.com), and you have the makings for a surprisingly bike-friendly city. Hundreds of Citi Bike kiosks in Manhattan and parts of Brooklyn house the iconic bright blue and very sturdy bicycles, which have reasonable rates for short-term users.

To use a Citi Bike, purchase a 24-hour or seven-day access pass at any Citi Bike kiosk. You will then be given a five-digit code to unlock a bike. Return the bike to any station within 30 minutes to avoid incurring extra fees. Reinsert your credit card (you won't be charged) and follow the prompts to check out a bike again. You can make an unlimited number of 30-minute check-outs during those 24 hours or seven days.

Ferry

Hop-on, hop-off services are offered by **New York Waterway** (www.nywaterway. com) and **New York Water Taxi** (www.nywatertaxi.com). The **NYC Ferry** (www.ferry. nyc), which launched in 2017, runs year-round commuter service connecting a variety of locations in Queens and Brooklyn with Manhattan. The fare is the same as a subway ride (and uses a MetroCard).

Another bigger, brighter ferry is the commuter-oriented **Staten Island Ferry** (www.siferry.com; Whitehall Terminal, 4 South St, at Whitehall St; ⏰24hr; ⓢ1 to South Ferry) **FREE**, which makes constant

TRANSPORTATION SURVIVAL GUIDE **237**

Subway Cheat Sheet

A few tips for understanding the madness of the New York subway:

MetroCard All buses and subways use the yellow-and-blue MetroCard, which you can purchase or add value to at one of several easy-to-use automated machines at any station. You can use cash or an ATM or credit card. Tip: if you're not from the US, when the machine asks for your zip code, enter 99999. The card itself costs $1.

Numbers, letters, colors Color-coded subway lines are named by a letter or number, and most carry a collection of two to four trains on their tracks.

Express & local lines A common mistake is accidentally boarding an 'express train' and passing by a local stop you want. Know that each color-coded line is shared by local trains and express trains; the latter make only select stops in Manhattan (indicated by a white circle on subway maps).

Getting in the right station Some stations have separate entrances for downtown or uptown lines (read the sign carefully). If you swipe in at the wrong one – as even locals do on occasion – you'll either need to ride the subway to a station where you can transfer for free, or just lose the $2.75 and re-enter the station (usually across the street).

Weekends All the rules switch on weekends, when some lines combine with others, some get suspended, some stations get passed, others get reached. Locals and tourists alike stand on platforms confused, sometimes irate. Check www.mta.info for weekend schedules. Sometimes posted signs aren't visible until after you reach the platform.

free journeys across New York Harbor.

Bus

Buses are convenient during off hours – especially when transferring between the city's eastern and western sides. The bus network uses the MetroCard; prices as per the subway.

Taxi

Hailing and riding in a cab are rites of passage in New York – especially when you get a driver who's a neurotic speed demon, which is often (don't forget to buckle up). Still, most taxis in NYC are clean and, compared to those in many international cities, pretty cheap. Meters start at $2.50 and increase roughly $5 for every 20 blocks. Tips are expected to be 10% to 15%, but give less if you feel in any way mistreated; be sure to ask for a receipt and use it to note the driver's license number. See www.nyc.gov/taxi for more information.

Boro Taxi

Green Boro Taxis operate in the outer boroughs and Upper Manhattan. These allow folks to hail a taxi on the street in neighborhoods where yellow taxis rarely roam. They have the same fares and features as yellow cabs, and are a good way to get around the outer boroughs (from, say, Astoria to Williamsburg, or Park Slope to Red Hook). Drivers are reluctant (but legally obligated) to take passengers into Manhattan as they aren't legally allowed to take fares going out of Manhattan south of 96th St.

Car Service

These services are a common taxi alternative in the outer boroughs. Fares differ depending on the neighborhood and length of ride, and must be determined beforehand, as they have no meters. These 'black cars' are quite common in Brooklyn and Queens, however, it's illegal if a driver simply stops to offer you a ride – no matter what borough you're in. A couple of car services in Brooklyn include **Northside** (☎718-387-2222; www.northsideservice.com; 207 Bedford Ave, btwn N 5th & N 6th Sts, Williamsburg; ☺24hr) in Williamsburg and **Arecibo** (☎718-783-6465; 170 Fifth Ave, at Degraw St, Park Slope; ☺24hr) in Park Slope.

Behind the Scenes

Acknowledgements

Climate map data adapted from Peel MC, Finlayson BL & McMahon TA (2007) 'Updated World Map of the Köppen-Geiger Climate Classification', Hydrology and Earth System Sciences, 11, 1633–44.

This Book

This 2nd edition guidebook was curated by Regis St Louis and was researched and written by Michael Grosberg. The previous edition was researched and written by Regis St Louis, Cristian Bonetto and Zora O'Neill.

Destination Editors Evan Godt, Lauren Keith, Trisha Ping

Product Editor Jenna Myers

Senior Cartographer Alison Lyall

Book Designers Nicholas Colicchia, Clara Monitto

Assisting Editors Katie Connolly, Ali Lemer, Gabbi Stefanos, Amanda Williamson

Cartographer Julie Dodkins

Assisting Book Designers Ania Bartoszek, Virginia Moreno

Cover Researcher Wibowo Rusli

Thanks to Liz Heynes, Ester Kim, Alison Ridgway, Tony Wheeler

Send Us Your Feedback

We love to hear from travellers – your comments keep us on our toes and help make our books better. Our well-travelled team reads every word on what you loved or loathed about this book. Although we cannot reply individually to postal submissions, we always guarantee that your feedback goes straight to the appropriate authors, in time for the next edition. Each person who sends us information is thanked in the next edition, the most useful submissions are rewarded with a selection of digital PDF chapters.

Visit lonelyplanet.com/contact to submit your updates and suggestions or to ask for help. Our award-winning website also features inspirational travel stories, news and discussions.

Note: We may edit, reproduce and incorporate your comments in Lonely Planet products such as guidebooks, websites and digital products, so let us know if you don't want your comments reproduced or your name acknowledged. For a copy of our privacy policy visit lonelyplanet.com/privacy.

A — Z
Index

Lower Manhattan

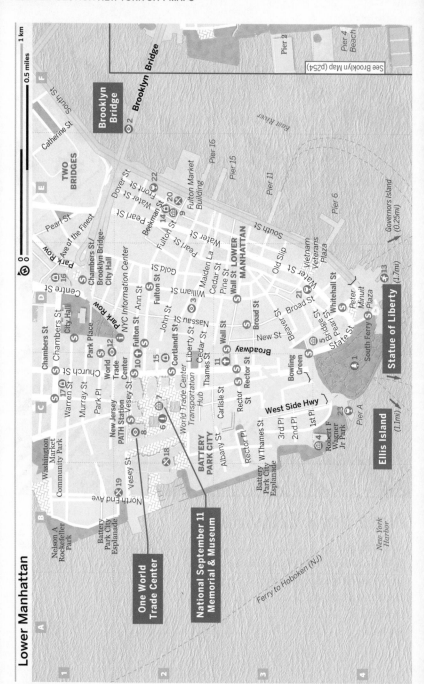

One World Trade Center

National September 11 Memorial & Museum

Brooklyn Bridge

Statue of Liberty

Ellis Island

Washington Market Community Park

Nelson A Rockefeller Park

Battery Park City Esplanade

TWO BRIDGES

BATTERY PARK CITY

LOWER MANHATTAN

New Jersey PATH Station

World Trade Center Transportation Hub

NYC Information Center

City Hall

Brooklyn Bridge City Hall

Fulton Market Building

Bowling Green

Robert F Wagner Jr Park

Battery Park City Esplanade

West Side Hwy

Broadway

East River

New York Harbor

Governors Island (0.25mi)

Statue of Liberty (1.7mi)

Ellis Island (1.1mi)

Ferry to Hoboken (NJ)

See Brooklyn Map (p254)

Vietnam Veterans Plaza

Peter Minuit Plaza

South Ferry

1 km
0.5 miles

Lower Manhattan

SoHo, East & West Villages and Chinatown

SoHo, East & West Villages and Chinatown

Times Square & Midtown Manhattan

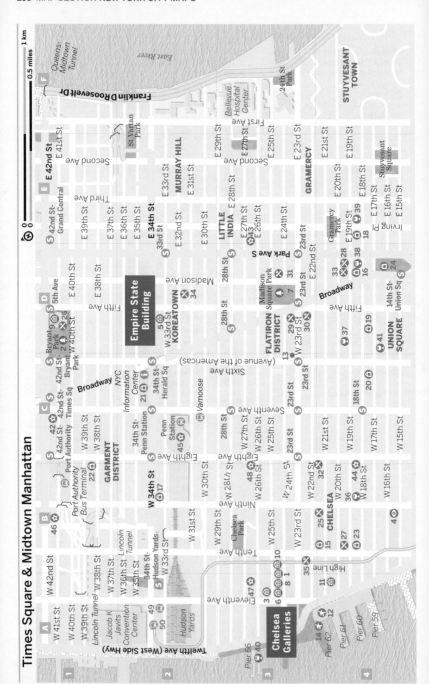

Empire State Building

Chelsea Galleries

Hudson Yards

Jacob K Javits Convention Center

Lincoln Tunnel

Port Authority Bus Terminal

GARMENT DISTRICT

Penn Station

34th St-Penn Station

NYC Information Center

34th St-Herald Sq

KOREATOWN

Bryant Park

Times Sq

42nd St-Port Authority

42nd St-Times Sq

MURRAY HILL

LITTLE INDIA

Madison Square Park

FLATIRON DISTRICT

CHELSEA

Chelsea Park

High Line

GRAMERCY

Gramercy Park

UNION SQUARE

14th St-Union Sq

Stuyvesant Square

STUYVESANT TOWN

Bellevue Hospital Center

St Vartan Park

24th St Park

Queens-Midtown Tunnel

East River

Franklin D Roosevelt Dr

Broadway

Fifth Ave

Madison Ave

Park Ave S

Third Ave

Second Ave

First Ave

Sixth Ave (Avenue of the Americas)

Seventh Ave

Eighth Ave

Ninth Ave

Tenth Ave

Eleventh Ave

Twelfth Ave (West Side Hwy)

Lincoln Tunnel

Hudson Yards

Pier 66
Pier 62
Pier 61
Pier 60
Pier 59

W 42nd St
W 41st St
W 40th St
W 39th St
W 38th St
W 37th St
W 36th St
W 35th St
34th St-Hudson Yards
W 33rd St
W 31st St
W 29th St
W 28th St
W 26th St
W 25th St
W 24th St
W 23rd St
W 22nd St
W 21st St
W 20th St
W 19th St
W 18th St
W 17th St
W 16th St
W 15th St

E 42nd St
E 41st St
E 40th St
E 39th St
E 38th St
E 37th St
E 36th St
E 35th St
E 34th St
E 33rd St
E 32nd St
E 31st St
E 30th St
E 29th St
E 28th St
E 27th St
E 26th St
E 25th St
E 24th St
E 23rd St
E 22nd St
E 21st St
E 20th St
E 19th St
E 18th St
E 17th St
E 16th St
E 15th St

Irving Pl

Broadway

0.5 miles
1 km

A B C D E F
1 2 3 4

Times Square & Midtown Manhattan

Central Park & Uptown

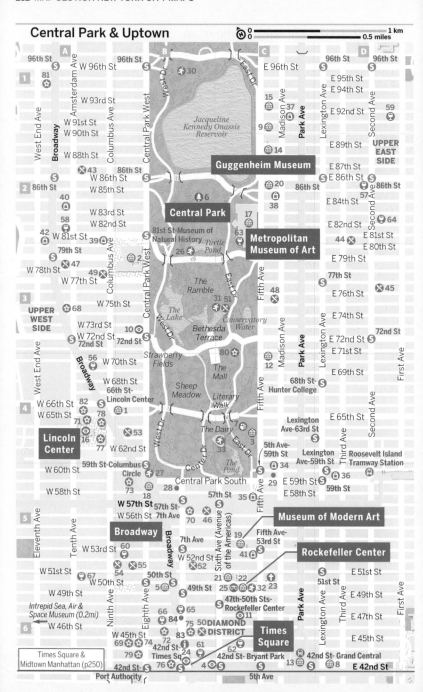

0 1 km
0 0.5 miles

Jacqueline Kennedy Onassis Reservoir

Guggenheim Museum

Central Park

81st St-Museum of Natural History

Metropolitan Museum of Art

Turtle Pond

The Ramble

The Lake

Conservatory Water

Bethesda Terrace

Strawberry Fields

The Mall

Sheep Meadow

Literary Walk

The Dairy

UPPER WEST SIDE

UPPER EAST SIDE

Lincoln Center

59th St-Columbus Circle

Central Park South

The Pond

Hunter College

Roosevelt Island Tramway Station

Museum of Modern Art

Broadway

Rockefeller Center

DIAMOND DISTRICT

Times Square

Intrepid Sea, Air & Space Museum (0.2mi)

Times Square & Midtown Manhattan (p250)

47th-50th Sts-Rockefeller Center

Port Authority

Central Park & Uptown

Brooklyn

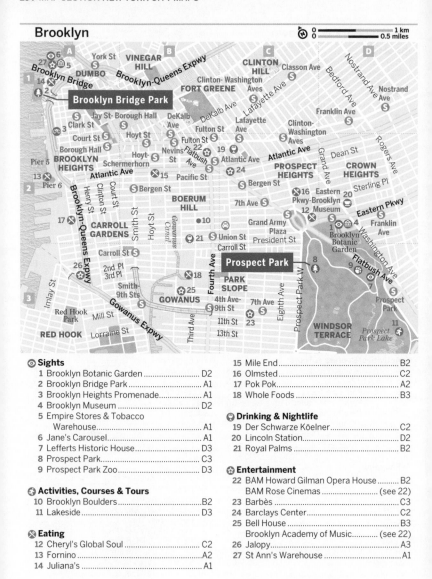

0 ——————— 1 km
0 ——————— 0.5 miles

Williamsburg

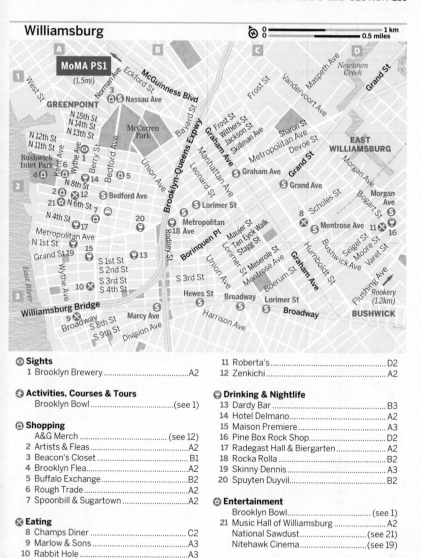

MoMA PS1
(1.5mi)

GREENPOINT

McCarren
Park

Bushwick
Inlet Park

EAST
WILLIAMSBURG

East River

Williamsburg Bridge

BUSHWICK

Rookery
(1.2km)

Newtown
Creek

◎ Sights
1 Brooklyn Brewery A2

✦ Activities, Courses & Tours
Brooklyn Bowl ....(see 1)

🏠 Shopping
A&G Merch .... (see 12)
2 Artists & Fleas A2
3 Beacon's Closet B1
4 Brooklyn Flea A2
5 Buffalo Exchange B2
6 Rough Trade A2
7 Spoonbill & Sugartown A2

✕ Eating
8 Champs Diner C2
9 Marlow & Sons A3
10 Rabbit Hole A3

11 Roberta's D2
12 Zenkichi A2

◖ Drinking & Nightlife
13 Dardy Bar B3
14 Hotel Delmano A2
15 Maison Premiere A3
16 Pine Box Rock Shop D2
17 Radegast Hall & Biergarten A2
18 Rocka Rolla B2
19 Skinny Dennis A3
20 Spuyten Duyvil B2

✪ Entertainment
Brooklyn Bowl .... (see 1)
21 Music Hall of Williamsburg A2
National Sawdust ....(see 21)
Nitehawk Cinema ....(see 19)

Symbols & Map Key

Look for these symbols to quickly identify listings:

- ◉ Sights
- ✪ Activities
- ⊖ Courses
- ◔ Tours
- ✪ Festivals & Events
- ✖ Eating
- ◎ Drinking
- ✪ Entertainment
- ◎ Shopping
- ❶ Information & Transport

These symbols and abbreviations give vital information for each listing:

- ✍ Sustainable or green recommendation
- **FREE** No payment required

- ☑ Telephone number
- ☺ Opening hours
- Ⓟ Parking
- ☺ Nonsmoking
- ✳ Air-conditioning
- @ Internet access
- ☎ Wi-fi access
- ☒ Swimming pool
- ▣ Bus
- ☒ Ferry
- ▣ Tram
- ▣ Train
- ▣ English-language menu
- ✒ Vegetarian selection
- ♦ Family-friendly

Find your best experiences with these Great For... icons.

 Art & Culture
 History
Beaches
 Local Life
Budget
Nature & Wildlife
Cafe/Coffee
Photo Op
Cycling
Scenery
Detour
Shopping
Drinking
Short Trip
Entertainment
Sport
Events
Walking
Family Travel
Winter Travel
Food & Drink

Sights
- Beach
- Bird Sanctuary
- Buddhist
- Castle/Palace
- Christian
- Confucian
- Hindu
- Islamic
- Jain
- Jewish
- Monument
- Museum/Gallery/Historic Building
- Ruin
- Shinto
- Sikh
- Taoist
- Winery/Vineyard
- Zoo/Wildlife Sanctuary
- Other Sight

Points of Interest
- Bodysurfing
- Camping
- Cafe
- Canoeing/Kayaking
- Course/Tour
- Diving
- Drinking & Nightlife
- Eating
- Entertainment
- Sento Hot Baths/Onsen
- Shopping
- Skiing
- Sleeping
- Snorkelling
- Surfing
- Swimming/Pool
- Walking
- Windsurfing
- Other Activity

Information
- Bank
- Embassy/Consulate
- Hospital/Medical
- Internet
- Police
- Post Office
- Telephone
- Toilet
- Tourist Information
- Other Information

Geographic
- Beach
- Gate
- Hut/Shelter
- Lighthouse
- Lookout
- Mountain/Volcano
- Oasis
- Park
- Pass
- Picnic Area
- Waterfall

Transport
- Airport
- BART station
- Border crossing
- Boston T station
- Bus
- Cable car/Funicular
- Cycling
- Ferry
- Metro/MRT station
- Monorail
- Parking
- Petrol station
- Subway/S-Bahn/Skytrain station
- Taxi
- Train station/Railway
- Tram
- Tube Station
- Underground/U-Bahn station
- Other Transport